# THE DAY THE NAZIS CAME

# THE DAY THE NAZIS CAME

My childhood journey from Britain
to a German concentration camp

## STEPHEN R. MATTHEWS

JOHN BLAKE

Published by John Blake Publishing,
80–1 Wimpole Street,
Marylebone
London W1G 9RE

www.facebook.com/johnblakebooks
twitter.com/jblakebooks

First published in paperback in 2016
This paperback edition published in 2020

Paperback ISBN: 978-1-78946-207-4
Ebook ISBN: 978-1-78606-336-6
Audio ISBN: 978-1-78946-250-0

British Library Cataloguing-in-Publication Data:

A catalogue record for this book is available from the British Library.

Design by www.envydesign.co.uk

Printed and bound in Great Britain by Clays Ltd, Elcograf S.p.A.

1 3 5 7 9 10 8 6 4 2

John Blake Publishing is an imprint of Bonnier Books UK
www.bonnierbooks.co.uk

# DEDICATION

This book is dedicated to the bright and cherished memory of my parents, Cecil and Eileen Matthews, whose fortitude, humour and dedication carried us all through those difficult and troubled times.

To the immense courage of Franz 'Otto' Laib, the German deputy commandant who saved my life, and to Helen 'Goldilocks' Roschmann, the camp administrator and interpreter, whose devout values sustained many of the British prisoners in her charge; and to sister 'Annie', the German nurse who cared for all her patients, including my mother, in the camp hospital, irrespective of their race or creed.

And, finally, to all those extraordinary Channel Islanders who touched my life, including my steadfast and lifelong friend Neville Henry Godwin, from our traumatic days in Dorsten and Biberach concentration camps.

# CONTENTS

# FOREWORDS

*'Of all gifts that fortune grants us, there is none greater than
friendship – no greater wealth, no greater joy.'*

So in the spirit of this quotation from Epicurus of Samos, I
am delighted to write a foreword for this book.

Here, close to the town of Biberach in southern Germany,
the Lindele camp was located. When the French liberated
the camp on 23 April 1945, they found internees from many
nations. Though the camp was supervised by the International
Red Cross, I do not want to euphemise the situation: the
people interned here were robbed of their freedom.

Despite the close quarters, the lack of privacy, the cold
and the continuous supervision, a spirit of humanity existed
between the internees and the population of Biberach; for
me, this is a very positive sign. Stephen Matthews reports
about Franz Laib, the deputy camp commandant, who saved
his life, entries in his mother's diary about Helen Roschmann,
a translator at that time, and also contacts between women
having their babies at the hospital, which led to friendships

between people from Guernsey and Biberach, which have been fostered for generations. They sowed the seed for today's friendship between the island of Guernsey and the town of Biberach. Every year reciprocal visits take place, and former internees bring their families to Biberach. Both here and on the island there are people dedicated to perpetuating this friendship.

I would like to thank Stephen Matthews for his initiative in recalling so graphically this humane aspect of the Second World War and wish all the readers of this book the wealth and joy of friendship in the spirit of Epicurus's words.

Norbert Zeidler
Lord Mayor of Biberach

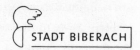

Most of the people who will read this book have lived through a time of peace in Western Europe and have not had to experience the World Wars during which our parents and grandparents suffered. Many of us will have heard first-hand accounts of World War Two from those who lived through it. Often, the stories will be of the bravery and courage of the men and (in some cases women) who fought for the freedoms we have enjoyed.

# THE DAY THE NAZIS CAME

Those of us who have had the pleasure of living in the Channel Islands have heard from those civilians who suffered as the result of enemy occupation of their homes. I have heard many extraordinary and often heart-wrenching, as well as heart-warming, tales. Sadly, most of those who lived through the occupation never wrote down their experiences, often because the memories were too painful. Consequently, many stories are no longer remembered and will never be recalled.

Those, such as Stephen Matthews, who have recorded and preserved their memories have made a valuable and beneficial contribution to our understanding of all that war entails. We all need not only to remember the bravery of those who fought but also to realise the suffering endured by ordinary civilians. In doing so, we ensure that future generations will learn about the horrors and futility of war and will grow to realise that we must strive to maintain the peace and freedoms we currently enjoy.

We also learn that the hatred and evil encouraged and perpetrated by the leaders of nations are not always shared by their citizens. Compassion and humanity are not the characteristics solely of one side of the battle.

In this book, Stephen Matthews conveys the memories of his own, and his family's, experiences of enemy occupation on the island of Guernsey, followed by deportation and internment in Germany. It is a personal tale not only of the horrors of war but also the love and compassion that human beings on both sides of the conflict were able to show to each other.

Such mutual respect for our fellow beings underpins the

contacts that now exist between the communities of the Bailiwick of Guernsey and the town of Biberach. Through such friendships, understandings are able to grow between different communities; and, through those contacts and by remembering the suffering of our predecessors, we hope that we and our subsequent generations can continue to live in peace.

Sir Richard Collas
Bailiff of Guernsey

*'To the living we owe respect but to the*
*dead we owe only the truth.'*
Voltaire

# CHAPTER 1

# THE LULL BEFORE
# THE STORM

*T*he stooped old man stood on the glistening cobbled stones of the *Marktplatz*, wrapped up in a warm overcoat and holding an umbrella close to him in a relentless battle against the driving rain and the bitter cold. He was here in the German town of Biberach an der Riss, to celebrate his liberation by Free French Forces from the nearby German concentration camp where he had been imprisoned with his parents some seventy years ago as a young boy. Standing there, he realised he was now one of only a few survivors – literally a dying breed – and, more poignantly, it was unlikely he would ever stand here again. He mused about the passing years: how did the intervening decades pass so quickly and when did hatred and anger on both sides become deep friendship and love, so that the raucous noise of war could be soothed.

Was this how it felt to be an ageing dinosaur, at a time when a third of the population didn't know anything about the Battle of Britain and a quarter of them thought the Germans had been on

1

*the Allied side in World War Two? Perhaps this was the right time to leave quietly. Pulling his coat snugly around him and tightening the woollen scarf around his neck in a vain attempt to stop the rain dripping down his neck, he smiled to himself as he was reminded that all his aches and pains were merely God's way of telling him he was still alive, and with that he shuffled off into the gloom of the late afternoon.*

So where did it all start? On reflection, it must have begun with my birth on 7 June 1938, when I finally made an appearance as the younger son of Cecil and Eileen Matthews. My parents resided happily in the upper-country parish of St Martin on the calm and feudal Channel Island of Guernsey, where my maternal forebears had lived and prospered for many hundreds of years. It has been said that our own personal traits and characteristics are formed between the ages of three and seven, and, by the time I reached my seventh birthday, I had been imprisoned, terrorised, threatened, starved, beaten, had my hand broken by a German guard, bombed, shelled, shot at, spat upon and finally stranded in a minefield.

The Channel Islands had formed the very last vestige of the medieval Dukedom of Normandy, where all the laws were promulgated in the ancient Norman French language, and where, culturally, Norman French was the predominant tongue used throughout the islands until the late nineteenth century. The winding roads and quaint country lanes all carried French names and the islanders owed staunch allegiance to the British Crown, or, rather, to an ancient Norse warrior, Rollo, the first ruler of the principality known as Normandy.

# THE LULL BEFORE THE STORM

After the Norman Conquest of 1066 it was the name we Channel Islanders gave to all the kings and queens of England and have continued to do so to the present day. Guernsey comprises ten parishes, each administered by an elected 'Douzaine' of twelve good men and true, assisted in their day-to-day administrative duties by two constables. These positions have always been totally honorary and unpaid, and rely on the participants' dedication and commitment to serve their island and their parish.

In the summer sunshine, uncles and aunts, cousins and friends enjoyed a plethora of regular family events, such as charabanc trips to the seaside with picnics held on golden sands; lazy afternoon teas held under flowering cherry trees, where only the best starched and embroidered table clothes were used and where cucumber-and-salmon sandwiches were served alongside a continuous supply of Darjeeling tea, dispensed from highly polished silver teapots. Farmers ploughed and planted their fertile and sacred soil and the world-famous golden Guernsey cow calmly munched the cud and thrived in such a pastoral environment. All in all, it was a magical time, when the sun shone down brightly on British islands caressed by the warmth of the Gulf Stream.

I have always felt that my arrival took place at a rather unpropitious moment, because my elder brother, Alan, was also in hospital at the same time suffering from pneumonia, a condition invariably considered to be life-threatening in those ancient times. Contemporary medical treatment dictated he should have one lung removed, which was a tricky operation, especially for a young lad of only seven, to suffer.

After some family deliberation, I was named Stephen after my grandfather, Stephen Rabey, who was an elected Deputy in the island's Parliament, and had also been a parish constable from 1910 through to 1912. Family life on Guernsey at this time still had a semblance of normality about it, and most of the islanders, if they had but known it, lived an almost idyllic life. Indeed, Victor Hugo, a former long-time resident of Guernsey, had once described the Channel Islands as being 'fragments of France which fell into the sea and were gathered up by England'.

All the same, by June 1938 the unmistakable shadow of war was beginning to manifest itself across most of Europe, but, even then, as families and tourists swam in the clear warm waters or walked the picturesque cliff paths, emblazoned with golden gorse flowers, they could never have envisaged the time would come when the bays would be seeded with thousands of treacherous German landmines and the sides of our glorious cliffs, laced with antipersonnel roll bombs and barbed wire, for we were, after all, British and part of an illustrious and invincible empire – and didn't we bravely sing 'Rule, Britannia!' with gusto, especially the line 'Britons never will be slaves'? It wouldn't be long before this myth would be dramatically shattered for many; nonetheless the islanders were no strangers to wars and upheaval, and throughout they had always loyally supported both king and country in time of need. All the Channel Islands had suffered enormous and devastating casualties in World War One – the Great War – as witnessed by the fullness of the war memorials erected in each island parish, emphasising the significance that, for instance, the Guernsey Light Infantry had suffered a 47 per cent casualty rate during some of the bitterest fighting of that conflict.

My father had been born in Portsmouth on 20 April 1898 of Guernsey parentage, and during World War One he joined the armed services at a very young age and served with the Royal Field Artillery, eventually reaching the rank of sergeant after he had been sent out to fight the Germans in France and Belgium. There, he had been wounded and listed as missing in action for several months. He very rarely spoke of his combat experiences, except sometimes to me many years later, when I was home on leave from the Colonial Police Force in Northern Rhodesia, following the Belgian Congo débâcle. I think he talked to me then only to reassure me and emphasise the point that we had both experienced exceptionally dangerous moments in our lives, and in spite of everything, and all the near misses, we had both survived. He told me once, on a late morning somewhere in Belgium – when the British heavy guns were firing at some distant German targets – that he had been ordered by the colonel of the regiment to go down below into the heavily reinforced dugouts and bring back another set of army maps, as the regiment had received orders to realign the direction and range of its artillery to seek out a new set of German military targets.

The underground dugout had been constructed with a welded framework of steel railway lines, supported above and on three sides by heavy oak railway sleepers covered with a goodly depth of soil, and the whole complex was probably some thirty feet deep. He had just retrieved the maps when the whole ground shook violently beneath his feet for several minutes, causing him to lose his balance. As he lay on the earthen floor, dirt and debris cascaded down from the gaps between the railway sleepers and, after a pause, he dusted himself down, grabbed the maps and returned to the artillery emplacements above ground. As he emerged into the bright sunlight, he was faced by a scene of total carnage, with guns overturned or destroyed, mounds of earth, ammunition strewn everywhere, shell holes, broken human bodies and dead horses. It was evident that, while he had been away, the regiment had been devastated by salvo after salvo of incoming German shells. At this precise moment as he surveyed the slaughter before him, German heavy-machine-gun fire erupted all around him, so he took off, running quickly down the side of the nearby railway embankment. As he crossed over the railway line, a bullet passed through his right hand and another bullet clipped his boots and neatly removed one of the heels.

Walking for several days in the direction of the nearest large Belgian town, he eventually fetched up in some small enclave, where he was taken in by a family who owned the local brewery. They gave him food, dressed his wounds and hid him from the opposing forces, which meant he had little choice but to stay with them for several weeks until he had fully recovered from his ordeal. The owner of the brewery had three extremely rotund spinster daughters, and it was suggested to my father that he might like to select one of them, to settle down with and help run the brewery after the war. My father told me he had very politely declined this very kind offer, because the sight of the three daughters actually frightened him far more than having to face the German enemy. After several weeks' recuperation he was provided with an ancient but valiant carthorse, and, wearing an old straw hat kindly donated by one of the daughters, he set off back to find the remnants of his regiment.

My paternal grandparents were born on Guernsey but moved to England, where my grandfather was inducted into the Royal Naval School of Music. The family resided in Portsmouth, where my grandfather died in 1922. My own father talked to me only once about my grandfather, to say that, when my father was about ten years of age, it was his regular duty to visit various local public houses in the late evenings, where he had to stand outside and wait until my grandfather appeared. My grandfather would then place one hand on my father's head to steady himself and then my father would have to guide him safely home. I notice from family records that Grandmother Matthews was some eight years older than my grandfather, which must have been quite unusual during those times. Anyway, she was regarded by all accounts as a very fine and remarkable woman, and my mother was often to repeat one of her sayings: 'We may be poor but we don't have to *look* poor.'

My mother was born on Guernsey, on 26 January 1908, being the youngest of five daughters of Stephen Rabey and his wife Ada. She was christened Eileen Florence, and lived with her sisters at Clovelly on the Rue Maze, in very close proximity to all the Rabey clan. Unfortunately, Grandma Ada died when my mother was very young and, after a suitable period of mourning, my grandfather eventually married a local widow. Nonetheless, it was a happy enough childhood for my mother, with vivid memories of the whole family renting cottages for the long and sultry summer months on the nearby island of Herm, which lay just a few miles off St Peter Port harbour. It was here they could all play or laze on the famous Shell Beach, and ride the large farm-horses down into the surf.

At this time my UK grandma had her younger spinster sister, Great-Aunt Emily, living with her, who was also a remarkable woman in her own right. There was a family anecdote, always talked about in hushed tones, involving Great-Aunt Em. It was apparently some time after she found employment as a nanny, with a member of the British Royal Family in London, and through this connection she had in due course come to the notice of a rising Irish diplomat who was then living and working in London. Although already married, he had declared his undying love for Emily and stated he was going to seek a divorce so he could ask her to marry him.

There was a secret signal arranged between these two lovers that was to take place at a pageant and celebration parade to mark the Diamond Jubilee of Queen Victoria in 1897. Great-Aunt Emily, at the age of twenty-seven, was to be included as a servant in the royal party and the signal to be given to our worthy diplomat as he rode by in the parade was twofold. If the answer to the proposal of marriage was yes, Emily was to wave her handkerchief wildly in the air. If, however, the answer was no, then she would turn away and not wave her handkerchief at all. She knew very well that any divorce would create a great scandal, demolish a promising political career and destroy a reputation, perhaps leading in turn to ruin and abject misery. On the day of the great event, as everyone stood together on a raised dais, enthralled by the excitement and full majesty of the occasion, Great-Aunt Em let the handkerchief fall from her hand as she turned away and walked off into obscurity. She was never to marry.

We now fast-forward to 1929 when, during one lunchtime in Portsmouth, Grandma Matthews was just sitting down to the Sunday roast lunch with her whole family. This made a very welcome change, as Alfred, her younger son, was only recently home on leave from the Royal Navy in Hong Kong. As they all sat down around the table, Grandma told them an old cousin of hers from Guernsey was going to visit them that very afternoon and would be accompanied by a Miss Eileen Rabey, a Sunday School teacher from St Martin's Methodist Chapel, who had also been given the great honour of representing the Girl Guides Association in 1921, where she presented a traditional Guernsey copper milk can to HRH Princess Mary.

Grandma added – bearing in mind the importance of the visit and the fact that she had taken the trouble to make sandwiches and cakes – that the family should all be very supportive and attend. Alfred said he would very much like to be there but had been called away to the Royal Naval Club. Aunt Edith said likewise but that she was due to play piano at the local church hall. Cecil couldn't think of an excuse in time, so merely stated he would be upstairs working and shouldn't be disturbed on any account, especially by an ancient cousin and a decrepit Sunday School teacher from Guernsey.

Sharp at the appointed time of half-past three, a taxi drew up at the gate. My father, watching from upstairs, groaned inwardly to himself as an ancient old biddy clambered laboriously backwards out of the vehicle. The next moment he was nearly bowled over by the sight of a beautiful young girl with dark wavy hair and dressed in a gaily patterned summer frock also alighting from the very same taxi. Grandma had only just reached a point in the introductions where she was explaining the reasons for the absence of her family, and had said Cecil was out playing football, when he miraculously appeared and announced he and Eileen were going for a walk in the nearby park. Later in the afternoon, tea passed quite happily, although by then it was obvious the 'ancient relic' who was accompanying Eileen was beginning to feel the full responsibility of being a chaperone in an almost dark and foreign land.

Early the next morning, Cecil hotfooted it around to the Temperance Hotel in Gosport, where the ancient relic and Eileen were staying, only to find the birds had flown, apparently in some disarray and consternation at his unwelcome attentions. Not to be outmanoeuvred, he turned his considerable charm on the Christian lady who owned the establishment and she reluctantly gave him the couple's forwarding address in the London suburbs. My father was always one for quiet but decisive action, and he soon remembered he had several friends from his army days now working on the railways. Through one of them he was able to obtain a free passage on the footplate of a steam engine going to London later in the morning, provided he would be willing to help shovel the coal on the journey, which he did with great enthusiasm.

Once in London, he soon found a friendly taxi driver who took him to the Temperance Hotel in the suburbs, where he found a rather astonished but secretly pleased twenty-one-year-old Eileen and a somewhat disgruntled and truculent old biddy. Brushing aside all protestations from the chaperone, who up to that time had been congratulating herself on her skilful and diplomatic departure from Portsmouth, my father once again suggested a quiet evening stroll in the nearby park. We now come to what was really my father's first big mistake and one that could have been disastrous. When they reached the park entrance my father had first seen through the windows of the taxi, he realised it was in reality the entrance to the local cemetery. Undaunted and with the last throw of the dice, he walked Eileen through a myriad of headstones, then finally picked her up and deposited her, quite unceremoniously, on a cold and damp tombstone. He then got down on bended knee and proposed, whereupon, to his utter astonishment, he was immediately and enthusiastically accepted.

Later, back at the hotel when the old biddy had been told the exciting news, she had a fit of apoplexy, realising she had signally and dismally failed to carry out her duties as chaperone. After reluctantly agreeing to meet with my father again the next day, she decamped forthwith, and, taking my protesting mother in tow, caught the very next boat train from Waterloo to Southampton, and then the midnight mail-boat back to Guernsey. While my father was carefully planning his next move, the full horror story was being reported by the old relic to my grandfather in his dining room at Clovelly in the Rue Maze. The riposte was a short, erudite letter demanding my father's immediate presence on Guernsey with a plausible excuse and explanation for his unwarranted, discourteous and unbelievable behaviour.

After a week or so had passed, my father duly arrived on Guernsey. The short lapse of time had been opportune, for it provided my mother with the opportunity to use her considerable wiles against my poor old defenceless grandfather. As the pair of antagonists met formally for the first time in the main dining room, my grandfather's anger gradually dissipated, and he found he was actually taking an instant liking to my father, probably seeing in him the son he had never had but always wished for. When my father left the dining room later in the morning, the engagement had been agreed and my grandfather said he couldn't quite understand what all the fuss and nonsense had been about in the first place.

My Guernsey grandfather was certainly no easy pushover. He led a very active and dynamic life both in his own business and in political spheres. After a close cousin suffered a serious accident that necessitated her leg being amputated on grandfather's dining table, he became a prime mover for the development of a local cottage hospital. He also insisted the whole family, comprising his five daughters, should all sit down to have their meals together, and at breakfast time the post would be placed on a silver salver in the dining room and couldn't be touched until he had personally handed out the letters to the recipients. It was also part of our family folklore that he insisted the morning newspapers had to be ironed before he read them!

So the wedding was set for a year hence with the ceremony planned to take place at Les Camps Methodist Chapel, and, on a beautiful autumnal morning of 23 September 1930, father and daughter found themselves in the front garden of Clovelly, waiting anxiously for the wedding transport to arrive. Up to this point, tradition had dictated the use of a liveried horse and carriage, bedecked with flowers, bows and ribbons. However, this modern miss had decided early on in the planning stage to have an ultramodern wedding using a highly polished limousine and a resplendent uniformed chauffeur. On this morning of all mornings, not only was the car late in arriving but it immediately broke down on the spot, and everyone's anxiety didn't improve when all they could see were the chauffeur's big feet sticking out from under the front end.

A little time passed until Eileen fretfully announced enough was enough and she was going to hoist up her white bridal gown and stride out the mile or so to the Chapel. However, at that very moment a knight in shining armour rode gallantly to the rescue, in the form of one Bill Green. Well, a gallant knight, certainly, but not in shining armour and certainly not on a big white charger. Bill was riding by on his old and somewhat dilapidated motorcycle with an attendant battered sidecar full of bread, which he was in the process of delivering throughout the neighbourhood. My mother ran out into the road and, after some discussion, the bread was offloaded and stacked up in someone's front garden. My mother-to-be hitched up her wedding dress and clambered onto the pillion seat, and, being left with virtually no other option available to him, my grandfather was gently eased and shoehorned into the ramshackle sidecar, and off they all set for the chapel in great haste. This, then, was the start of a long and very happy marriage in which my parents' deep love for and loyalty to each other always played a pivotal role in our family life.

In May 1939, my Uncle Alfred, now warrant master-of-arms on the China Naval Station, died while on active service in Hong Kong, and my Guernsey grandfather fell terminally ill at home on the island. On 1 September 1939, German shock troops, sent by Hitler, swarmed across the Polish borders, unleashing the first *Blitzkrieg* the world had ever witnessed. This act was soon to be followed by an announcement broadcast by the British Prime Minister, Neville Chamberlain, on the morning of 3 September 1939 declaring that a state of war now existed between Britain and Germany.

Thus the stage was set and everyone would gradually learn of their future roles through terror and suffering. This war would drag on for a further six years, being the most extensive and costly of all military ventures, demanding as payment the lives of tens of millions of people worldwide.

I often sensed my father had an overriding sense of *déjà vu*, having already fought the Germans once before in Belgium and France during World War One, and now, almost twenty-five years later, the same aggressors were yet again marching through Belgium and still singing their battlesongs of hate.

I only recently found my mother's diary and notes, secreted away in an old leather-bound family Bible, held with a large metal clasp, which described these violent times as the German armies swept inexorably onwards through the Low Countries and France towards Dunkirk. Rumours and counter-rumours abounded in the islands and finally, on 15 June 1940, the British government declared the Channel Islands to be a demilitarised zone, as the islands were not thought to be strategically important, and, in any event, they could not be adequately defended. Unfortunately – and tragically – it would seem nobody thought to apprise the advancing German military of this important edict.

At this dire stage, my father was exceptionally tired, dividing his time between the family building company in the Rue Maze, St Martin, and his responsibilities as a constable of St Martin's, at the Parish Hall, a post he held from 1940 until 1942. Generally arriving home in the late evening, totally depleted, he would periodically forget about the regulation 'blackout' and switch on the bedroom lights without having drawn the curtains, only to be forcibly reminded of his grave error by the shrill whistle of the local ARP warden (ARP stands for Air Raid Precautions). My father always said he was amazed that the warden, who was under five foot tall, could summon up such a cacophony of sound from so small a frame.

On one particular day in mid–May 1940, my mother had decided to give their bedroom a really good spring clean and, as part of the process, the bed and other pieces of furniture were completely rearranged. My father came home extremely late and exhausted as usual, after a very trying day, but this time he remembered the blackout. As he started to undress in the dark and had reached the stage of loosening his trousers, he sat down where he thought the edge of the bed would be, and suddenly found himself stretched out full-length on the cold linoleum floor. My mother, hearing the commotion, woke up and automatically switched on the light, whereupon almost immediately the ARP warden, standing outside in the roadway, started blowing on his whistle. My father, who was normally very slow to anger, girded his loins and walked very slowly and deliberately to the window, throwing it wide open. Looking down somewhat disdainfully at the diminutive figure of the warden clad in an outsize steel helmet, he said in a loud voice, 'Eileen, come here quickly – I think that dammed tortoise has escaped again.' Then he shut the window, retired to his bed and switched the light off. Nothing more was ever heard of this affair again and the warden was soon moved on to other more worthwhile duties.

# CHAPTER 2

# THE STORM

A t the outset of war, the population of Guernsey had been estimated to be about 40,000. However, as young men and women left the island to join the forces and some of the older ones went to work in the war factories in England, the population rapidly decreased to some 22,000. Eventually, the Guernsey government took the difficult but bold decision that all children of school age should be evacuated with their teachers to the mainland of Great Britain. The morning of 19 June 1940 dawned and my mother and father were called to my brother's school to receive their instructions for his evacuation by mail-boat on the following day. Already the dull crump of explosions on the nearby French coast could be heard, and this seemed only to add a sharper edge to a deplorable and frightening situation.

The next day, all the schoolchildren gathered at their school in the early morning and walked in line with their teachers the several miles from the outskirts of the island capital, down the long and winding hills to the harbour. Parents had been forced to say their goodbyes at the school because barriers had been placed across the road leading into the harbour area, and these had been installed quite a long way from the quayside. This had been done because of a very real fear of an air-raid or a possible low-level attack by the German air force, the Luftwaffe. All the parents and friends waited patiently by the barriers until the boat finally left St Peter Port harbour, and many a fervent prayer was offered for his or her child's safe arrival in England.

On Saturday, 22 June 1940, my mother spent the whole day agonising over the decision to send my brother Alan away, bearing in mind his poor state of health, and wondered whether they had taken the right course of action. It was the what-if scenario. 'What if he were ill again? What if the Germans attacked the boat? What if . . .?' In retrospect, it was certainly the right decision. Of that I have no doubt whatsoever, because, with all that would subsequently befall us, my brother would not have survived the war. Nevertheless, this must have been one of the hardest choices my parents had to make in sending their child away, in an endeavour to keep him safe from harm, but it would haunt them for many years as they continually agonised as to whether they had been right or not.

On this very same day, France signed an armistice with Nazi Germany, which in effect divided the country into two independent zones. During this part of the conflict, 390,000 of its sons fell defending France, whereas German losses were placed at only 35,000. The following morning, Hitler visited Paris for only three hours, and, by 9 a.m., the tour was over. Hitler said at the time: 'It was the dream of my life to be permitted to see Paris. I cannot say how happy I am to have that dream fulfilled today.' Then he left abruptly, never to visit the city again.

While parents and family still fretted over the safety of their loved ones in England, more devious German military minds were already hard at work, conjuring up even more diabolical terrors to be inflicted on the unarmed population of the Channel Islands. Once his forces reached the French coast in double-quick time, Hitler had personally instructed his army to begin planning for a frontal assault on the Channel Islands. The codeword used for this incursion was to be '*Grüne Pfeil*', or 'Operation Green Arrow'. It was to involve two battalions of troops from the German 216 Infantry Division with attendant fighter aircraft and naval forces. The initial assault was to be preceded by a heavy naval bombardment and Stuka (from *Sturzkampfflugzeug*, 'dive bomber') fighter aircraft, because reconnaissance flights had already mistakenly identified the long lines of what appeared to be military convoys and troop carriers, clustered around the main harbours. In reality, these perceived military convoys were only civilian lorries full of potatoes and tomatoes still being exported to markets in England.

Friday, 28 June 1940 on Guernsey had started as any other day, but was to finish as no other day in its history. People went about their normal activities, if living in those days could ever be called normal. The mail-boat and cargo-boats continued to ply their trade and long lines of lorries full to the brim with tomatoes were quietly discharging their precious loads onto the quaysides ready for export, and it had been only eight days since all the schoolchildren had been evacuated from the very same quaysides to England. By late afternoon on this day, my father had cycled into the capital of St Peter Port on business, and to see what progress was being made on some building work being carried out by his company in the dock area, where he would also hand out the week's wages to the building team.

After completing his business, he exchanged pleasantries, discussed the deteriorating international situation with friends and acquaintances, and then set off for home, cycling past the weighbridge, then along the inner harbourfront and finally continuing up the steep incline of Les Val de Terres, and on towards St Martin and home. Finding the hill outside of the town a little too steep, he walked a good bit of the way, taking time to appreciate the wonderful views across the calm blue sea to the nearest outer islands of Herm and Jethou, with Sark in the distance. Halfway along the Fort Road, he heard the sound of approaching aircraft followed by the screaming of engines at full throttle and then the rapid thudding of machine-gun fire and resonant explosions. The time was 6.45 p.m. He hurried home, pedalling as fast as he could, with planes swarming overhead, so low he could see the clear German insignias on the wings, as the Stukas turned and wheeled. Rushing through the front door of our house, Dallington, he eventually found my mother, my Aunt

Maud and me all huddled together under the stairs in the dark, shaking and absolutely terrified.

The raid itself lasted a mere fifty minutes, and in that brief span of time thirty-one men, women and children were unjustifiably and wilfully murdered by German forces and a further forty-seven severely injured. Six German aircraft took part in this assault and many of the lorry drivers at the harbour were killed or wounded. The shrieks of the dying blended with the screams of the diving fighter engines at full power, and many civilians who desperately sought shelter by crawling underneath the lorries were burned to death as petrol tanks exploded and salvoes of bombs rained down, causing further death and destruction. It was also a day of raw courage, as members of the emergency services rushed to the scene of the disaster only to come under heavy fire themselves. An ambulance clearly marked as such and carrying some of the terribly injured was machine-gunned and the driver, Private W.A. Nicolle, was severely wounded.

The Guernsey lifeboat proudly displaying its livery was also strafed at low altitude and the son of its coxswain killed outright. Houses, shops, hotels and guesthouses all along the seafront of St Peter Port were machine-gunned and a few bombs fell on some of Guernsey's outlying country districts. Apart from the mail steamer, SS *Isle of Sark*, there were two other ships in the harbour armed with light machine-guns, and they all tried to divert the attacking aircraft, and through this action were in some part able to lessen the full impact of the offensive. Captain Hervy H. Golding, captain of the *Isle of Sark*, was later to be awarded the OBE for his actions during this attack, and for his calmness under fire. However, I do wonder why the courageous actions of others who came to help and who went into this maelstrom to assist the wounded and the dying on that day were not officially recognised for their outstanding acts of bravery.

It is an undoubted fact that this atrocity was part of the German *modus operandi* to instil a deep and lingering fear in the minds of the Islanders in advance of their anticipated military landing. The first order, issued some time later by the newly appointed German commandant, stated: 'Should anyone attempt to cause the least trouble, serious measures will be taken and the town will be bombed.'

On Saturday, 29 June 1940, my mother visited Great-Aunt Rachel and the nearby butcher's shop in St Martin, and on her way back the wailing air-raid siren sounded again, so she ran pell-mell for home from the Old Post situated at the top of the Rue Maze and the Grande Rue, and there she lay with the baby (me) trembling on the sitting room floor for most of the remaining day.

The following day, as the German army was preparing to launch the planned land assault on the island, a reconnaissance pilot from the Luftwaffe overflew Guernsey Airport, and, not seeing any activity, decided to land, only to find the airfield completely deserted. So this was the real start of the invasion. While all that was taking place, my parents were sitting down to lunch in Dallington. My mother states in her diary:

> The Germans had only landed at the airport that
> evening and in looking out of the sitting room

window I saw a German army motorcyclist, with tin helmet and a rifle slung across his back, stop outside our front gate, look in towards the house, then he turned his motorcycle around and went back towards the aerodrome.

She then wrote in her diary: 'Oh Boy did I have a fright!' with each of those seven words heavily underlined. A real fright it must have been, because she never again underlined any other words in her diary.

By the next day the Germans were totally entrenched in the island. Their orders went out to all islanders that they should go about their normal duties and they would be treated properly if they behaved themselves. The German ultimatum for the surrender of the Channel Islands had contained the promise, 'In case of a peaceful surrender the lives, property and liberty of peaceful inhabitants are solemnly guaranteed.' The German authorities signed this undertaking. *Feldkommandantur* (or Field Commander) Friedrich Knackfuss, commanding officer of all German forces in the Channel Islands, was always overly concerned about his honour and self-esteem and realised it was his duty to act within the real meaning of the promulgation. This was to cause him untold worry and the effects of this would haunt him for many years to come.

Over the course of the next few days, heavy Junkers Ju 52 aircraft transported large numbers of German Army and Navy personnel into Guernsey. These were three-engined aircraft known colloquially by the German armed forces as 'Iron Annies'. They were really ugly transporters with a characteristic corrugated 'duralumin' metal skin, usually painted black with the swastika and the German cross edged in white. Our home in Dallington appeared to be on the general flight path and, when these low-flying planes flew over the house, the vibration from the droning engines caused severe shaking throughout the whole building. Doors and windows shook violently, crockery rattled, and even a vase fell off the mantelpiece. Throughout one day and evening alone, my mother counted more than 150 sorties, amounting to a virtually nonstop performance by the Luftwaffe. It may well have been a frightening experience but there was also the sense of the bizarre about it, because, on the very first day of occupation, my mother went out with me in the pram to visit old Mrs Fallaize, who was rather 'poorly', and then, accompanied by my Aunt Gladys, she went to see my Aunt Bet and help her thin the grapevines. Finally, later in the evening, my mother was safely back at home and busily making jam.

Gradually, the German occupying forces introduced more draconian laws. Listening to the BBC was a serious offence. Nazi law was now paramount and stringent race laws were structured and especially designed to persecute the Jews. In the Channel Islands some seventeen Jews were soon traced and sent to their deaths in German concentration camps. A curfew was imposed between 11 p.m. and 6 a.m. and a strict nightly blackout was instigated. The use and sale of alcohol was prohibited, and even owning a pigeon was an offence punishable by death. Very quickly it became a hostile occupation with vehicles being requisitioned, and the islanders were soon given a stark choice: either they had to use their bicycles to get about or they would have to walk everywhere. Clocks were changed in line with Central European Time, and gradually place names were changed. The German language became mandatory in schools and the British national anthem couldn't be played or sung without prior permission, rarely given.

Within a short space of time the cliffs and beaches so loved by islanders and tourists alike were screened off with minefields interlaced with barbed wire and roll bombs suspended by threads of wire, so anyone trying to climb up the cliffs would soon have live shells falling down on them. Walking along the scenic cliff pathways was forbidden, and the shops in St Peter Port were soon ruined and their precious stocks purchased by the invading troops with worthless German marks; the invaders immediately sent the goods home to Germany. In the meantime, the new German commandant took over the residency of the absentee lieutenant governor, where previous royal events had been celebrated and specially invited islanders entertained at glorious summer garden parties.

By early July 1940 my grandfather's health was fading fast and, although he hated the idea of his beautiful island being overrun by the 'Krauts', he was grateful he had lived long enough to see the emergence of the next family generation. Even though he was now extremely weak, he would still slide his feet out from under the bedsheets so I could play with 'gan–gan's toe-toes'. On Thursday, 11 July, the family had their last dinner together at Grandfather's house and then stayed with him all through the night. Later in the evening he spoke with my mother and told her he had no worries and there was nothing on his mind and he was now ready to go and join his Maker.

As my grandfather lay dying on Guernsey, Adolf Hitler issued his Directive Number 16, setting in motion his proposed invasion of England under the codename of 'Operation Sea Lion' ('*Unternehmen Seelöwe*'). Hitler stipulated several prerequisites for the invasion, and top of the agenda was the elimination of the British Royal Air Force, followed next by the total destruction of the Royal Navy. It then teemed with rain for several days, accompanied by thunder and lightning, and to many this must have seemed like nature's bugle call, sounding the alarm for the start of the Battle of Britain.

On the very same day, over in Portsmouth, Grandma Matthews and her sister Emily sat in their small back garden at 2 St Swithin's Road. The house was a brick end-of-terrace cottage and the latest innovation had been the recent installation of an Anderson air-raid shelter. The shelter was of a regulation design supplied by the Government free of charge to the poor and at a cost of £7 for anyone else. Grandma, though, had insisted on paying her full share as part of a contribution towards the war effort. The shelter used both straight and curved galvanised corrugated sheets, all bolted together. The shelter was six foot high, four foot six inches wide and six foot six inches long, and was buried some four feet into the ground; then fifteen feet of soil was placed on top for further protection. On 11 July 1940, the two old ladies had taken tea in their garden just after lunch, and were enjoying the warmth of the afternoon sunshine when the air-raid sirens sounded for the first time.

German aircraft appeared over Portsmouth, intent on a surprise raid, and dropped a line of twenty to thirty bombs on the city centre, killing eight civilians and wounding a further sixty. Simultaneously, as an opening gambit in the Battle of Britain, the Luftwaffe, under the command and direction of the unique Reichsmarschall Hermann Göring, launched the first ferocious attack against shipping in the English Channel and then followed this up by bombing RAF aerodromes in southern England, in an attempt to completely annihilate the Royal Air Force. However, one good thing came out of this otherwise disastrous day, which was that British radar had worked properly and had proved to be really effective.

My grandfather died, quietly and peacefully on 18 July, and on the 22nd, which was also my brother's birthday, the whole family went to the afternoon funeral service at Les Camps Methodist Chapel, and then followed the cortège to the cemetery near Saints Road, St Martin. My mother wrote in her diary that she found the days following the funeral very trying but at least normal, until Friday, 9 August, when a bomb dropped and exploded nearby during the family dinner, doing very little damage. However, then a real air-raid conducted by the RAF developed at about 7.30 p.m. at the aerodrome, causing quite a lot of damage. A Mr Brockway and several other people came to the house as they were passing by, so they too could take shelter under our stairs, well out of the way of flying shrapnel.

One thing I find really surprising about these turbulent and dangerous times is the implied criticisms levelled by many local residents at the British government of the day, accusing it of neglect, betrayal, isolation and exposing islanders to mortal danger. No one appears to have realised or taken into account the fact that Britain was staring at a massive national defeat and virtual annihilation, and was in the very midst of endeavouring to retrieve the defeated armies of British and French troops from the beaches of Dunkirk. During this time, from 25 May until 5 June, hundreds of thousands of soldiers, many of them wounded, had been rescued by the Royal Navy and those flotillas of small private ships while under heavy enemy fire. Putting matters into perspective, how could a resident population of fewer than twenty thousand people, however deserving, realistically expect to take precedence over a whole nation?

Island roads were soon blocked by convoys of German heavy lorries filled to overflowing with armaments and materials for building large-scale fortifications. Tanks, cars and motorcycles moved along at high speed, knocking down walls and gateposts and sometimes even cutting through hedges and gardens. Civilian cyclists or pedestrians were given scant consideration and several people were knocked down and injured. Regiments of German soldiers and swathes of European slave-workers belonging to the Organisation Todt (the Reich's engineering group) started to arrive, and soon the neat cobbled streets of St Peter Port were littered with rotting rubbish and thronged with starving and downtrodden foreign labourers from many East European nations.

Most of my father's building yard had been stripped of plant and equipment, with all of the cement-mixers and handcarts being commandeered by the Germans. The only transportation left for the civilian population was their bicycles, and these soon became known as man's best friend. The local newspapers were strictly censored and were mainly full of German war news so exaggerated and biased they became a feature of ridicule when compared with the news being received illicitly from the BBC in London. Local libraries started to significantly increase their lists of members and there was a growing demand for self-sufficiency books on horticulture and rabbit- and goat-keeping. However, the German forces seized and destroyed a number of British books of a more political nature, including several written by Winston Churchill.

In September 1940, there was great excitement in the islands when overflights by the RAF dropped leaflets during the night. The first drop contained the following message from the King: 'The Queen and I desire to convey to you our heartfelt sympathy in the trials which you are now enduring. We earnestly pray for your speedy liberation, knowing that it will surely come.' There followed several extracts from Winston Churchill's speeches as well as a photograph of the King and Queen inspecting the damage done to Buckingham Palace by German bombers. The leaflet then continued: 'We shall continue to bring you news from England as often and as regularly as we can.'

As soon as dawn broke, German soldiers were out and about scouring the countryside in search of the leaflets, and of course the next day's newspapers contained the following notice:

> The attention of the public is drawn to the fact that leaflets which were dropped on this island by a British plane on the night of the 23rd–24th September 1940, come within the definition of 'enemy propaganda material' as contained in the German proclamation dated 29th July 1940.
>
> It is therefore an offence to hand on such leaflets or to communicate their contents to others and it is the duty of persons in possession of such leaflets to deliver them to the Feldkommandantur, Grange Lodge Hotel.

The end result was most of the islanders fortunate enough to have found or retrieved a leaflet felt truly delighted, and soon the jungle telegraph moved swiftly into overdrive and these precious documents were surreptitiously passed around to other eager hands throughout the island. (Days later, there was a more sinister activity taking place in Berlin, when Germany, Italy and Japan signed a tripartite pact, giving birth to the Axis powers.)

Even though most of the population were at times downhearted, they often went out of their way to tease the occupation forces whenever they could. Years later, one of my father's oft-repeated stories told how Hitler had a great liking for Bavarian and Irish folk music and he would often sit in his residence in the Berghof near Berchtesgaden, high in the Bavarian Alps, listening to local musicians. Hitler had made it a prerequisite that such music and education should be heavily promoted in the ranks of the Hitler Youth movement, and in this he was supported by many dedicated Nazis. So it was no surprise when quite a few German musical groups were established on the island, and some of them played regularly on their evenings off for their comrades and patrons in various Guernsey hostelries.

There was a humorous story, widely circulated throughout the island, to the effect that one group of German soldiers who enjoyed playing their traditional Bavarian folk music in a local pub enlisted the help of one of the pub's more frequent customers, who was a noted musician. They had enquired if he knew any special English folk songs they could play and, if so, could he kindly teach them? After many days of intensive tuition the German group finally, and proudly, managed to produce a very fair rendering of 'God Save the King'; however, this part of their repertoire didn't last very long.

## CHAPTER 3

# LIVING WITH
# THE DEVIL

At an early point in December 1940, an isolated and single act of sabotage was carried out by a number of local Guernseymen, who cut through the German military communication cables running from the airport in the Forest parish to the German communication centres in the capital of St Peter Port. As far as I remember the story, often repeated for my benefit by my mother, the attack was perpetrated near Les Caches corner in St Martin, very near our own home, and, as a direct result, all the men of St Martin's parish, starting with my father as the elected constable, were forced to take turns in standing on guard for a period of nearly three weeks. The guardroom was situated near the airport and, as a further reprisal, all radio sets were immediately confiscated by the Germans; fortunately, these were returned to their rightful owners just before Christmas Day, although not for long.

On one particularly dark night, the German guards gave

my father and another member of the parish community a specific stretch of the communication lines to be patrolled, along the very sector that had previously been sabotaged. The orders were for them to start at opposite ends of their designated boundary with the notion they should cross over at the midway point and then continue to the end of their respective beats. The German guards told them quite unequivocally that, if the line was cut or even damaged in any way within their boundary, it would be regarded as a capital offence and an insult to both the Führer and the Third Reich, and they would be shot forthwith.

Part of the difficulty in this operation was that the communication lines crossed over hedges and ran alongside fields. After stumbling along in the dark for quite some time, my father realised he should have already met his compatriot coming the other way, and he could only fervently hope his fellow countryman hadn't deserted his post or, even worse, cut the cable and run away. At the end of the line, after my father arrived, the Germans gave a marvellous display of total panic and consternation when they realised one of their captives had gone AWOL. My father was then forced to retrace his footsteps accompanied by shouting armed guards until they eventually found that the poor man had fallen down a German slit trench in the dark and broken his leg!

During the occupation organised resistance was all but impossible, especially for an ageing population, for within a short space of time there was almost one German soldier for every two islanders. Guernsey is condensed into an area of only thirty-one square miles and surrounded by sea, and we had German troops living cheek-by-jowl with the local residents. My mother often wrote that our family couldn't sleep properly because of the noises made by German soldiers 'running around next door all night'. Resistance was for the most part passive in nature and relegated to painting out road signs and drawing V-for-victory signs on the walls of houses occupied by German officers.

However, by all accounts, Christmas 1940 was quite a happy occasion in spite of being the first festivity to be held under strict German domination. It seems everyone in the extended Rabey clan had decided to completely ignore the presence of the 'Hun' over the holiday period. Aunt Harriet Rabey had kindly donated a half-tin of precious icing sugar so my mother could bake a very small Christmas cake for me and she had also been able to store some fruit preserves to make several miniature Christmas puddings. A lovely lady, a Mrs Luscombe from St Martin, had especially given the family two plump chickens, as a token of her family's appreciation for my father's many kindnesses in extremely difficult circumstances. So friends and cousins came for lunch, bringing with them whatever produce they had been able to save. According to the family records the guests included Auntie Nance, Hilda, Doris and Uncle George, and 'everyone had a nice quiet time really'.

On Boxing Day, everyone once again decamped to Auntie Glad and Uncle Alf (Gladys and Alfred Rabey), who lived two doors down from Dallington – with some German soldiers billeted in between in the middle house. In the afternoon everyone played cards and charades and quite forgot the time until someone realised it was well past the curfew time. There was nothing for it but for my mother and me to stay with Uncle Alf and Auntie Gladys for the night, while everyone else had to creep back to Dallington commando-style. They crawled across the lawns and pathways past the German quarters in the dark, hardly breathing for fear of arousing the sleeping enemy. At one point on the journey, and with the moon gently rising in the sky, my father, seeing how ridiculous they all looked, started to giggle, then Auntie Nance followed suit and soon everyone was giggling, shushing and chortling. My father always said it was a miracle they didn't wake up the whole parish or end up turning out the German guards with all the noise they were making.

It was New Year's Eve, and, once again, the whole 'gang', as they were now called, turned up at home for supper. The evening was billed as a very special meal of fresh eggs and chips and ended up with everyone 'just dancing around and listening to the music from the gramophone records'. At the end of the evening my father and my Uncle George duly escorted all the ladies back to their respective homes and they just managed to return to Dallington before the later-than-usual curfew began at 3 a.m. This, then, was an evening 'never to be forgotten'.

Although they probably didn't realise it at the time, they had in reality formed a mutual support group. Auntie Nance's son and daughter were already in the United Kingdom and Uncle George had to face the occupation alone without his wife (Aunt Leila) and their son Malcolm, who were now living in England. Uncle Alf's and Aunt Gladys's two sons,

Colin and Brian, were with my brother and the rest of their school companions in Oldham. So the gang were held together by strong bonds of kinship and friendship born of deep suffering and worry.

New Year's Day dawned, a trifle early for some, and the time was spent with Great-Uncle John and Great-Aunt Rachel. Everyone played cards and prizes were awarded to the winners. Everyone had hot roasted chestnuts. The main topic of discussion was making New Year resolutions for 1941, and pondering what the coming year would hold in store for all of them.

In the early spring, my father managed to buy eighteen one-day-old chickens and five fowls. He built the chicken runs and fowl house from old scraps of wood and my mother wrote, 'It was really grand fetching the eggs – while it lasted – but it did mean a lot of very hard work.' The gang used to spend their days going out with the pram – with me happily ensconced within – gathering sacks of wood from various places in the parish, where trees had been specifically felled. As my mother said, 'All the island men employed in this work were always very kind and understanding and usually helped to fill the sacks.' Later, the gang would all go *en masse* to the British Legion Hall by the Old Post, and collect their ration of potatoes from the main food depot there.

At harvest time, everyone spent many hours gleaning, which in itself was very rewarding but uncommonly tiring. After gleaning, it was then necessary to carry out the threshing, which my mother found to be an eminently comical sight.

She had found the best way to proceed was for my father and her

> . . . to sit on low stools in the kitchen, with our trepid [a Guernsey French word for a pot on short legs] going and surrounded by tin baths and a sieve to rub it through. For several nights after that, the girls and George came to help and it was all great fun. Then we had to wait for a windy day to do the winnowing and after that, we all had a great time picking out the knobbly bits – and that alone lasted three more nights!

Later the next day whilst out and about in the parish, my mother met two friends, an Elsie Brockway and another acquaintance called Jean (Petruske), who were making their way to the local hospital to see a wonderful and gentle cousin of ours called Hilda. She wrote at the time:

> It was so distressing to meet Elsie Brockway and Jean going to the hospital to see Hilda who was there for a rest and had suddenly become very ill. I hurried after them, but Hilda was passed {sic} all help and soon passed away early on the Wednesday morning. Jean and I fetched Elsie from the hospital and she spent the whole day with us. On the Saturday we all went to her funeral which was very sweet and lovely and we have missed her ever so. She did very useful work, helping Mrs Burlingham prepare potatoes for

the evening meal at the soup kitchen and I too spent many evenings serving the evening soup.

It was a capital offence to listen to the BBC and, with radios being confiscated, then returned and then finally confiscated once more, my father decided it was time to build his own one-valve set into the water cistern of an outside toilet. The set was carefully assembled and the cistern emptied. The power came from the ceiling light fitting and the cable was attached to the socket and later removed as required. Noise levels were isolated by using only a single headphone and, again, this was shielded within the cistern at the end of the drill. Piece by piece, the unit was carefully installed until my father could spend many happy hours sitting in splendid isolation, with his single headphone clasped over one ear, while he listened to the BBC, and with the door securely locked. At the end of each period the accoutrements were then safely stored away in the cistern and he was careful to relock the door when he left, although everyone in the family knew exactly where the key had been hidden.

It wasn't long before stocks of various trade goods started to run out on Guernsey, and even postage stamps became a rather scarce commodity. As these precious stocks diminished, the postal authorities had an inspired brainwave, leading them to cut the stamps in two from corner to corner, thus making two triangles and thereby doubling their existing stocks. During the forthcoming weeks, my father's prizewinning garden gradually changed dramatically from being a picture of vibrant-coloured flowers to a more mundane but essential vegetable plot. My father would sometimes work in the garden in the early evenings, often hindered by me, but greatly assisted by Great-Uncle John Rabey, an elder brother of my grandfather and one of the founders of the building company. Even then Great-Uncle John must have been well into his seventies but he was fit and wiry with snowy-white hair and flowing beard. Surely this is what a latter-day Moses would have looked like, because no one was more religious in outlook and belief.

However, about this time, my mother had taken an afternoon off to go 'wooding', or, more likely, to engage in pillaging the locality, as my father was wont to say. I had been left in his care, and, probably because I slowed him down somewhat, we arrived back home a little late. Great-Uncle John was already waiting for us and had made a good start, but how good a start we soon found out. The first thing he said to my father, albeit in a jocular fashion, was, 'Cecil, you call yourself a builder when even your own plumbing doesn't work? Anyway, not to worry: I've fixed it and it's all going perfectly well now!'

My father never said anything either then or afterwards, but the radio was already floating in the cistern and was far beyond repair, and so illicit BBC reception was finally abandoned for the duration. Probably this was a good thing in the long run, because our home security was extremely lax, as witnessed by my mother's diary entry: 'But the news today was so grand, none of us could concentrate. Mr Eden announced in the House of Commons, that the second front has been agreed.' If ever found by the Gestapo this item alone would have been sufficient evidence for a signed death warrant.

On 22 June 1941, my father had needed some relaxation and a chance to escape from his onerous parochial duties, so he had started playing bowls again. My mother went off to her singing lessons and thought she was getting on really well. Uncle Reg spent the whole afternoon queuing at the Gaumont Cinema in St Julian's Avenue for tickets for a film called *Captains Courageous*, while, far away on another continent on this day, Hitler authorised the commencement of 'Operation Barbarossa', whereby 4.5 million Axis troops launched a brutal invasion against the Soviet Union.

In the autumn of 1941, Britain decided to intern those German agents and citizens who were deemed to be working against British interests in modern-day Iran. Sitting in his eyrie at Berchtesgaden, in Bavaria, Hitler was personally incensed at this act, and instantly directed his Foreign Office to contemplate effecting reprisals, as a matter of some urgency. The German Foreign Office, with usual Teutonic efficiency, soon realised the country held a captive audience in its recently acquired Channel Islands and, more importantly, the islands contained a large group of British nationals. In the meantime, Hitler had decided to teach the British a serious lesson and personally specified he would take ten hostages for every one German interned by the British.

In the middle of September 1941, the Bailiffs of both Jersey and Guernsey were required to furnish Berlin with a list of all British-born males aged over fifteen. This directive was amended shortly afterwards to include all males born in Britain between the ages of fifteen and fifty-six and a further list detailing those aged fifty-six to sixty-eight.

It soon became apparent that the potential number of prisoners available would not be sufficient to meet the Führer's mandate, so, on 22 October 1941, the *Feldkommandantur* demanded the lists should be revised without delay to include dependent women and children. However, at this point great confusion existed between the German Foreign Ministry and the country's armed forces, the Wehrmacht, which in particular didn't want to see women and children held in operational areas of war. The overall effect of all this confusion was to afford the Channel Islands a very brief reprieve.

In October 1941, Hitler personally ordered the Channel Islands to be turned into impregnable fortresses as part of the giant Atlantic Wall fortifications stretching from Norway to Spain. Festung Guernsey was to be one of only twelve European fortresses, which Hitler expected to be defended to the death. Most bunkers and fortifications on Guernsey were to be of fortress standard, meaning their walls of ferroconcrete would be at least two metres thick, and the bunker systems would be specially designed to be mutually supporting. It was Hitler's stated intention that, once the war was over, England would never be allowed to take back the Channel Islands.

According to my mother, not a great deal happened on Guernsey in early December 1941, and life continued in some dreary form or other, as usual. However, on the other side of the world it was a totally different matter, as a drama was taking place that would set in motion a tide of events that would change all of our lives for ever. On 7 December 1941, the Japanese armed forces launched a surprise attack on the US naval base at Pearl Harbor. The United States then entered the war as Allied countries declared war on Japan.

Over the course of the next few years, the Channel Islands were to be transformed through an extensive complex of defences quite out of proportion to their strategic importance on the world stage. Thousands upon thousands of foreign slave-labourers, mainly from East European countries, were brought in to build these heavy bulwarks, and many died in horrific circumstances as a result of brutal treatment, planned starvation and overwork. Over on the nearby island of Alderney, most of the islanders had been evacuated, allowing the Nazis to build four evil concentration camps, mainly to house hordes of Jews and foreign slave-labourers who were forced to build the massive concrete defences throughout the island. The main camp, known as Lager Sylt, was a true place of horror where prisoners of war trying to escape were crucified on the camp gates. Half of the prisoners brought to Alderney by the Nazis died there after being mercilessly beaten and otherwise mistreated.

Around this time I had been given a tricycle that had originally belonged to my brother, and, although it may not have been new, as far as I was concerned this unlocked a door to a great new and exciting world, and one I was keen to explore, even if I didn't know what the words actually meant. The family have often told me I tended to view life outside our green garden gate as part of an exhilarating universe.

Apparently, I decided to go and see for myself, and so, one afternoon, just after lunch when my father had gone back to work and my mother had decided to have a short rest, I was told to stay and play in the garden, and, just to make sure, my mother shut the old garden gate and then bolted it.

Undaunted, and dressed in my blue-and-white sailor's outfit, I must have taken my trike through a narrow gap in the hedge that divided us from my step-grandmother, onto her pathway and thence to her front gates. With little traffic over the lunchtime period I had no difficulty crossing the road onto the pavement opposite and so merrily set off on my next adventure. According to my mother, I must have soon pedalled past La Quinta Hotel, by now a local German military HQ, trundled up the road and passed my father's building yard and offices, then the numerous houses owned by members of the Rabey clan. Probably because my head didn't stick up over the garden walls, my progress was unnoticed and unimpeded. My mother always said that, having reached the Old Post and turned right onto the Grande Rue pavement, I must have been pedalling quite fast. On the main road military trucks were continually passing by with vehicles containing German soldiers, staff cars and lorries with all the materials of war on board. However, no one seemed to give me even a backward glance. I then rode by Aunt Ethel Langlois at Rosemount, a lovely granite house with a Victorian conservatory holding her precious grapevines. All in all, I was having the time of my life.

As the story goes, the dream started to fade when a Mrs Watson, still wearing her pinny, came running along the pavement and finally stopped my progress. She had seen me go by on the tricycle and had telephoned my mother, who was absolutely sick with worry. So we trundled back to the neat row of cottages and stood by her front gate to wait for my mother. To be fair, Mrs Watson did go inside her cottage and soon returned with a piece of lovely fruitcake and a glass of lemonade for me. Minutes later, Dad arrived on his cycle and, seeing me with the cake and lemonade, just said, 'Well, you've certainly had a good afternoon! Now, let's go back for tea as Mum's waiting for us.' No more was ever said about the incident.

The last escapade I was involved in with my tricycle included various elements of the occupation forces, who were holding a military parade of sorts in the field alongside our building works. It was probably the playing of the small military band that first attracted my attention, so I set off on my trusty trike, and gradually meandered through the building yard until I reached the parade. The parade was already formed up in the field, but, undeterred, I was so completely mesmerised by the large shining chrome headlights of the highly polished black German staff car that I totally ignored the group of important uniformed staff officers standing around it.

According to family folklore, one of the officers, seeing me and probably in an attempt to ingratiate himself with some of the local inhabitants who were also watching the parade, picked me up and carried me over to the car for a better look – and, more than that, he gave me a lovely sweet as well. That was all right as far as I was concerned, but within seconds a whirlwind of fury erupted around us as my mother suddenly appeared jostling and heaving her way through the bemedalled ranks until she reached us. Then, snatching me from the arms of the officer, she retreated in some haste and I was left in no doubt that 'these people were really bad and horrible'. To make matters much worse, my tricycle was locked away for a good length of time and I was grounded.

New Year's Day 1942 dawned but it started rather badly, as my parents' gas ration had run out. So the gang, who had contributed as generously as they could to the proceedings, put all the food in the pram with me and wheeled it around to Uncle George de Garis (one of the gang), who lived some little way away on the Grande Rue. There they proceeded to cook the victuals and have quite a party in the process. Apparently, it was rather a hilarious time, compounded by my father, who spilled all the fat from the oven down the front of his clothes. Then, putting the food in tins and bowls and wrapping it all up in newspapers to keep it warm, they all set off again back home. Auntie Nance took charge of the cabbage, Uncle George was looking after the pudding, while everything else was piled all around me in the pram. At home, Auntie Doris had everything ready, so the meal went ahead as originally planned, albeit with a slight delay.

After the meal they all sat around drinking coffee – well, not quite. What they were drinking was the result of roasted and ground acorns percolated to form a hot drink, which required vast imagination to convince anyone it could really be called coffee. Later in the afternoon the party left together to visit Great-Uncle John and Great-Aunt Rachel for afternoon tea.

My mother's diary for 1942 continually mentions foraging parties, accompanied by friends and relations and their being absorbed with such euphemistic words as 'gleaning', 'wooding' and 'sticking' throughout the length and breadth of the parish (once the owners had granted permission, of course). The foraging parties soon came to mean something totally different to me. I had a lovely black Pedigree baby carriage, newly bought for my arrival in far happier times. This had quite a spacious interior but, more importantly, it also had a commodious hold, designed originally to contain soiled nappies and baby accoutrements, and it had a hidden, secret, fitted cover.

The image created for the world, including the inquisitive German military, was one of a young mother parading her baby son, dressed in all his finery, to be greeted by his adoring family and friends throughout the parish. In truth my mother used the pram as her main means of transport and, luckily for her, it was well-sprung. With it she was able to transport and move large quantities of produce and wood, in fact anything of use that had suddenly become available on these regular jaunts. My father would say in later years I had inevitably developed a funny walk, through enduring endless hours spent sitting on mounds of knobbly potatoes and piles of hard Brussels sprouts.

On 26 March 1942, the gang descended 'as one' on Auntie

Nance to play a few energetic rounds of table tennis, and, as my mother wrote,

> The hilarious evening 'wound up' with a large air-raid but fortunately we all got back home to our respective houses just before the curfew expired. Since then we have learnt that the planes were going over to bomb the Germans in France.

On the very same day as the gang enjoyed their time together, a small flotilla of boats, led by an obsolete destroyer called HMS *Cambletown*, left Falmouth Harbour in England for the coast of France. A few days later, on 28 March, Royal Navy and Army commandos mounted a major seaborne attack on the dock gates of St Nazaire in France. They rammed the *Cambletown*, loaded with high explosives, into the dock gates and the commandos then destroyed much of the dock area, making it unusable until well after the war. During this raid no fewer than five Victoria Crosses were earned by British forces. Back on Guernsey on this particular Saturday, my mother had gone into St Peter Port to collect the family rations. She visited the family grocer's, called in at Luff's for her bread and then had to queue for buttermilk. Meanwhile, my father remained at home and worked hard in the garden.

My father's birthday was on 20 April, and it was also that of Adolf Hitler, Der Führer, who had been born in 1899 and had served with some distinction in the German armed forces during World War One, being invested with the

Iron Cross First Class for actions under fire. He was to die eventually in the Führerbunker in Berlin, by his own hand, on 30 April 1945. Hitler's birthday was a major celebration in Germany from 1933 until 1945 and the day was declared a national holiday. Joseph Goebbels, the sycophantic Minister of Propaganda, stated that, although the German people were on holiday, their 'beloved leader' was working as usual. Proving the point, Hitler was photographed attending the first demonstration of the awesome Tiger tank, whose main claim to fame was the power of its guns and the extra layers of armour protection. Assembly lines had been set at Kassel ready to commence production and, although there would be teething troubles in manufacture, by November 1942 some forty-two Tiger tanks had been completed for service.

On Guernsey, and with very little food left, my mother had decided to lay on a special birthday spread for my father, with the *pièce de résistance* being a boiled vegetable pudding! This was followed by a very small fish salad with an egg and an even smaller birthday cake, all saved from their meagre food rations. As she said in her writings, 'This was all such a very great treat.'

One week later, 27 April, was a remarkable day in many ways. The *Guernsey Evening Press* was the local newspaper avidly read by islanders, who by tradition usually turned to the births, marriages and deaths columns first, before moving on to island news. Since the occupation the, press had been subjugated by Goebbels's propaganda machine and was forced to carry heroic stories of German victories in Europe.

# THE DAY THE NAZIS CAME

On this day the newspaper carried banner headlines and this story:

HERR HITLER ASSUMES SUPREME COMMAND

HERALDS THE FINAL BLOWS IN BRITAIN'S DOWNFALL

THE FÜHRER SPEAKS

'Britain can win nothing in this war, she will lose and this fact will be recorded in history. The destiny of peoples and states should be entrusted neither to cynical drunkards nor to the feeble minded; in this conflict Germany will be victorious.'

With these words the Führer yesterday concluded an historic declaration to the German Reichstag which, on returning from the Eastern Front, he summoned to a special meeting.

At this time my mother's thoughts, normally so positive and bright, took a sharp tumble into the realms of despair. She wrote:

We had a good dinner for these times and then spent all morning and afternoon in the kitchen for warmth, with rugs wrapped around us. Our tea was three slices of bread and some cheese and two cups of tea. Our rations are very low now and we are all feeling the pinch, with the scarcity of food and four weeks without sugar.

That was the last entry for nearly four weeks, when she appeared to be back to her old cheerful self again.

One mid-afternoon towards the end of May 1942, a German army field car pulled up at the front gate of the house and two rather imposing and immaculately uniformed German officers alighted and marched up to our front door. My father received them in the front room and it was very clear from their attitude they were far from happy and were fiercely demanding immediate action from him, in his capacity as constable of the parish, as he was after all the representative of the local civil administration. It transpired they were billeted in very comfortable accommodation at the top of Burnt Lane, in St Martin, which ran down to the Rue Maze, just opposite our own house. Their accommodation had been duly commandeered by the occupying forces from local residents who had been evicted and thrown out into the street, and, according to the officers, it was a very pleasant property with a small but delightful wooden fence in the front garden.

They informed my father that, when they had left for duty in the morning, all was well. However, when they returned for their lunch, they found part of the wooden fence was missing. After their lunch they duly reported the matter to the Feldgendarmerie, but afterwards, when they returned to the property a little later, they found to their astonishment and annoyance that the remainder of the fence had also been stolen. They eventually left my father with much wagging of fingers and stamping of feet and made it obvious to him that they expected him to locate the miscreants forthwith, who in their opinion must be islanders and must therefore be found and severely punished.

My father immediately realised the seriousness of the situation and put on his hat and coat with the intention of going back to the Parish Hall straight away to start work on the investigation, but first he went out into the garden to tell my mother where he was going. He found her there with me in the backyard just behind the house busily sawing up what remained of the German's 'liberated' wooden fence. As she cut up the wood, it was my job to stack it neatly around the side of the garden shed. Being totally astounded by the sight, all he could say was, 'One day, Eileen, you are going to get me shot.' And one day he was nearly proved right.

Some time later, on 8 June, the day after my fourth birthday, the very same German officers returned to the house and demanded a list of names of all the persons who lived in the Rue Maze, with their addresses and full details of how many lived in each house. After weeks worrying about this sinister request, nothing further happened, and the matter was soon forgotten.

Days later, another memory – and I recognise now that most of my earliest memories were brought about through fear, noise or very vivid colours. One sunny, peaceful morning I was standing at the front gate, probably waiting for my father to come home for his lunch, when I spotted a local tinker pedalling along the road from the direction of Les Caches and the Beaulieu Hotel towards our home on the Rue Maze. He was riding a rickety sort of tricycle with a towbar fixed behind the saddle, which, in turn, held a small two-wheel affair containing his wife, albeit with only a modicum of comfort. Old pots and pans were tied down all around the tricycle and, although his name was Mr Davidson, I must have heard neighbours and schoolchildren call him by his nickname, 'Can Can'.

As the couple passed I very politely wished Mr and Mrs Can Can a very good day and was then scared out of my wits by his angry, bright-red face and a mighty bellow of rage as he brought his machine to a grinding stop. Pots and pans fell off his tricycle onto the road with a terrible clang and, not waiting for anything else to happen, I was off up the path like a rocket and rushed around the side of the house. Here I sought the sanctuary of the rabbit hutch. I pushed our poor pet rabbit, Mr Hawkins, out into his run as I tried to make myself totally inconspicuous by lying crouched on his straw bedding.

If ever I thought of my mother as a formidable and courageous woman, she certainly proved it that day. Hearing the commotion from one of the upstairs bedrooms, she rushed down, seizing a long-handled broom in passing, and met Can Can head-on as he came around the side of the house. Wielding the broom like a martial-arts expert, she trounced him sorely about the head and shoulders, forcing him back down the pathway. Mrs Can Can, herself a formidable woman in her own right, decided on this day that discretion was very much the better part of valour, and remained cocooned in her basket chair. They both subsequently left in high dudgeon, with much swearing and commotion accompanied by the clattering of pots and pans.

Ever after, in the years that followed, when Can Can was regarded as a rather colourful and cheerful local character about town on Guernsey, I would endeavour to avoid him, although he did eventually get his revenge. Many years later and just after Can Can's death, when my father was a member of the Guernsey Rotary Club, he was asked to assist friends from the Red Cross Society to help clear out a rundown and seedy property in Pedvin Street, on the edge of the capital of St Peter Port. As I was on my school holidays I went along to help move the mountains of rubbish, stale food and dead mice. As we cleared through, we realised from some of the faded photographs displayed on the mantelpiece that this had been Can Can's last abode.

When we had finished these chores and were on our way home, we both started to itch. At home my mother met us at the door and, knowing full well where we had been, refused to let us in. She insisted we go around to the back door, where we had to strip down to our underwear. It was then we discovered we were covered in fleas, and, adding insult to injury, my mother immediately turned the garden hose on us both, dousing us from head to toe with stinging streams of icy-cold water.

I also think that, at this time during the occupation, my mother and friends adopted the disposition of either totally ignoring the presence of the German military in their midst or resorting to more dangerous methods in teasing them. The Germans may have strutted around Guernsey and declared themselves the master race and they may well even have seemed to be winning the war – for the moment. But who did they think they really were? So in the minds of my mother and friends, and as far as was possible, the Germans didn't exist, and, if by some mischance they did come into vision, then they could be made fun of – a dangerous game.

One evening after choir practice, the gang all finished up at Great-Aunt Harriet's house in the Rue Poudreuse, St Martin, where they all had a lovely game of cards and where 'real' toffees were passed around – and, oh boy, were they good! But my mother thought that best of all was 'the great fun everyone had in walking back home in the dark. It was a dreadfully foggy night and the "Jerries" kept flashing their torchlights on us from every gateway – my, how we all laughed and cheered.'

# CHAPTER 4

# THE SWORD OF DAMOCLES

The family were soon made aware from time to time that the 'Jerries' from next door would wait until darkness fell, then they would creep up and stand in the shadows just outside our front door and listen to the hilarity and frivolity going on inside. It was firmly fixed in my mother's mind that this was spying and had to be ignored and firmly discouraged at every opportunity. This meant that, whenever they saw a German phantom skulking in the darkness, the noise levels inside would be increased and ridicule would be brought down upon the head of the unfortunate in particular and the Teutonic nation in general. Sometimes they would play games such as one of Uncle George's favourites, in which he would announce in a loud voice:

'This is the BBC in London and here is the news read by George de Garis. Mr Churchill said in a speech given in the House of Commons today there had been reports from

Guernsey that members of the Third Reich have developed cauliflower ears and housemaid's knee, as a result of spending too many hours on their knees listening at Guernsey keyholes.'

Uncle George's other most vaunted trick was to approach an unsuspecting German soldier in the street and raise his arms as if in the Nazi salute. At the same time he would utter the word '*Heil*' as if in greeting and, just as the German gratefully responded, Uncle George would change his salute into a dismissive gesture and the words would be converted into 'highly unlikely'. He said it never failed to work but the secret was not to use it too often. In retrospect, I think some of the soldiers were just decent young men who didn't want to be involved in the war, and simply missed the warmth of their own homes and the loving companionship of their families.

It is easy to see during these desperate times that the Rabey family, as with most islanders, were like diamonds showing many shining facets. They may have been occupied by Teutonic bullies but they were never going to be cowed or defeated. Their traditional stubborn natures resisted subjugation while undergoing a period of passive coexistence. As the months and the years dragged on, with all the attendant food shortages and lack of those small, everyday luxuries, there was more and more of a movement towards positive thoughts and actions. Friends and family came together to help and share what little they had. The old, the infirm and the sick, whoever they might be, received care and such nourishment as was available, and they were never forgotten.

In the capital's indoor fish and vegetable markets, Mrs Lucas and the other Guernsey stallholders would converse together in the ancient Guernsey French patois, which couldn't be understood by the Germans. They would smile benignly at their German overlords while accepting their worthless money, then berate them in their patois for being the illegitimate offspring of Hitler's loins – or even worse.

We must go back in time a few months for one of the greatest days to illustrate the positive side of family involvement, 28 January 1942. This heralded the Golden Wedding anniversary of Great-Uncle John and Great-Aunt Rachel. According to her diary, early in the morning my mother, father and I went around to their house to deliver the presents. This took the form of a rose-pink bedspread to match the eiderdown given to the happy couple by their own grandchildren and some cakes made by my mother for the afternoon tea party. Already some of the Rabeys were hard at work in the kitchen 'preparing for the great afternoon's event', after which we all trudged back home for lunch. Then promptly at 5 p.m. my parents returned once more, and the whole family started to assemble. As my mother wrote:

> We arrived just on 5 o'clock, and by gum what a treat, as Uncle John had a great fire going. In waiting for tea, the Bridegroom told us lots of his reminiscences about his childhood days and then we were all called in to the next room for tea. The table looked a picture and it really was a marvellous spread.

There was beef and tongue, HP Sauce and Heinz Tomato Ketchup, hot black-current [sic] tart, trifles, fruit salad, and Guernsey biscuits. [No sell-by dates to worry about here, then!]

The Bride and Groom then entered to the strains of the wedding march amidst all the singing and clapping of hands by all of those present. With food being so very scarce I must mention all the hard work put in by all members of the family, which was really a great credit to all concerned. There was cold tinned meat, and Guernsey Gâche [a Guernsey delicacy]. Home-made cakes and plenty of bottled fruit but best of all a Grand Golden Wedding Cake including the almond paste, which was all beautifully iced by cousin Aggie. The cake had been given by Alf and Glad Rabey and Glad also made some doughnuts, just as Grandma had made for the wedding fifty years ago.

At the end of the tea, the bride made a wonderful speech, which brought back wonderful memories to all present. By God's help they had been sustained through the passing years. Uncle John also made a very lovely speech. Then Alf spoke on behalf of the family, praising his mum and dad for their loving care to them all and for all the help, which they had given. Then we all went into the drawing room and Mr Toms took our photos and the rest of the evening was spent in playing those real old games. Auntie Rache played the accordion and we all sang which was grand. Then at about 11 p.m., we had supper.

This was pancakes, which Wilson Falla had made and were quite beautiful and after another good meal we all went home after having had a most wonderful time, with the [start of] curfew being extended until midnight especially for the party. We arrived back home to find Nance and Doris sitting around the fire and we talked until the early hours of the morning, the girls being kind enough to have looked after Stephen.

Many years later, my mother told me this had been one of the highlights of those dark years, when the whole family joined together to save up those invaluable items from their jealously guarded prewar stocks and from their meagre food-ration allowances for many, many months to ensure the Golden Wedding was such a marvellous event.

On this same day, while the family celebrations were in full swing, on another continent the first 100,000 men and 50,000 women were being deported by train from Germany to the recently established network of concentration and extermination camps called Auschwitz, which had been built inside German-occupied Poland. Auschwitz had been designated by SS Reichsführer Heinrich Himmler as the focal point for the so-called 'final solution' of the Jewish question in Europe. From this time forward transport trains delivered Jews to the camps' gas chambers from all over Nazi-occupied countries. The camps' first commander, Rudolf Höss, subsequently testified at the Nuremberg trials that some 1.1 million people had died there and that 90 per cent of them had been Jews.

On Guernsey, local entertainment figured prominently in people's lives and certainly my parents and the gang went out on average once a month. Their trips to the cinemas or theatre were usually undertaken on foot and a highlight was walking back home in sufficient time to beat the curfew. It provided a means of brief escapism: as my mother wrote, they often all walked back to St Martin in the moonlight singing all the latest hit songs. The shows were varied and entertaining, and the films must have been left behind before the Germans arrived. There was a visit to the Regal Cinema to see *Variety Pie* (not a bad show, according to my mother). Then to the Lyric Theatre in St Peter Port to see *Indoor Fireworks*, although the snow made the walk difficult. Then *It Pays to Advertise* – a real success – which was soon followed by *French Without Tears*. On 25 June 1942, the gang had a 'marvellous' and very special tea at home, which consisted of fried eggs, and then they all went off to the Gaumont Cinema again to see *Captains Courageous*. On 4 July there was a rendering of *Hiawatha*, but no comments from my mother. However, the real success of the night was a surprise: late fish supper organised by my father, who had arranged for a Mr Greenway, a local fisherman, to deliver some freshly caught mackerel. The last visit to the Lyric was on 8 September 1942, when the owner, Freddie Williams, put on an extravaganza called *Café Continental*. My mother says the show was rather wonderful but she felt so very tired having been out all day gleaning in the fields. None of them knew then that the next time they would see *Café Continental* – produced again by the same Freddie Williams – they would all be in Germany and caged behind the barbed-wire fences of a German concentration camp.

It is clear, too, that home entertainment played an important part in their lives during these dark and depressing times. It involved all the family, cousins and friends with highlighted visits to each other's homes. They held table-tennis tournaments and darts matches, card evenings and sometimes musical evenings, where they all stood around a piano singing, or sometimes just played gramophone records. Then there was always chapel on Sundays. For my mother there was choir practice and regular singing lessons, and her group took the decision, war or no war, and in spite of the 'bloody Krauts', that no one was going to stop them having their regular bridge afternoons every Thursday.

Then came the inauguration of the communal parish soup kitchen, supervised by the redoubtable Mrs Burlingham, who lived on the Grande Rue, just opposite Les Camps Methodist Sunday School. In spite of increasing hardships and the fact that she had a growing baby to consider, my mother provided both the time and energy to support this endeavour, as did many others in the parish. As far as I can ascertain from her writing, she went along to the soup kitchen at the Parish Hall on at least two evenings each week. There is one particular entry in her diary dated 13 September 1942, which I find both distressing and enlightening: 'Today was Maud's [my aunt's] Silver Wedding. Knocked off my cycle by a German soldier today as I was going to help in the soup kitchen.' A statement pure and simple, and typical of my mother's courage. Unknown to everyone at the time, including the devoted Mrs Burlingham, within a matter of days we would all be marched off to the quayside at St Peter Port harbour and forced aboard totally unsuitable and filthy transport boats for deportation to Germany – so much for all the previous German promises.

On the evening of 14 September, my mother was involved in gleaning once more and threshing in the kitchen, and a Mr Bougourd called to take measurements for recovering the settee in the drawing room at Dallington. However, on 15 September, the order for the deportation of British nationals and their families was finally issued by the German authorities in Berlin and then received by the German military in the islands. Notice to this effect was published in the *Guernsey Evening Press*, and my mother wrote in her diary that she

> . . . felt very worried about the German orders in the paper today about the evacuation of British subjects and their families to Germany – did some more threshing this evening. Reg came in to give a hand and George and the girls arrived for an hour or so. We had a few dances but everyone is really worried about the new orders.

The editors of the *Guernsey Evening Press* didn't correct the grammar contained in the orders and printed them exactly as they had received the notice, mainly as a measure of solidarity with the deportees and in order to show their abhorrence of such a treacherous act.

The direct order read:

NOTICE

Guernsey, den 15, September 1942

By order of Higher Authorities the following British subjects will be evacuated and transferred to Germany:-

Persons who have their permanent residence not on the Channel Islands, for instance, those who have been caught here by the outbreak of the war,

All those men not born on the Channel Islands and 16 to 70 years of age who belong to the British people, together with their families.

Detailed instructions will be given by the Feldkommandantur 515.

Der Feldkommandant,

gez. KNACKFUSS,

Oberst.

The saddest thing about all this was that, by now, Hitler had lost complete interest in the deportation issue because his attention was now firmly fixed elsewhere: on the Russian conflict. The battle for Stalingrad (now Volgograd) was reaching a crucial stage in what was to become known as the bloodiest battle in human history with over two million combined casualties. However, in relation to Channel Island deportations, the all-powerful head of the German people had given an order, so consequently the German war machine had no alternative but to execute the order and pursue the expulsions.

# THE DAY THE NAZIS CAME

At St Martin's Parish Hall, my father had the dubious honour and duty of handing himself his own deportation order, which included my mother and me in the detail. This was in spite of the fact that the deportation of non-combatant British subjects from their homes in the Channel Islands was expressly forbidden by the Hague Convention, to which both Britain and Germany were signatories. I still wonder, even today, why the British government and the Channel Islands' authorities failed to take action to secure reparation or compensation from Germany on behalf of islanders after the war – although I recently saw documents in Germany showing that a sum of money equating to approximately £1 million was paid by the German government as reparation, but this was used by the British to offset the costs of having to support Polish ex-servicemen who couldn't return to Russian-occupied Poland. The family deportation order was issued on a flimsy single sheet of paper and read:

```
Feldkommandantur 515 Jersey, den 18th
Sept 1942
Cecil Frederick Matthews and two family
members
Dallington, Rue Maze, St Martin.

On account of the Notice of the
Feldkommandantur 515 dated Sept 15th
1942 you have to report yourself/
yourselves at 12 noon on Sept 23rd 42 at
the Gaumont Cinema.
```

You have to take with you this order together with papers proving your identity.

It is necessary that you fit yourself/ yourselves out with warm clothes, solid boots, some provisions, meal dishes, drinking bowl and if possible a blanket. Your luggage must not be heavier than you can carry and it must bear a label with your full address.

It is left to you to get, for each person, a trunk ready packed with clothes and locked for shipment to you. You must mark your full address on each trunk.

It is also left to you to take with you an amount of money up to Reichsmarks 10 German notes of Reichskreditkassen for each person.

Should you fail to obey this order, you must expect to be punished by a martial court.


Der Feldkommandant


gez. Knackfuss Oberst.

So the die was cast and we would shortly be deported to Germany, although the full implication of all this was placed far above my level of understanding. Much has been written about the lack of any organised resistance to the German occupying forces: I personally believe this has largely been conducted by people with a mischievous bent, seeking to create disharmony and discord where none previously existed. I often think the difficulty in criticising others is not that you may make mistakes about them but that you will inevitably reveal the truth about yourself. Within all of this carping is the implied smear that the islanders lacked sufficient courage during the occupation years to mount any resistance to German authority. I would refute this entirely and am reluctant even to demean the islanders' reputation by deigning to defend the position, because any defence is totally unnecessary. During the German occupation some 1,400 people were arrested for sabotaging the German war effort and, of these, 570 Guernsey folk were sent on to Continental prisons or camps where at least nine died in captivity in despicable and appalling conditions. However, seventy-five Guernseymen managed to escape from the island, and not one islander joined any German military units, unlike the case with many other occupied countries.

As an aside, in 1943 it was reported in *The Times* that more than 10,000 Channel Islanders who had been evacuated prior to the German invasion were now serving in the British armed forces. I also know that those serving earned more awards for gallantry, including Victoria Crosses, than those from any other location within the United Kingdom, in relation to geographical size. In addition, many islanders reached some of the highest ranks in the armed forces and served with outstanding distinction during this period, as they have invariably done in many previous conflicts over the centuries.

The Channel Islands had more than 26,000 Aryan occupying troops and over 20,000 foreign slave-labourers. We even had quite a few Germans billeted next to us in St Martin. This was the time when the Hun would frequently commandeer houses at a moment's notice, ejecting the occupants out onto the street. As most of the young men and women had already left Guernsey prior to the outbreak of war in order to join the armed forces, it was often the elderly who were left to cope. Because of Guernsey's compact size, there was little room to establish hideouts or storage facilities, and all vehicles had been requisitioned by the enemy, so how on earth would they have received and distributed arms and ammunition?

As I write this, I am reminded of those unsung heroes and heroines who hid or surreptitiously gave food to many of those brutalised slave-workers and were subsequently sent to their deaths in German concentration camps. I am reminded, too, of those who were caught with radios or in passing illicit news bulletins to the island people and who suffered torture and imprisonment and sometimes met their end in horrific circumstances. I would ask the question: if we are, rightly, able to maintain a war memorial for the casualties of the Boer War, why in heaven's name can we not have an official memorial, and not just a metal plaque, for those civilians who gave their lives so unselfishly for the good of humanity throughout these islands?

As in all German-occupied territories, there would be instances of collaboration and acts of betrayal, carried out mostly, but not always, by foreign nationals. Petty jealousies, personal grievances and the settling of old scores all played their part. However, the vast majority of islanders suffered the full rigours of the German occupation with courage and fortitude, stoicism and resignation. Fraternisation between local women and members of the Wehrmacht was not only discouraged but also vehemently opposed. Those few girls who became involved with German soldiers were soon the object of anger and ridicule and were known locally as 'jerrybags'. Looking back now from the comfort of an armchair, I find that it's possible to see that emotions took a firm hold. It must have been difficult at times for young girls to find male companionship in the islands, especially as most of the eligible young men had left before the outbreak of hostilities. It is also an inescapable fact that many of the German soldiers were in themselves decent and upright young men who had been coerced into joining the Wehrmacht even though they had no stomach for the war. Unquestionably several relationships were formed between islanders and soldiers that were genuine and caring, and surely we shouldn't feel any antagonism towards those involved.

Even some time after the war I can still remember being told not to play with or visit one or two of my young friends because their 'mother is a jerrybag'. As youngsters we soon developed a much more temperate approach whereby, if the friends were good sports and amiable, we continued to play together and it was just that we never told our parents about it. There was also a measure of double standards involved, because, if the girl had been, say, a distant cousin, a member of the family or a close friend, she was described only as being 'rather keen on the Germans'.

I am not overly concerned with the British government's dictum that 'The Channel Islands should adopt a passive co-existence to the German occupying forces', but would prefer to emphasise what I consider to be the islands' greatest contribution to the war effort. Hitler had decreed early in the occupation that over 10 per cent of the cement, steel and armaments scheduled for the creation of the Atlantic Wall should be diverted for use in fortifying the islands.

By the end of September 1944, Guernsey alone had, largely through the efforts of those poor, brutalised slave-workers, created more than 700 tunnels, reinforced bunkers and miles of coastal walls, and laid more than 76,000 mines. The slave-workers were part of the Organisation Todt, whose taskmasters wore khaki uniforms and red swastika armbands, in contrast to the German field-grey uniforms worn by the regular troops.

The slave-workers could be seen from time to time marching along the island roads, from one location to another, often with cement bags tied about their feet instead of shoes, or with the cement bags over their heads and shoulders to ward off the worst of the rain and bad weather.

The slave-workers' endeavours also encompassed the creation of fourteen coastal batteries and thirty-three anti-aircraft sites, and on Guernsey alone they used over 270,000 cubic metres of ferroconcrete. If you add to this the vast amounts of ferroconcrete used in Jersey and Alderney, the figure is quite extraordinary. Some of the largest pieces of artillery ever installed in the whole of the Atlantic Wall defences were located on Guernsey. These gargantuan guns had been taken by the Germans from a captured World War One Russian battleship, and could lob a shell over a distance of some thirty-two miles.

Looking today from afar and back over the long intervening years, I can see that Guernsey's real triumph was interwoven irretrievably with Field Marshal Erwin Rommel's final misfortunes. Rommel – known colloquially as the 'Desert Fox' – moved his Army Group B to Normandy in November 1944 with full responsibility for the defence of this part of the French coast against the long-awaited Allied invasion. Considered by friend and foe alike to be one of the ablest of military commanders of his generation, he had originally wanted to be an engineer and throughout his distinguished military career he displayed an extraordinary technical aptitude.

As soon as he had established his HQ he toured the Normandy coastline with great energy and total commitment. He was dismayed by the lack of completed construction works and infuriated by the slow pace of building. Rommel immediately started to invigorate the fortification effort along this part of the Atlantic Wall but with very special attention being given to the Normandy beaches. Although Field Marshal Gerd von Rundstedt and many other generals of the

High Command thought Pas-de-Calais would be the Allied invasion point, as it represented the shortest sea journey from Britain, Rommel had no doubts whatsoever that Normandy would be the likeliest.

Rommel's energy during this anxious period of the war was quite electrifying and he was constantly to be found on the French coast supervising the installation of tank traps and beach obstacles, disrupting possible glider landing sites and seeing to the laying of landmines. How very fortunate for the Allies that the Channel Islands had finally denied him access to all the necessary paraphernalia of war, including ferroconcrete, the slave-workers, heavy guns and the troops all contained on the islands. Had he been given this 'Pandora's box', then the task facing the Allies in eventually moving off the Normandy beaches would have been greatly hindered, coupled with the added certainty of sustaining far higher casualties.

Rommel finally committed suicide at Hitler's insistence on 14 October 1944, several months after the D-Day landings.

D-Day was scheduled for 6 June 1944, and it should have been an easy task to collate the Allied casualty rates for that momentous day. In practice, it has proved almost impossible to arrive at an indisputable figure, except to say many historians believe the numbers lie somewhere in the region of five thousand Allied troops killed and some six thousand wounded on this first day alone. It has also been calculated that, if all the German material, armaments, troops and ferroconcrete from the islands had been utilised in Normandy, there would have been a further two thousand or more Allied casualties incurred just in getting off the Normandy beaches. It is not known how many members of the French Resistance were involved in supporting the Allies from 6 June onwards, nor their casualty rates, but it has been estimated that, during this period, some fifteen to twenty thousand French civilians lost their lives, while the number of wounded remains a complete mystery.

# CHAPTER 5

# DEPORTATION

After a short period of time, sufficient to collect her troubled thoughts, my mother described how she first heard the anticipated and chilling news of our family deportation:

> I came back on the Monday afternoon after wooding and gathering food for the rabbits and I saw Alf, uncle John and Cecil in deep conversation. In a very light-hearted manner Cecil said to me, Have you seen the article in the Press about people having to be deported? Well I read it and made some comment and then said, I'll make you all a nice cup of tea, which was really quite special for September 1942; and when I returned with the tea he (Cecil) showed me our deportation papers with all the instructions,

and I said 'Oh well, God will look after us I am sure.'
We also had to be bright for dear uncle John's sake.

Since the islanders had received the dire deportation notice, the need for a realistic and practical approach soon became very apparent. No other members of the gang were in fear of being deported, so they all rallied around and helped us to move the more valuable and useful items of our furniture that had to be stored with various friends and relations for the duration. A large proportion of the effects went to Great-Uncle John. It seemed unbelievable to everyone that it was at Uncle John's house that they had all celebrated his Golden Wedding Anniversary, such a happy occasion, only seven months previously. But, as my mother wrote, 'everyone had such great fun moving all the furniture'.

While all this hubbub was going on, I was told we were all going on a lovely long holiday; but, as I told my mother, if it was going to be such a lovely holiday why was all our furniture being taken away and everyone crying all the time?

It was also the time for the last supper, where all the gang were present and united for this, the final meal. Everyone was conscious they had reached a milestone and their future lay in the hands of others elsewhere. I can just vaguely remember this meal because this was the first time I hadn't been packed off to bed, and I was allowed to stay up with the adults. It was also a special occasion because we had the meal in the front room on the ancient kitchen table, and there we all sat on a variety of odd chairs, although I was comfortably propped up on cushions. During the meal, apparently someone complimented 'the chef' on how well-cooked the rabbit was, and I, quite innocently, asked if this was the remains of our pet rabbit Mr Hawkins. My mother told me years later that, at this point, everyone suddenly fell very silent, laid down their knives and forks and stared far off into space.

On 18 September 1942 some of the furniture was still being moved, although by now it involved the much heavier pieces. Uncle George, Uncle Frank Le Page, Reg and my father huffed and puffed and eventually manhandled the piano and sideboard across the garden and into my step-grandmother's home for safekeeping while we were away. On the 19th there came the final assault on the heavy goods, which was rounded off with afternoon tea at my step-grandmother's home. These were the concluding notes in my mother's first diary, and on this day it was placed inside the old leather-bound family Bible secured by a metal clasp and left there hidden until rediscovered sixty-eight years later. However, when all these momentous times were eventually finished with, nothing in our lives would ever be the same again.

On Monday, 21 September 1942, all those families designated for deportation had to assemble in the early morning at the parish church, where buses would take them into the island capital of St Peter Port. There were sixty-three people listed as deportees from our parish of St Martin. My parents took along a blanket for me, and Nick Parker, who had once been in the Royal Navy, gave us three of his kitbags. My mother wrote:

We took Bovril, tea, cocoa and lots of stuff besides medicinal things; and although Stephen was only four years old he had to carry a very heavy kit-bag. We also had to take enough clothes for him plus shoes and then we had to be at St Martin's Church by 11 am. It took Uncle John, Alf, George and Reg to carry what Cecil, I and Stephen had to cope with alone.

She then went on to say:

The morning of departure arrived and anyone living here will tell you the guns in France were continually banging away and this had kept me awake all night thinking we were going right into the enemy camp. Before we left we went into next door and knelt down with Glad and Alf and said our prayers. Then we left and everyone in the roadway from the Rue Maze to the Church were all weeping and it was we who had to tell them not to worry and that we would be fine!

Little did my parents know that, within two years, Uncle Alf would be dead, never to see his dear island free from the yoke of German domination, nor ever again to hold his two beloved sons.

From my point of view, I was beginning to become more than a little frightened, and my parents told me when I was old enough to fully understand that, when we finally left home in the morning, I somehow knew it was for the last time, so I went to say goodbye to my cat Dinky and stroked his glossy fur coat for the final parting. All the family friends and relations were waiting at the front gate to see us on our way and many of them walked with us to the parish church. Everyone was crying and someone carried my sack, which I could see was almost as tall as I was, part of the way – so this was going to be some 'holiday' all right, and that was for sure. It gradually became worse as people started coming out of their houses to wave to us as we went by, and everyone was crying as they said goodbye, so what sort of holiday was *this* going to be?

The deportation centre was situated at the Gaumont Cinema in St Julian's Avenue, just outside the main harbour facilities. However, before reaching the Gaumont, we had to go through the horticultural premises of Messrs Geo. Munro in the Truchot, St Peter Port, forming part of a dark warren of wooden storage sheds. It was all very frightening and the situation was made much worse by the shouting and cursing of the German soldiers, and I could see their angry red faces and bulging veins standing out on their foreheads. They pushed and prodded everyone along, not giving people time even to catch their breath.

Here we were forced to leave our luggage and parcels en route to the cinema building, where we all had to undergo a medical examination. I have one fearful, lingering memory of this day, and that is coming out of the cinema onto St Julian's Avenue, where the bitterly cold wind blowing along the avenue was so strong I had the greatest difficulty in breathing and carrying my heavy kitbag – or, rather, dragging it along

– at the same time. Still, I didn't mind too much, as my sack contained a fair number of my precious tennis balls.

On our return to Munro's stores to collect our luggage, each family was given a traditionally produced, Guernsey wooden tomato box with a handle, containing food for the forthcoming journey, a most welcome and thoughtful gesture from the local Guernsey government. The box contained a loaf of bread, butter and a tin of sardines or liver pâté, chocolate, cheese, and toilet and shaving soaps, while the men also received an extra allowance of tobacco from Messrs Bucktrout & Co. This tomato box stayed with us throughout the war and during our confinement in Germany and features in an original pencil drawing of our barrack room, which I have kept. I think it eventually became a symbol of another life and happier times in a Guernsey that existed long before the outbreak of the war.

The Germans kept us waiting around for most of the day, and then, at about 5 p.m., we had to walk in line from the Gaumont Cinema all the way down the avenue to the quayside at the White Rock ready for embarkation. My mother wrote later:

Imagine all the men women and children walking down the avenue, it was all so ghastly as a barrier had been put up at the Weighbridge and the crowds were there to say their final goodbyes. It was a very moving but sad departure. I must say that the Germans had their work cut out to control the 'singles' as we called them as their wives and families were all in England.

# DEPORTATION

> We just had to learn to be patient, but the lads would
> all start singing 'Why are we waiting?'

I can remember feeling very scared and upset, mainly
because everyone seemed to be crying, and the German
soldiers continued to shout and harry us. It was here we
received our last hot meal for a very long time, prior to our
anticipated departure. Guernsey government officials had
thought up the idea of the hot meal and they turned to 'Uncle
Frank Stroobant', who was also on the deportation list, to
cater for everyone leaving Guernsey that day. The States of
Guernsey provided the meat, potatoes, vegetables, milk and
bread, and Uncle Frank gave some enormous tins of meat he
had secretly hidden away in anticipation of the long-awaited
liberation of his island. He even attempted to buy eggs, but,
because of island shortages, prices had moved to an exorbitant
rate and were often well above the controlled prices stipulated
by the local government. Nevertheless, vendors accepted either
the controlled price or a much lower price, and many others
refused to take the money at all, but made a gift of the eggs as
their own personal contribution for the deportees.

Another States of Guernsey official and a stalwart friend
of our family, Louis Guillemette, persuaded the Germans to
provide two field kitchens so Frank Stroobant and his band
of helpers could provide a hot, appetising meal for everyone.
He was assisted in this endeavour by Clement and Germaine
Pommier, and even well after the war our family would
buy their meat delicacies and sausages from Pommier's. One

of Uncle Frank's last acts that day was to try to find milk supplements for the babies and children having to make this arduous journey. A certain local Dr Sutcliffe knew exactly where he could obtain a supply of lactin (sugar derived from evaporating milk whey) and the two of them became embroiled in a stealthy operation whereby Frank had to hide under a blanket in the back of Dr Sutcliffe's car. They sped around St Martin's parish looking for my Uncle George de Garis, who was also manager of Le Riches Stores, one of the largest grocery organisations in the Channel Islands holding these vital supplies. It was well after curfew when the matter was resolved satisfactorily and, although Dr Sutcliffe had a German pass, authorising him to be out and about on medical matters, Uncle Frank would have been placed in an invidious position if he had been caught lying under the blanket in the back of the car.

Uncle George would often regale us with his view of these events by saying one of his worst experiences of the war was seeing the ghostly and dishevelled apparition of Frank Stroobant suddenly appear white-faced before him from under the blanket in the back of Dr Sutcliffe's car.

While all this was going on, the German Feldgendarmerie carried out searches on many of the deportees, confiscating cameras, photographs, jewellery and any money over and above the stipulated ten-Reichsmark allowance. Once they had been relieved of their possessions the deportees were cleared for embarkation. The two German transport vessels in question were called the *Robert Muller* and *La France*, and a courageous Guernseyman called Frank Falla, who was a journalist working on the local *Star* newspaper at the time, wrote of the *Robert Muller*:

> 'It was a cleaned-up coal boat totally unfit for human habitation; not a suggestion of sanitation, crawling with lice and fleas and, into the bargain quite unseaworthy. It had been used to transport Nazi slave-workers.'

Frank Falla was later betrayed by a foreign national called Paddy for being involved with the distribution of prohibited BBC news bulletins. Frank, in collaboration with others, produced a secret daily news-sheet called *G.U.N.S..* This betrayal very nearly led to his death in any of the worst German penal establishments, where he was held in two main jails, Frankfurt-am-Main and Naumburg-an-Saale.

Frank Stroobant, in his book *One Man's War*, stated, 'In fact the transport was so unbelievably primitive, that I was sure many of the deportees couldn't possibly survive the journey.' At this time, the normal September southwesterly storms were reaching a zenith and many people were becoming greatly agitated over the prospect of having to embark on such dilapidated transport ships. Even some of the Germans themselves held grave concerns but, nevertheless, we were all herded together like cattle and forced to climb the steep gangplanks onto the vessels. Our ship was called *La France* and my parents considered us lucky to be on board, because many of the other deportees were confined to the *Robert Muller* with little or no protection from the elements.

My overriding memory of all this was the frightening, dark,

chasm-like holds of the ship and the bright-orange colour of the metal sides and what looked like enormous mountains of metal chains. In truth I was probably looking at many years' accumulation of rust, and we must have been forced right down into the bowels of the ship by the Germans. I can still see the long wooden benches we were supposed to sit on and I could feel the alarm swelling up from the other deportees surrounding us. I could also hear the distressing crying of nearby children.

There was another saviour that day, in the form of Mr Fred Benham, who was being deported together with his wife and son John. He tried to keep all the children happy and amused and I would have dearly liked to have thanked him, years later, for his efforts during that stressful period, but that is unfortunately another missed opportunity I cannot now put right.

In the meantime the German military command in St Malo had already notified the German Channel Island authorities that the weather was far too rough for vessels to consider making the passage there. So it was decided they would remain in St Peter Port for the night, but the deportees would have to remain on board. It seems a great pity that no one thought it necessary to tell the deportees themselves this vitally important piece of news.

On this particular disturbing nightmare day I learned one very important lesson in life: if everyone around you is frightened and crying but your own parents remain calm and smiling, you have nothing very much to worry about! Of those times my mother explains:

# DEPORTATION

We were taken right down to the bottom of the ship and then locked in. Many of the men had to lie between the rafters and the water seeped in. There we met a wonderful man Freddie Benham, who looked after the children and so we all settled down. By early morning when we thought we were in St Malo, we were bitterly disappointed to find we were still on Guernsey. Rumours started to fly, there were submarines outside and very rough seas. The doors were finally unlocked and we were told to go home but had to leave everything behind.

The next day dawned and, although the weather had marginally improved, it was still deemed too dangerous to get under way. Then, at about 11 a.m. on the Tuesday, the deportees were told to disembark and return to their homes, if this was at all possible, and await further instructions. My mother and father celebrated their twelfth wedding anniversary on the Wednesday, back in Dallington and in a state of absolute limbo, knowing they were definitely being deported but not knowing exactly when. After several false starts the whole process was re-enacted almost a week later, as we all had to re-embark on Friday, 25 September. By this time, the disgraceful transport boat the *Robert Muller* had been replaced by a slightly improved version of a liner tender called the *Minotaur*, but our family were still scheduled to travel on *La France*.

The two vessels finally set sail in the very early hours of Saturday morning, but the sea crossing was exceptionally bad, and *La France* and the *Minotaur* used to transport us to St Malo were totally unsuited for their task. The seas were still mountainous, even after the storms of the previous week had passed, and many of the young mothers and their babies suffered terribly. There were further delays going through the lock gates at St Malo and it was just after seven the next morning when the two vessels finally docked.

Mercifully, I remember nothing of the difficult sea journey to St Malo, although it soon became apparent, to everyone's relief, that I would turn out to be a very good sailor in the most harrowing of circumstances! I do, however, remember being herded onto the train at St Malo by angry and agitated soldiers holding rifles, some with fixed bayonets, and dressed in grey uniforms and black jackboots, who kept shouting and waving their arms about, and I noticed just how mottled-red their faces were with anger. Looking out of the dirty carriage windows, I was able to see groups of local French women, who had been so disheartened to see pregnant women and young children, besides many of the old and infirm, being treated in this way that they approached the carriages clutching bread, and cold-meat sausages, which they proffered to the dazed prisoners. Even though they were being continually harassed and chased by the German troops, they still managed to evade them and ensure the food reached the right recipients. Such a display of tremendous courage!

I think it was this one marvellous and isolated incident that started a love affair between the French people and me to the point that I now live part of the year in France, where

# DEPORTATION

I am proud and privileged to regard many of them as friends and some of them as part of my extended family. I am always astonished and somewhat amused to hear a few British people say they detest or intensely dislike the French and, without fail, I find on further questioning that they have probably never visited France. The totally illogical answer to the question 'why not?' is consistently 'I have not visited France because I dislike the French.' There is certainly a cultural difference between the French and the British and, over the years, I have endeavoured to determine what the difference is. The one solution I have that satisfies me and enables me to feel comfortable is the explanation that, 'The British think with their heads while the French think with their hearts.'

If part of the deportation process was calamitous, then the next phase would surely be a journey into hell. My mother penned her notes concerning the appalling journey:

Having arrived at St Malo at dawn, we were given a thin watery soup, stale bread and part of a mouldy sausage and then forced onto a waiting train to take us on a long journey. Rumour had it we were going to pass through Paris in the dark and then on to Luxembourg until finally we would arrive at Cologne. But what a devastating experience to see so many lovely places bombed out and flattened and we were all scared stiff the British wouldn't know we were on the train and bomb us as well. After travelling for three days in miserable and wretched conditions, we were at one of the German railway stations near Cologne, when a train pulled in, with long open trucks packed full of Jews. They were being taken to one of the concentration camps in Germany and they were just crying out for food or cigarettes and so I threw all of mine to them, not realising that we would soon need every morsel very badly ourselves. But that sight will always remain with me, it was just so very dreadful.

Again, I have a vivid and haunting memory of looking out of the dirty carriage windows at those open railway trucks filled to overflowing with men, women and children, some of them my age, and all without shelter from the cold and driving rain. My father said he thought they were Jews, but I didn't know then what the word meant. It was bitterly cold and I could see this was a group of miserable and dejected humanity, crying out for food, and I think today that even our own pathetic gesture in giving away the small amounts of food and cigarettes – small because we didn't have very much ourselves – was probably the last act of kindness and consideration these people would ever receive before being annihilated in one of the notorious and brutal death-camp gas chambers.

As I sit comfortably in the shade of a flowering cherry tree, basking in the warmth of a summer sun, I ponder the following words as condemnation of that period:

> Who will hear me when I cry,
> Or understand my final sigh,
> And hold my hand when I should die?

# DEPORTATION

When underneath the sod I lie,
Who will stand to say goodbye?
My God will.

So here the world waits, and more than seventy years later nothing much appears to have changed. People are still oppressed and still starving. Ethnic cleansing and religious intolerance stalk the land, followed in turn by death, destruction and starvation; and through all this we seem to have learned nothing whatsoever from history.

My mother wrote in her diary:

> We had no idea where we were going and we were all tired, hungry and dirty. At one stop we were told we were heading to Dorsten on the Dortmund Canal and when we reached Essen we had to stay all night on the train at the station and there was a dreadful air-raid. The next day we were separated from the men, and all the women and children had to walk away. Spirits were very low as we didn't know if we would ever see our men-folk again; oh what a walk we had.

The Germans were totally unprepared for the arrival of such high numbers of prisoners and consequently had provided no additional food for the women and children.

> The long line of prisoners had a German guard leading from the front and when we at length entered one of the wooden buildings I saw three German officers sitting

at a table and taking everybody's personal jewellery. I happened to say to Joy Godwin, 'I haven't very much, only my ring and watch which is of great sentimental value.' And a voice behind me said 'Just put it in your pocket and I will take you through.' This was one of the German guards and it transpired later, he had worked for a long time in Australia but the Führer invited many Germans to visit their homeland but once they were in Germany they were forbidden to leave again.

Dorsten is situated on the very edge of the industrial Ruhr area of Germany near the towns of Essen, Dortmund and Düsseldorf, and can be found on a low-lying, flat tract of land alongside the Wesel–Datteln shipping canal. Our situation was quite precarious because constant bombing raids by the RAF had dislodged the enormous adjacent lock gates only days before our arrival. The warped thinking of the German High Command led them to believe that, by placing British prisoners of war in a highly industrialised war zone, they would encourage the British military to seek alternative targets. Some hope!

## CHAPTER 6

# DORSTEN TRANSIT CAMP

We eventually arrived at Dorsten Camp, otherwise known as Stalag VIF (Oflag VIE), only to find the place completely deserted but in such a terrible condition, as it had been evacuated only some forty-eight hours previously by Polish and Russian prisoners, who left the site in an abominable and filthy state, and there had been no time for the German authorities to have the place even fumigated or deloused.

My mother described Dorsten in the following terms:

Afterwards, a dreadful shock awaited us, because on entering one of the dilapidated buildings we found four rooms, so we bagged one of the smaller ones and took stock of our surroundings. We just couldn't believe we had to live in such filth, but I soon had twigs tied together to make a broom and then I sacrificed a pair of my 'knicks' and cleaned the table after which we were more or less organised. After that we inspected some of the other dirty wooden buildings and on opening the main wooden doors we walked into a large room with about 150 bunks all jammed together and leaving only a very narrow corridor and that led into another room with about 200 more bunks and then you had to pass through even another room until you reached the wash-ups and the 38 toilets. There were no partitions and no privacy – and it was quite a long walk to 'spend a penny', but we soon discovered that it was quite an achievement in the early hours of the morning to get back to your room safe and sound while hearing people snoring, talking and laughing – it was really ever so weird. Then there were rats and mice sliding about everywhere besides two German guards who were always smoking cigarettes at the entrance to the toilets. My word I was in and out like a shot and high-tailed it back as if old nick was chasing me! I was glad I had pyjamas with me so I could tuck them into my socks and so keep the mice out.

Poor Helga [Mrs Webb] was on a top bunk and the mice and rats used to run along the ledge but we never told her. She was in the first room and had to climb over others to get to her bunk but I felt I was so lucky to be in a smaller room. We were also given a ration of black treacle, and I used mine to put around the cracks and holes in the skirting boards to catch our little friends but I was ever so frightened.

At about 5 o'clock that evening, the men arrived at the camp and what a joy to see them come in, and for me all was well, just to see Cecil come in. I could not find a name for that camp, it was worse than filthy but we were so tired after our three days journey that we just flopped down on our bunks.

On our second night in Dorsten, there were terrible air-raids in the Essen district and we worried about the men and they of course worried about us. It was on our third night we began to hear noises. Joy Godwin didn't mind mice but I did. After a while she said 'Eileen are you asleep?' I mumbled something and she said 'I can hear and feel a lot of things crawling!' So I got off this high bunk and put the light on, I found an old dirty jar and we went around and filled it with what we were soon to come to know as bugs. I was really very dim on this sort of thing. The Russians had been here since coming into the war and we were sleeping on their dirty old straw sacks.

I can well remember the sandy soil, which made walking for a four-year-old extremely difficult, and it was almost impossible to bounce tennis balls on it when playing outside. The predominant picture in my mind is one of dilapidated, single-storey, wooden buildings with peeling paint and a few with shutters hanging off at weird angles. To say this was hell on earth would be an understatement, especially with the overpowering stench emitted from the unsavoury toilet facilities, which were virtually non-existent for in reality the toilets were mere slits in a concrete base, which in turn was suspended over a vast open chasm.

I remember at first being very absorbed by the sight of large barrage balloons in the far distance, which just appeared to hang in the air; but once I was told we couldn't play with them I lost interest in them very quickly. Two other features stand out in my memory. One was the yellow fog that seemed to blot out the sunlight at times, and was all-pervading. It was quite strange, because the fog tended to cling to both skin and clothes. Much later, we discovered this was caused by the extremely high sulphur emissions from the nearby chemical and industrial factories.

The other surprise for me was in looking through the tall barbed-wire fences out onto the lush green grassy banks and trees beyond, and suddenly having this surreal vision of a small barge moving slowly along the country fields, as if on wheels. The picture had been created and conjured up because the canal was on a much higher level than the camp, which in itself created a considerably greater danger for the prisoners should the canal ever be breached during the regular RAF bombing raids.

I recall, too, being perpetually hungry during this time, and certainly there was little or no food, apart from the meagre rations, which were so unsubstantial as to be almost non-existent. We were given one slice of stale bread each day together with a ladle of watery soup, and things became so awful that one day a woman prisoner grabbed the German commandant by his lapels and lifted him right off his feet in sheer frustration. We had little choice but to rely, sparingly, on the food we had brought with us.

So, all in all, this was a most parlous state to be in and, as a result, the health of many of the inmates began to rapidly deteriorate. Red Cross parcels were not available, mainly because the German authorities had failed to inform the International Red Cross of the large number of British subjects being deported to Germany from the Channel Islands. However, the herculean efforts of the German camp commandant to obtain parcels certainly helped to ease conditions in the camp, and, as a result, he probably saved many lives. Apparently, he contacted a British officers' camp nearby, which very kindly donated some Red Cross parcels from its own meagre stocks, and this was very well received and appreciated by the new Dorsten intake.

Hygiene must have been a serious problem, but I must have been too young to realise this because, in her diary, my mother wrote:

[With only] Cold water, it was all so very difficult, but my small bowl was very useful to use in my room. After about a month Mrs Stuart, Mrs Hartley-Jackson and Mrs McCloud had to find someone to make up a fourth to use the cold showers. They said they felt sure Mrs Matthews would join them and they were right, although I felt a lemon sitting on a box and waiting for the shower to come on, I had never had to bath with an audience before however, it was great to get a good wash in spite of the two watching Germans sitting on the roof. Stephen came in shouting for Mum and when he saw us, he was out of there again like a shot.

Our time here passed slowly, as we had to endure constant *Appells*, or roll calls, when the guards appeared to have a complete mental block about matching the numbers on parade with the established register of the inmates. Air-raid warnings were also a never-ending threat and, at each sounding of the sirens, we were all herded back inside our barracks – and, in addition, there was so very little food.

At this very young and vulnerable age I had no comprehension of just how much my mother's faith meant to her and how it sustained her through all of this terrible ordeal, but I am beginning to learn of it now when she wrote:

Each Sunday we could have our [church] service in the big hall, with the picture of Hitler taking up the whole wall. Reverend Flint took the first Sunday service with a German soldier on either side of him and he had to submit his sermon to them beforehand. That first Sunday was very emotional for us all, singing all our lovely hymns, renewing our faith and being thankful to God for bringing us safely there on our journeys both by sea and land. And thinking of everybody who would be in our lovely Chapel at Les Camps [Guernsey]. Reverend Flint was marvellous as it was Reverend. Ord and his wife who had been notified to come with us but they were in such very poor health, so Rev. Flint had offered to take their place.

We enjoyed Rev. Flint spending each day with us, in our room as his barrack was terrible and alive with vermin. All had to sleep in the main hall for a few nights while his barrack was fumigated, and that meant sleeping on a stool or lying on a dirty floor. I suggested he slept in my bunk during the day, but he was grateful to us for making this possible, and we all tried to be as quiet as possible. The men would never let us see where they had to sleep.

There were of course several tragic deaths while we were incarcerated during our relatively brief stay in Dorsten, and this included a baby from the Skipton family from Guernsey. My mother also wrote, 'Had a surprise one night as I always made a point of saying goodnight to several of the very old people. I peeped in to see Mrs Manning, God bless her, and the very next morning they told me she had died soon after I had left her.'

This, too, was my first introduction to Jesus, because, apparently, when I asked where all the dead people and babies went when they died, my mother told me they all went to stay with Jesus, who would soon make them better. This was quite a mystery to me because I couldn't understand why no one ever came back, and I held the firm opinion, expressed to my mother at such a tender age, that, whoever Jesus was, I could see he was going to be kept extremely busy in the future.

To be fair to the Germans, some of them were extremely kind and humane and utterly appalled at our condition and that we had ever been interned in the first place. Several of the officers spoke immaculate English, as they had previously lived and worked overseas before the outbreak of hostilities. The camp commandant was particularly kind and often purchased milk as gifts for the women and children out of his own pocket.

We must have stayed in Dorsten for some six or seven weeks, during which one interesting fact emerged: I was never bitten by fleas, lice or bedbugs, unlike almost everyone else in the camp. This has always been the case since then. However, in regard to mosquitoes it was quite another matter, as I was to find out to my cost many years later in the wilds of Central Africa.

On 12 November 1942, after seven weeks' enforced stay, all the British families vacated Dorsten and headed to another camp called Biberach, which was to remain our prison camp for the duration of the war. All I can remember about leaving the camp was being herded onto the dirty train by shouting and bullying soldiers in jackboots and one in particular who slapped me around the head as I boarded the train. I still had to carry a heavy kitbag about the same height as I was, and, as I struggled to cope, I was slapped again, causing me to fall over the bag and bang my head hard against one of the compartment doors. It didn't help me much when my mother told me something that was often repeated during our imprisonment in Germany: 'Brave soldiers don't cry.' But I knew they did. Besides, many others fared much worse than I did, as the guards weren't averse to using their rifle butts in urging the prisoners to get a move on.

Thank goodness we left Dorsten when we did, for, apart from the significant and routine bombing raids, there was the eventual catastrophic breaching of the nearby Möhne Dam by elements of 617 Squadron of Dambusters fame, commanded by Wing Commander Guy Gibson VC. The Möhne Dam was only some twenty-five miles east of Dortmund, and the serious flooding aftermath of this raid caused the deaths of more than 750 prisoners of war and slave-labourers. Furthermore, about four months after we had departed from Dorsten, the German Gestapo rounded up more than 300 prisoners of war, slave-labourers, anti-Nazis and various resistance fighters. These people were from a wide variety of countries and included many Dutch, Belgians, French, Polish, Russians and Yugoslavians. They were all herded into the fields surrounding Dortmund and there shot to death; and, in the years after the war had ended, only twenty-seven of the perpetrators were ever brought to trial.

Throughout my relatively long and eventful life there have been constant reminders and coincidences in relation to the time I spent in these German camps. It feels as if tendrils from the period have been extended outwards to take hold of me from time to time and drag me back again into the full horror and devastation of war-torn Germany. For instance, in the late 1950s I was working in the Contract Department of Messrs Maple and Co. of Tottenham Court Road in London. We had received a commission to design and produce a carved oak chair as a gift from the British government to the government of Ghana to be used by their speaker in the African parliament. The talented carver worked out of Maple's furniture factory in Drummond Street, Euston, and, after many meetings and discussions, I found that previously he had made the large-scale models of the Ruhr dams for the Dambusters. He was so taken aback to learn I had been in Germany, and in the same place and at the same time as he was making the models. He gave me a sample of his animal carvings, which I cherish to the present time.

The round-the-clock bombing raids in July and August 1942 had reduced nearby Düsseldorf to ruins. These large-scale attacks caused more than 6,000 civilian deaths and the total destruction of 176,000 buildings, leaving over 10 million cubic metres of rubble with only 10 per cent of the buildings remaining undamaged. In the spring of 1943, the British launched the first Battle of the Ruhr, with some 450 British aircraft attacking the giant Krupps armament factories in Essen. This took place on 2–3 March and then again 12 March. In March 1945 more than 6,000 bombs fell on Dorsten alone, and destroyed 80 per cent of the town, which meant that more than 3,000 buildings were flattened. The resulting debris took about three years to clear away after the end of the war. Thank goodness we were no longer in residence there!

While we were enduring the nightmare train journey southwards towards Biberach, another scenario was being played out back in the Channel Islands. One of the so-called deportees, an Irish national known as Dennis Cleary, had *apparently* been repatriated from Dorsten back to Jersey on the grounds of ill-health. On 13 November 1942, an interview with him was published in the *Jersey Evening Post*, only to be followed a week later by a similar one in the *Guernsey Star*. Two newspaper reporters had been taken under duress by the German authorities from Guernsey to Jersey in order to meet up with Cleary. These reporters had no alternative but to reproduce the stage-managed interview and, even today, the distortions, lies and innuendoes are still as transparent as they were all those years ago. Whether Cleary was also acting under duress, we will never know.

It was evident even at the time that this was a misguided publicity exercise, created in the warped minds of the propaganda-conscious occupiers. In the first place, Dennis Cleary was an Irish national and wouldn't have been deported in any event. Having examined all subsequent lists of deportations from both islands, followed in turn by a list of those later repatriated, I can report that Cleary's name does not appear on any document or schedule.

I also have the distinct feeling that Cleary's report left a lasting legacy of appalling proportions leading to the creation of a 'them-and-us' attitude within the islands. I sense the people who remained on Guernsey and Jersey believed part of the 'Cleary advertising campaign' and retained the thought that the deportees led a fairly comfortable and cosseted life in pleasant countryside surroundings. On their return, I also believe, many of the deportees themselves assumed life had continued in the islands in exactly the same way and with the same conditions as when they had left, and they failed to recognise the impact that severe starvation had inflicted on the residual population, who had no access to Red Cross parcels until the final stages of the war.

I have a copy of Cleary's sanitised statement, printed in a Guernsey newspaper, albeit covered with my mother's hieroglyphics, angry scribbles and expletives, but it reads as follows:

## WITH THE GUERNSEY COLONY IN GERMANY

How they are settling down to camp life

By Dennis Cleary

(As recounted to *The Star* in a special interview)

There falls to my lot one of the pleasantest tasks any man could wish for. I am able to give to the Channel Islands the first account of how people who were transferred to Germany seven weeks ago are living, how they are being treated and how they are settling down in their new surroundings.

For a month I have shared their daily life and routine, and I can speak from actual personal experience of what is happening there, and let me say at the very outset that, allowing for the changed circumstances and environment all of them are carrying on very much the same as they do at home.

When I returned I was assailed on all sides by two

questions: 'Where are they?' and 'How are they?', so I will answer them straight away. At first half of the party went to Western Germany and half to Southern Germany, but by now all have been assembled together in the same camp.

How are they? Well, when I left all had become accustomed to the new life and were rapidly adapting themselves to it. Everybody was cheerful and in the best of spirits. Those who were sick or ailing were being looked after, and the rest were all OK.

I gather that since our departure a number of silly stories and rumours have got about. One – that the men had been sent to forced labour – has been officially denied by the German Government, and others I can contradict here and now myself.

Do not believe that families have been separated. Do not believe that our people are being treated like prisoners. Do not believe that they have been sent to 'danger areas'. Each and every one of those tales is a fabrication. The true facts will emerge as I tell my story, and I hope they will serve to reassure all relatives and friends, both on Guernsey and Jersey.

So let me begin at the beginning. You all know what arrangements were made at this end for transport and rationing, and you saw for yourselves that every man, woman [and] child had sufficient clothes for a long journey, which it proved to be. The arrangements worked smoothly and well.

# THE DAY THE NAZIS CAME

We left our home ports at night. The sea trip was a normal one, and subject to no more discomforts than usual – that is to say, it depended whether you are ordinarily a good sailor or not so good.

In due course we reached St Malo. There our train was waiting, only a very short distance from the boat. There were parties of German soldiers on the quay, ready to give all the help they could with luggage and parcels. There was no confusion, and in quite a short time we were all settled on the train. Six or seven people occupied one compartment. There was plenty of room and they were second-class carriages.

Before we moved a meal was served – soup, coffee, and for the children gruel, supplementing, of course the ample allowances of food which everybody carried with them. German field kitchens travelled with us, and for several days we lived on that train – eating, drinking, sleeping, singing and generally amusing ourselves.

. . . and so on and so on, *ad nauseam*.

The report continued in much the same vein for many more paragraphs. Even after such a long passage of time, I am still incensed and nauseated by the sheer fabrication and tissue of lies promulgated by Cleary's report. And I have two important questions that need answering. One is: what happened to Cleary after hostilities ended? And the other is: why was no action ever taken against him by either local authorities or the British government? On a more personal note, if Cleary was a willing party to these gross lies, I would have much preferred to have just had him hanged, drawn and quartered.

I have no objection to calling Dorsten a transit camp, because it was exactly that. I do, however, take umbrage at having been chided for using the term 'concentration camp', especially in describing Biberach. I have been informed on several occasions that I should have really used the words 'internment camp'. *The Oxford English Dictionary* describes a concentration camp as being a camp where 'non-combatants of a district are accommodated, such as one for the internment of political prisoners and foreign nationals'. *The Random House Dictionary* is probably a little clearer in describing a concentration camp as 'a guarded compound for the detention and imprisonment of aliens, members of ethnic minorities and political opponents'. This strikes me as much more appropriate to the circumstances, and I too regard the words 'internment camp' as a mere euphemism for the real situation. I think there has been an erroneous merging in some people's minds of concentration camps and the barbarous and tyrannical death camps. Even renowned Holocaust scholars and the Germans themselves made a correct distinction between concentration camps and extermination camps.

I have often offered up a prayer of thanks for the fact I was blessed with the parents I had. My mother was not only courageous but also sustained by a powerful faith and a strong sense of duty, which upheld her during these extraordinary times. There is an ancient Chinese proverb that says, 'Where there is faith there is always hope.' My mother was energetic, fiercely determined and intensely loyal. My father was invariably a caring and gentle person, slow to anger and with a generous, almost wicked sense of humour. He was without fail the optimist and would make the best of any desperate situation; yet, when circumstances demanded it, he could become a man of direct and effective action. He had a motto, I think derived from his military service during World War One, which was to the effect, 'One should never volunteer for anything but always answer a call for help.'

Anyway, we were now embarking on another miserable journey from Dorsten to the next concentration camp, a journey fraught with anguish and distress. One episode of major world significance that occurred during our time in Dorsten, although we wouldn't know about it for several more months, was the battle of El Alamein in the Western Desert. From 23 October until 5 November 1942, British and colonial troops of the 8th Army, under the command of General Bernard Montgomery, defeated the German forces of the Afrika Corps, and forced them into a full-scale retreat. Winston Churchill said of this battle, 'Before El Alamein we never had a victory; after El Alamein we never had a defeat.'

But there was a lot more to this than we would know. One of our close family cousins, Annette Le Page, had left Guernsey to train as a nurse at St Bartholomew's Hospital in

London. At the outbreak of war she immediately joined the armed forces as a nurse and was eventually promoted to the rank of captain, after which she saw nursing service in the Sudan, Eritrea and Egypt. Because of the trauma of nursing the injured and the dying, together with the imposition of difficult work schedules, she found it impossible to keep a diary but she wrote letters to us all from wherever she was stationed in the desert, letters she knew she could never post home to Guernsey.

Perhaps this is a good time to reflect on what would have happened to the inhabitants of the United Kingdom if the Nazi-planned 'Operation Sea Lion' ('*Unternehmen Seelöwe*') had proved successful. The one thing most people seem to have forgotten is that the occupation of the Channel Islands was but a working blueprint for the military control of all the British Isles. It was an established truth that many of the serving German soldiers in the Channel Islands actually thought they were already settled in Southern England.

The outstanding courage and determination shown by all our armed forces deserves far greater credit than has already been given, because, if it had nor been for the rescue of our armies at Dunkirk or the success of our pilots during the Battle of Britain, surely German SS divisions would have goose-stepped down the Mall to German military music, at a victory parade where Hitler and his sycophants would have taken the salute on the balcony of a Buckingham Palace strewn with vivid Nazi banners and emblems.

With the Royal Family and the government of the day in exile overseas, the Nazis, with ruthless Teutonic efficiency, would have built concentration camps throughout the United Kingdom. The first camps appeared in Germany in 1933 to contain a variety of people seen as detractors and a hindrance to the Nazi cause, and this became a concept that was to spread throughout all the territories under German control, until, by the end of the war in 1945, there were more than 43,000 camps in existence with many being designated as death camps. All in all, some fifteen to twenty million people would be incarcerated within these heinous establishments: why would the United Kingdom have fared any better?

It is not difficult to visualise such camps being constructed in places such as Warrington, Manchester, Slough and Portsmouth, with death camps established in the likes of the Isle of Wight and Dartmoor. But what could Britons expect from their German conquerors? Well, certainly, street names would be changed and Greenwich Mean Time would have been abolished, with the country being forced to adopt Central European Time. Learning the German language would have been mandatory, all laws would have been promulgated in German and the German mark would have been the only accepted currency. Also, new draconian laws would have been imposed on the whole population. Schoolchildren would be compulsorily enrolled in the British section of the Hitler Youth movement and be forced to wear khaki uniforms with bright Nazi armbands.

And what of the proud British nation? The House of Lords would have been abolished and the aristocracy liquidated, whereas the House of Commons would have been converted into the new British Reichstag, with members approved and designated only by their German rulers. German and Italian internees would have been released and given priority work in the new order.

The SS and the Gestapo would see to the efficient and final eradication of all Jews, gypsies, homosexuals, the mentally impaired and the disabled. Intellectuals, Jehovah's Witnesses, Catholic clergy, common criminals and all dissenters would have been imprisoned for long periods of time with hard labour and then evaluated as to their suitability to live on, and many non-Aryans would have been press-ganged into slave-labour units to work on special projects for the Third Reich.

## CHAPTER 7

# JOURNEY TO
# DARK PLACES

The alarming migration by train from Dorsten camp may have started badly with some extremely rough handling by German troops, but much worse was to follow. The train was unquestionably not in pristine condition, and, although dirty and uncomfortable, it was far better than the cattle trucks normally reserved for the Jews and slave-labourers from Eastern Europe. Our trek started in the early morning of 13 November 1942 and, in the end, the journey took over thirty-six hours, which was endured without food or drink; to make matters so much worse, we soon realised the carriages were utterly disgusting and unsuitable, as they lacked corridors and access to toilets and washrooms. By the end of our travels, we were completely exhausted and utterly filthy. Our own carriage-compartment group consisted of 'Auntie' Joy and 'Uncle' Dave Godwin and their twin sons, Neville and Ralph; then there were my mother, my father and I.

# THE DAY THE NAZIS CAME

Auntie Joy was a teacher and Uncle Dave was the Guernsey secretary for the large wholesale and retail grocery chain Le Riches, which operated throughout the Channel Islands.

I remember the journey most vividly, of seeing a rudimentary blanket-curtain strung across the train compartment to provide a modicum of privacy; and I also remember lying down on one of the bench seats and looking across to the other side of the carriage and seeing Neville and Ralph, who were both covered with purple spots on their faces, arms and legs, where their flea bites had been daubed and treated with a gentian-violet solution.

There was one frightening period when our train was left unattended and in total darkness on a railway siding just outside Cologne. During these years Cologne was bombed a total of 262 times in separate air-raids and suffered the first thousand-bomber raid ever undertaken by the Royal Air Force. On the train at first light, there was a dramatic shaking of the carriages and I saw a large crack appear in one of the plate-glass windows of our own carriage. It also transpired later that the International Red Cross had erroneously notified the British authorities that there had been British casualties on the train, caused by RAF bombing at the Cologne station, and, regrettably, my mother, father and I (and presumably other prisoners) had been killed. The impact that this unhappy news had on my brother was extremely traumatic, more especially so as he was of such a young age.

At the age of eleven, he was brought to the headmaster's study at the school in Oldham – where two spinster sisters, Norah and Phyllis Bennett, were teachers – to be informed in quite blunt terms that they were all so very sorry, but his entire family had just been wiped out in a Royal Air Force bombing raid on Germany. However, everyone had to look to the future, so he would now be adopted by Norah and Phyllis Bennett. Alan told me many years later that it felt he spent days living in abject darkness and feeling totally alone. In the end, everything was resolved because, in a matter of a few weeks, the error was discovered and the situation rectified.

After some thirty-six hours we ultimately arrived at Biberach railway station by mid-afternoon, where we all disembarked amid the routine cursing and shouting by a detachment of armed German guards. Once again, there was no transport available, so all the prisoners had to walk the several miles up the steep and winding hill from the station to our new camp, with women struggling with their babies and men burdened with heavy suitcases and parcels. The ranks of prisoners soon became a line of pathetic stragglers with the old and infirm falling further and further behind the main group, only to be rounded up and verbally abused and jostled by the malignant German guards.

As we walked along, I took out one of my tennis balls and started bouncing it on the roadway and catching it smartly on the rebound. My mother told me I would most likely lose it this way but my father said, 'Why not let him play with it as long as it keeps him occupied?' Inevitably, though, the tennis ball did hit a rut in the road and flew off at a tangent and, before I could catch it, it bounced away down the road on the far side, with me running after it. With the steep gradient of the hill, the faster I ran the faster the ball went, until it stopped just beyond the guards at the rear who were chasing up the laggards and stray prisoners. The tennis ball was only a few tantalising feet away and, as I went forward to pick it up, I received a hefty clout on the side of my head from an angry guard. I was hustled back into the shuffling group and had to leave my ball lying there just out of reach. Later, I rejoined my parents near the front of the line and I was grateful no one said, 'I told you so.' The episode was never referred to again, although I was more concerned that my precious stock of tennis balls had now been seriously depleted.

Our arrival at Biberach Camp (Ilag VB, previously Oflag VD 55) was even less welcoming. The word '*Ilag*' is a shortened version of *Internierungslager*, being a place for the incarceration of civilians. I remember that the light was fading fast and it was freezing cold, with a bitter November wind whipping across the open parade ground. Those Channel Islanders who had arrived only a few days before us and were already settled in the camp had kindly prepared a hot meal for the new arrivals, but the German guards – who, we realised by this time, lacked even the basic concepts of humanity – forbade us to eat. It was important for them to complete a correct and accurate roll call, or *Appell*, as they preferred to call it. The main problem lay with the Germans themselves, as they always seemed to have problems counting correctly, and, indeed, even in dealing efficiently with confrontation where the figures actually tallied – and this first instance was surely a prime example.

We were very near the front of the assembly and, after

much time-wasting on the part of the Germans, my mother's frustration became far too great and her temper just snapped. She stormed up to the senior German officer on parade, and proceeded to berate the poor man, emphasising each point by jabbing him in the chest with her fingers. Undeterred by this onslaught, the officer merely took out his revolver, pointed it directly at my father and said in perfect English, 'Just tell her to be quiet or I shall shoot you.' For the first time in twelve years of very happy marriage, my father raised his voice, and said, 'For God's sake, Eileen, shut up or he will really shoot me!' I still believe today that my mother was more shocked by my father's rebuke than by the officer's pistol and threat of violence.

My mother later recorded:

I shall never forget the children were all crying with the cold and being hungry and tired. The men in our group started to get angry but the Germans soon showed us who were the masters. Guns were loaded and searchlights from every vantage point were switched on and trained on the square. Some of the German officers however were genuinely distressed for us because of the lack of food, especially for the children and babies.

Following this despicable episode we were inoculated against typhus and had our photographs taken, then we faced the registration formalities. At the end of the registration process, there was a brief moment of high drama leading on to a complete farce and finally great merriment. During the lull, my mother thought there would inevitably be a rush by the new arrivals to secure a good berth and a suitable position in the barracks, so, ever mindful of the fact that she had me in tow, she left my father on watch and we set off at the first opportunity and at a fair old lick to search for our new abode.

However, by a strange quirk of fate we somewhat hastily entered a barrack that hadn't been made ready for occupation by the new arrivals.

In the gloom of one room, and hampered by the fact that there was no electric light-bulb, I plainly decided I needed to relieve myself as a matter of some urgency, and, in answer to my ever-increasing demands, my mother, in some desperation, found an old and discarded enamel soup bowl. After completion of my toilet obligations, my mother managed to open the barrack-room window and jettisoned the contents of the soup bowl high into the night air. Unfortunately, the prompt and angry response sparked the realisation that she had thoroughly doused one of the, by now, irate German guards, who had been standing just outside the window enjoying a quiet smoke.

Without waiting for the full force of German retribution to befall us, we took to our heels and fairly skipped away down corridors and on into other barracks, criss-crossing our paths until we finally emerged onto the square once again. If it seemed that my feet hardly touched the ground, it was probably because my mother had a firm grip on my coat collar and propelled me along the stone floors at breakneck speed. Once we had reached the safety of my father and been absorbed into the milling ranks of waiting prisoners, both my parents started to laugh, although at the time I could see precious little to laugh about.

In the final analysis, we were allocated barrack rooms by the efficient German hierarchy and then issued with our personal eating utensils, which included a spoon, knife and fork together with an enamel bowl and an aluminium mug. At the end of all that, exhausted, cold and hungry, we were allowed to have our first hot meal after enduring such a long period of time without sustenance of any sort.

We discovered that Biberach (Beaver Brook) is situated on the River Riss, is some 1,800 feet (approximately 550 metres) above sea level and sits on a vast plateau with views across to the awesome Bavarian Alps. It may well have had a healthy environment with gentle and wide rolling hills, luxuriant green forests and fields where oxen and large shire horses still pulled the farm ploughs, but in winter it was not the best place to be. The daylight was clear and bright but, when the snow fell, the chilling cold would seep into the bones and penetrate one's whole being.

I can remember being numb with cold and wearing only short trousers and wet, broken-down shoes and looking in some despair at my legs, which displayed purple and dull-red patches brought about by the freezing weather. At some point during our captivity, I had no shoes at all and had to endure long and painful walks, generally in wet conditions and totally unshod. This created a lifelong and deep-seated abhorrence of snow and ice, which still lives with me to this day, to the point that I now spend some of the winter months being cosseted by the warm sunshine of Southern China's Pearl River Delta.

Up until the mid-1980s very little was known about the history of Biberach Camp. However, in 1983 a group of German students from the Biberach comprehensive school, under the direction of their teacher and local historian Reinhold Adler, took part in a competition organised by the President of the Federal Government of Germany. The object was to find out local historical facts of the area in relation to World War Two. They decided to investigate the camp at Biberach, as it appeared nothing was known about its history during the wartime period. Within a short space of time they all realised, even though it was thirty-eight years after the war had ended, that German people didn't want to talk about either the camp or what had actually happened there.

They eventually found some answers in the local newspaper archives of the period. They discovered that the camp was originally called 'Camp Lindele' and that the first barracks had been built in February 1939 on the orders of the Nazi government to house a full garrison of troops. This had been great news for the town after ten years of economic misery and they thought perhaps they could now expect some financial advantage from the garrison being stationed there. The first troops moved into the camp on 27 June 1939 at the time of the Biberach Schützenfest, which is a great annual carnival and celebration.

However, only a few short months later, these soldiers had already left for military duty on the Western Front and the townspeople soon realised they had been duped. The camp was then immediately converted into an Oflag VB prison camp for more than nine hundred British officers and orderlies who arrived on 28 August 1940. On 9 November 1941 the camp was renamed Stalag V-A and housed some eight hundred Soviet troops, and of this number 146 died of malnutrition and were unceremoniously dumped and buried in common graves in the woods near the camp. In March 1942 the camp underwent another revamp as Oflag 55D in order to accommodate Croatian, Serbian and French officers. Nonetheless, on 20 September 1942, the first contingent of Channel Islanders arrived. (On 19 December 1942 the camp would become Camp Ilag VB and, mercifully, fall under the control of the German civilian police administration and not the dreaded SS. We'll look more at this change in our fortunes in the next chapter.)

Biberach Camp was of the usual German military design and consisted of twenty-three barracks constructed in neat rows and with the whole conglomeration surrounded by the normal double fence of heavy-duty barbed wire. The fences were ten feet tall and the six-foot spaces between them were filled with short coils of razor wire, the whole arrangement forming a totally impenetrable barrier. At every corner or bend stood the classic German raised sentry box complete with machine-gun and searchlight, and a powerful floodlight was positioned every ten feet along. On the ground and just inside the camp was a single strand of wire, which was the nearest point that prisoners could approach the barbed-wire fence, and anyone crossing this wire was more than likely to be shot on sight.

Each barrack housed eighty-five prisoners and was subdivided into small rooms, taking up to eighteen people each. Men were billeted in separate barracks from their wives and children, although everyone could mingle during the normal, but specially designated, hours of daylight. The actual times when husbands were allowed to join their wives and families each day had been designated as 10 a.m. until noon and 2 p.m. until 6 p.m. In these extremely difficult periods my mother created a completely new way of life to cope with the uncertain future:

I used to say to Cecil, just how are we going to live through all of this? The first few weeks seemed like years, it was an absolute shambles and I almost despaired. Then Cecil and I decided we would think of this time as being an engaged couple all over again! It was then we realised what a great gift of humour God had given us both. In watching everyone saying goodnight, we had lots of laughs in spite of feeling so low. We found that we could help people who were so very distressed, to see the funny side of various situations and of course we had our faith.

Two of the barracks were designated as hospital wards for men and women respectively, and another block was used as a school. There was a large Red Cross store, cookhouse and canteen, showers and a concert hall. The main focal point of the camp was the sizeable German administration building, which was known by some as the Big House and by others as the White House. This was a substantial double-storey building with a terrace at the rear and a wing on either side.

My mother and I had been allocated Room 6 in Barrack 15, but the room already held quite a few occupants, so there was little chance of our selecting a prime position. We found ourselves positioned nearest the draughty door and against the far wall, which proved a boon to me as I could slip out quietly whenever I chose without disturbing any of the inmates or even being noticed by anyone. The room seemed to be filled with double bunk beds; some of the beds were made of metal and others of wood. My mother selected one of the top bunks and I was installed immediately below. An old and tattered blanket was draped from under my mother's straw-filled palliasse and allowed to hang down on the open side, so I could sleep and not be disturbed by the bare electric light-bulb hanging from the ceiling, whilst it also afforded the grown-ups some measure of privacy. This system was to serve me exceptionally well later, when I had built up my menagerie of the animals I kept in the dark, well away from parental interference. I had large green crickets, worms, beetles and a chrysalis. From time to time my mother would have a clean-through and any animals were subsequently released back into the wild unharmed.

The occupants of our barrack room were diverse characters in many ways. For instance, there was the delightful Fay Williams, who had been trapped by the Germans in Norway, and Bobbie, a young Polish lady who was married to a debonair doctor called Gabriel from Buenos Aries. Then there were Mrs Buchan and her son Gordon from Jersey. There was the young Patsy Flynn, who called my mother 'Mama', and Mrs Isobel Guy, who appeared to be in a perpetual state of ill-health; and several others, but I am sorry to say their faces have now dissolved into the mist of time and I just cannot remember their names. If we thought our conditions were excessively overcrowded, we would have done well to remember the more unfortunate sufferers in the death camps of Bergen-Belsen and Auschwitz, who endured a mass of five hundred people sandwiched into just one filthy barrack.

My father, on the other hand, had the most exciting room in Barrack 6, which faced southeast and had been positioned adjacent to a hillside that started to rise just beyond the barbed-wire fence. Numerous holes had been dug into the hillside, as witness to the energetic activities of the previous British POW inmates, but the most outstanding and intriguing feature was the tunnel constructed by former British prisoners digging down under the cast-iron stove. The present incumbents of the room were immensely proud of this jewel in their crown, and never tired of showing it off to all and sundry at the slightest excuse. I can recollect being totally mesmerised by the sheer ingenuity of it all, as the stove could be easily swung out while still alight, and the floor tiles removed to give the tunnellers room to descend; then, afterwards, at the end of their shift, everything could be replaced again and made to look as if nothing had ever happened. The tunnel opening was only one foot nine by one foot six, and I was told the reason most of us now had metal beds to sleep on was that the wooden ones had been used to shore up the long tunnel.

Only the year before, on 13 September 1941, the tunnel was used by a British prisoner of war, Lieutenant Colonel Michael Duncan MC, who, together with twenty-five other officers, managed to escape from Biberach. This resulted in four 'home runs', where these four army prisoners managed to reach the safety of Lake Constance on the Swiss border. Some time later, the Germans showed my father the grave of a British officer who was shot at Biberach railway station during an escape, and by sheer coincidence he recognised the family name as coming from the Portsmouth area. After the war he was able to visit the family and give them more information and a fuller account of those tragic circumstances.

There was also another notable escape from Biberach when an officer called John Paul MC, together with a companion, tunnelled out from under the camp latrines, while they were still in use! The two escapees made their way to the Swiss border, where they were ultimately captured and returned to Biberach. John Paul later went on to become Sir John Paul, and enjoyed a distinguished career in the British Colonial Service.

I was totally entranced by my father's room and the camaraderie evidently existing among all the prisoners, and I could see this was a calm, male-dominated environment, far removed from the petticoat government and antiseptic conditions of the women's barracks. I soon found out it would be possible for me to move across to join my father when I reached the age of seven, provided I could rehouse one of the present incumbents. I could hardly wait for my seventh birthday and I spent many of the daylight hours trying to work out who would have to leave the room in Barrack 6 to make way for me. In the meantime all the barrack doors were securely locked at 6 p.m. with lights out usually at 9 p.m., after which time guard dogs were then turned loose to patrol the entire camp throughout the nighttime hours.

Human nature is quite remarkable in its ability to learn, change and adapt to the most difficult of situations. For our part, the young ones soon learned through trial and error how to dodge the posturing guards and evade their usual hitting-and-kicking antics. Then we went on the offensive in so many ways. The older boys would chant, mimic and jibe at their captors, so I thought we younger ones should play our part as well. I gathered together a group of three-, four- and five-year-old boys like myself, and furnished them with broom handles and pieces of wood we had surreptitiously removed from some of the barracks, and used them to simulate rifles. We started marching up and down in formation on the square, and in front of several of the goons; and, as we went along, we sang one of the songs from Disney's *Snow White and the Seven Dwarfs*, but with some alternative words we must have learned from a few of the older boys. The song was 'Whistle While You Work', and the words went something like this:

> Whistle while you work,
> Hitler is a twerp,
> Göring's barmy, So's his army;
> Whistle while you work.

Luckily enough for us, the goons didn't understand English, so all they heard were the words 'Hitler' and 'Göring' and thought this was a rendition of approval. Their response was much waving of hands, beaming smiles and the words '*ja, ja*' as a signal of their approbation.

While all this was going on, my mother had another shock as a Mrs Langmead, one of the Guernsey contingent, hurriedly summoned her to come and see just what Stephen was up to. Of this event my mother later wrote:

We had many frights during our first few days, poor old Mrs Langmead came running in to find me one morning, so we all ran onto the square. Just imagine how scared we were, with the guards listening to all this going on and it was a jolly good job they couldn't speak English, otherwise it might have been quite a different story if they had. Anyway we made sure that would never happen again

All I can remember of the latter part of this event was that the performance didn't last very long, as a gaggle of horrified mothers soon descended on our group and we were hauled off in every direction by the scruffs of our neck – but we had enjoyed a wonderful time and felt we had scored a minor point or two over our German superiors.

For a time the guards patrolled the barbed-wire fence from inside the camp and, as dusk fell, some of the older boys would throw stones at the patrols passing by, and then run away, darting off in different directions through the maze of barrack buildings. This seemed such a good idea and such great fun, a few of us younger ones decided to follow suit and join in. Because of our age and smaller stature, we had to get much nearer to the enemy before loosing-off our missiles, in order to ensure a reasonable chance of a hit. Once, I heard a distinct ping followed by an angry bellow of rage, and realised I had achieved my goal by bouncing a pebble off a German steel helmet; but immediately I had to run away flat out into the gloom, to avoid being caught. As I ran I could hear the heavy tread of army boots chasing me, and it was just sheer fright that made me run even faster. At one stage I thought I could hear the footsteps and heavy breathing growing nearer and, in a blind moment of desperation, I ducked down behind one of the concrete washstands and held my breath as the German guard pounded on by, although I was still scared stiff he would hear my heart beating.

After a few moments' waiting nervously in the darkness, I shot back the way I had come, running into my barrack room, jumping into my bunk and pulling the blanket-cum-curtain down from under my mother's palliasse. I realised then I had just had a very narrow escape and vowed never to do it again. Shortly afterwards, we were all warned off by our camp leaders, who pointed out the inherent dangers if we continued with this type of action. Nevertheless, we felt completely vindicated afterwards when the guards were ordered by their superiors to leave the interior of the camp itself and to start patrolling along the outside perimeter wire.

# CHAPTER 8

# EARLY DAYS IN BIBERACH CONCENTRATION CAMP

Initially, not having enough food to eat was an enormous problem. Soup, such as it was, was provided once a day, but this was generally a watered-down cabbage composition tasting just as foul as it smelled. But when you are really starving you are inclined to eat anything within reach. Sometimes the soup recipe changed and we would find large, hard lumps of swede floating in the water. Some people called them pineapple chunks but, as I didn't know what pineapples were, it didn't worry me very much.

After some time we started to receive a very small portion of cubed, cooked meat, although this was mainly very low-grade fat and gristle. On one memorable occasion I was given a cube of meat with a portion of bone in it, as part of my meat ration. I sucked and sucked this small scrap of bone with maximum enjoyment, and I kept the shard for at least the next ten days until my mother found out and promptly discarded what was my most prized possession. Greens appeared rather infrequently, although Eddie Coll, from Guernsey, who represented the St John Ambulance in the camp, hinted publicly he strongly believed these were nothing more than graveyard cuttings from the local cemetery.

Supplementing this meagre fare was what was purportedly a loaf of bread, designed to last between ten and twelve days. My mother would give me her one slice of bread one day and my father would do likewise on the next day and so on. This bread was baked in Ulm, which was only some thirty miles away, but it was usually a month old by the time it reached us, being stale and mouldy into the bargain. The ingredients were nondescript and couldn't be vouchsafed as gradually the Germans were reduced to adding increasing quantities of sawdust and other equally obnoxious substances to the concoction, and eventually the bread would turn a light mauve colour when left in the darkness of a cupboard for any length of time.

Even in this parlous state, Christian faith and beliefs still took precedence for my mother. She commented:

Each Sunday we would attend a service, we had Rev. Foss who was really quite marvellous as poor Mrs Foss was very confused. Rev. Stuart was also very confused but very good in his confusion, he would always be kind and helpful to others, going around bartering from people without children, who would gladly swap some of their milk for meats. He would also stretch under the barbed wire to pick dandelions for the (Church) table on Sundays. His coat was always back-to-front and life for Mrs Stuart wasn't easy. Church of England ministers were represented by Rev. Wood, Rev. Laxton from Cobo Church, Rev James from Vale Church and Rev. Hartley-Jackson from St Stephen's.

Life in the barracks was noisy, cumbersome and it took major adjustments to cope with the myriad difficulties people faced. As my mother said:

There was a room in our barrack for 20 or so of the old folk, which was called 'The Ladies Room', and I never went in without knocking first. They were dears, and each night I was asked to take Stephen in to say goodnight, when he was ready for bed and in his pyjamas. He always cheered them up, but goodness knows what he was telling them but they always said he was a tonic.

Once a week we had a head inspection by Mrs Toplas and then the German woman commandant would come and inspect our rooms and lockers, as we all stood silently to attention. We were always very cold, NO HEAT, temperatures in the winter from October through to March were usually minus 20 degrees centigrade, with lots of snow. We would have a ration of 8 briquettes per month for each room (for the pot-bellied stove) but it would take that amount just to light it. Also we had morning cans of mint tea brought to our barrack, and we would go down the corridor, get our tea and skip back on our bunks and have a good old natter. If there was any left over we would take it and have a good wash!

Gradually the prisoners began to hone themselves down into viable units although still with major travails to overcome, according to my mother:

We started to feel a lot better after a few weeks in this new camp, getting to know the people you had to live with, eat and sleep. I was lucky in one way having Stephen to share the bottom bunk with me, so we didn't have the problems others had with rows galore. Mrs So and So wanted the windows closed, and others wanted them open, or it was too draughty. Mrs So and So snored all night, all those sort of things. The people without children were lucky as they only had themselves to please, it was the Mums with two or three or four children or even more who had a rough time. It really was hard for them, it was like a Sunday School treat every day with all the brew [brouhaha] and noise and that's the only way I can describe it. Also the mums always had the children even when they were ill, the men were always free as they had to be out by 9 p.m.

We had a very cold area where we had to wash in a very narrow concrete trough with high taps and of course cold water. The toilet accommodation was a

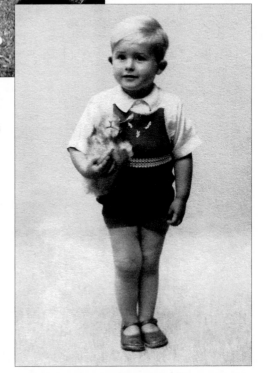

At the tender age of four years and three months, having just been told we were all going away on a lovely long holiday- some holiday! How could they send young children on such a journey into hell? But then, after seventy-eight years nothing seems to have changed.

Feldkommandantur 515

Jersey, den 18. Sept. 1942

*153*

An Mr. Cecil Frederick M a t t h e w s,
and two Family Members,

Dallington, Rue Maze, St. M a r t i n s.

Sie haben sich auf Grund der Bekanntmachung der Feldkommandantur 515 vom 15.9.1942 am 21.9.42 um 12 Uhr in Parish Church einzufinden.

Es ist mitzunehmen die vorliegende Aufforderung nebst persoenlichen Ausweispapieren.

Die Mitnahme warmer Kleidung, fester Stiefel, etwas Munavorrat, Essgeschirr, Trinkbecher und moeglichst einer Decke ist notwendig. Das Gepaeck darf nicht schwerer sein als Sie es tragen koennen und ist mit einem Zettel mit Ihrer Namensaufschrift zu versehen.

Ferner wird anheimgestellt, pro Person einen verschlossenen Koffer mit Kleidungsstuecken zur Nachsendung bereitzustellen. Auf dem Koffer ist genaue Anschrift anzubringen.

Es wird ferner freigestellt, Geld im Betrage bis zu RM 10.- in Reichskreditkassenscheinen pro Person mitzunehmen.

Falls Sie dieser Aufforderung nicht nachkommen, haben Sie kriegsgerichtliche Bestrafung zu gewaertigen.

On account of the Notice of the Feldkommandantur 515 dated Sept.15th, 1942 you have to report yourself / yourselves at 12 noon on Sept., 21st, 42 in Parish Church.

You have to take with you this order together with papers proving your identity.

It is necessary that you fit yourself / yourselves out with warm clothes, solid boots, some provisions, meal-dishes, drinking-bowl, and, if possible, a blanket. Your luggage must not be heavier than you can carry and must bear a label with your full address.

It is left to you to get, for each person, a trunk ready packed with clothes and locked for shipment to you. You must mark your full address on each trunk.

It is also left to you to take with you an amount of money up to Reichsmarks 10.- in German notes of Reichskreditkassen for each person.

Should you fail to obey this order, you must expect to be punished by a martial court.

Der Feldkommandant:

gez. Knackfuss

Oberst.

As Constable of the Parish of St Martin, my father had to hand himself his own deportation order, before a group of uniformed German officers. He received the document in his right hand, then transferred it to his left to prove execution.

*Left*: My precious aluminium mug, missing in December 1943, suddenly reappeared as my Christmas present, having been engraved by a camp inmate using only a hammer and a nail.

*Below*: A police officer, the late Michael Kraft, pictured emerging from the recently discovered hundred-metre long tunnel, through which twenty-five British POWs escaped after beginning excavating under the stove in Cecil Matthews' barrack room.

*Courtesy of Stefan Rasser*

*Above*: My fifth birthday card, drawn by internationally renowned artist Ethel Cheeswright. This is the only card depicting a Walt Disney character ever produced in a German concentration camp. A copy is held in the Walt Disney Museum.

*Below*: Goldilocks (second from left) pictured amongst the men she hated. Acting as the Biberach prison camp administrator, interpreter and eventually censor, she was similarly hated by her Nazi commanders. She was finally infected with typhus, although happily she survived. *Courtesy of Rheinhold*

--------------------

During the time I was looking after the 12oo
British Internees coming from the Channel Islands,
I have appointed several men for special work in our
camp at Biberach/Riss, South Germany.
Amongst those was Mr.Cecil Matthews, who was in charge
of the Red Cross, distributing parcels from the Red Cross
in Geneva and the YMCA as well as the YWCA. It was
a plasure to cooperate with Mr.Matthews, as he was an
outstanding character, absolutely reliable and righteous
in his work. He never said a word too much, he remained
calm when others got excited and was friendly to everybody.
I appreciated him as a perfect gentleman and wonderful
personality, so did Mr.Laib, who was the German official
in charge of the Red Cross. Also he regarded Mr.Matthews
a clever and capable man doing well whatever he was undertaking.
The International Red Cross Representatives from
Switzerland and Sweden, who visited the camp regularly,
assured me, that it was a pleasure for them to converse
with Mr.Matthews upon many subjects regarding the Red
Cross and the camp. He will always be in our mind
remembering the camp at Biberach/Riss during the war.

*Helen Roschmann*

Interpreter and Administrator
of Biberach-camp

Goldilocks's glowing testimony to my father, who asked for nothing more than
to be able to serve his fellow man in any capacity, without seeking glory or
looking for any reward save that of knowing it was a job well done.

*Above*: An illicit photo of part of General Leclerc's Free French Armoured Division, parked in Biberach's Town Square. Taken by a German camp officer with Nazi sympathies who should have surrendered his camera to the authorities once Germany capitulated.

*Below*: A targeting error by US bombers resulted in fifty-five civilian deaths and destruction of thirty-seven buildings, while I cowered under a concrete washstand in the camp as the ground heaved and buckled under my body.

*Courtesy of Rheinhold Adler*

No. 19995

The holder of this Card is / Inhaber dieser Karte ist: *MATTHEWS CECIL FREDERICK*

Residing at / Wohnhaft: *"Dallington" Rue Maze St Martin's*

Born on the / Geboren am: *20 – 4 – 1898* (at/in) *England*

**PARTICULARS — NÄHERE ANGA...**

*M* ....Single, Married, Widow or Widower
*verheiratet*....Ledig, verheiratet, verwitwet
*Brown*....Colour of Hair
*Braun*....Farbe des Haares
*Hazel*....Colour of Eyes
*Nussbraun*....Farbe der Augen

Controlling Committee of
the States of Guernsey.

Feldkommandantur,
Nebenstelle Guernsey.

No. 19996

The holder of this Card is / Inhaber dieser Karte ist: *MATTHEWS EILEEN...*

Residing at / Wohnhaft: *Dallington Rue Maze...*

Born on the / Geboren am: *25 – 1 – 1906* (at/in)

**PARTICULARS — NÄHER...**

*M* ....Single, Married, Widow or Widower
*verheiratet*....Ledig, verheiratet, verwitwet
*...Brown*....Colour of Hair
*Dunkelbraun*....Farbe des Haares
*Brown*....Colour of Eyes
*Braun*....Farbe der Augen

*Sept 1942*

Controlling Committee of
the States of Guernsey.

Feldkommandantur,
Nebenstelle Guernsey.

It was a huge indignity to pose for Nazi identification cards, but in spite of this, my mother's still holds the lucky four-leaf clover I found over seventy years ago, in the hope the leprechauns would come to spirit our family back home.

*Above*: After the occupation of Guernsey, and the departure of German troops, my eclectic and rare collection of working German military radio equipment lead to my becoming a Junior Associate of the Radio Society of Great Britain... and accidentally making contact with a commercial Pan Am flight.

*Below*: Upon my return to Guernsey, after serving with the Northern Rhodesia Police, it was a very moving moment for me to finally be able to shake the hand of Herr Laib (right), the man who had once saved my life in Biberach concentration camp.

welcome change from Dorsten but there were always shrieks of laughter as the Germans walked through to lock us in at night. Each Barrack chose its own leader, so any complaints or advice would go to her and she would also bring us any mail. She would also write anything of interest on a board in the corridor but it wasn't an enviable job to be a barrack leader, but in my barrack 15 we had Mrs Foot and her young daughter Ann and I think she did a very good job. Popped into our room very often to share the troubles, which were many.

One afternoon when the weather was so extremely cold, my father came visiting for a cup of hot afternoon bramble tea. He was wearing his coat but, in spite of this, he was shivering with the cold. So he could warm up and be more comfortable, he stretched out on my lower bunk, but no sooner had he done this than a great commotion erupted outside the barrack-room door. Within seconds the door was kicked wide open by a member of the dreaded SS troop, who began berating my father and made him stand to attention against one of the walls in the room. (This was before the running of the camp was entrusted to the German civilian police.) The SS guard started to gesture and pummel my father, and, as my mother wrote, 'We quite thought we were all for the high-jump!' I was shocked, too, but I waded into the fracas and started to pull at the German's uniform, for which I received a sound slap around the head and shoulders, sending me flying into the table and wooden stools.

My mother then grabbed hold of me and wrapped me in a vicelike hold so I was unable to move. My father stood stoically to attention, staring straight ahead and all the time the SS guard jabbed and pushed him around. Then the guard left just as quickly as he had arrived and we never knew what the disturbance had been about in the first place, but assume it was an endeavour to get my father to respond so further severe action could be taken against him. All I know is that, once again, I had a very sore head and a black eye for quite a few days afterwards.

Members of the International Red Cross and the YMCA and YWCA organisations visited the camp in that winter of 1942 and their initial reports gave a very depressing picture of a concentration camp massively infested with vermin and being bitterly cold. The barracks were impossible to heat and consequently twenty-eight people had already been admitted to the camp hospital because of the freezing conditions, primitive sanitation and the grievous shortage of an adequate and nutritious food supply.

Several weeks after our arrival in Biberach, all the inmates received the first emergency issue of Red Cross parcels, which helped to ward off near-starvation for many of us. It has been incorrectly written elsewhere that 'one of the most responsible jobs was the distribution of Red Cross parcels in Biberach, and this went to Mr R. W. Fletcher.' My mother's angry scrawl across the pages of one history book says otherwise, as she writes, 'total rubbish and even more rubbish as Mr Fletcher was not even in Biberach!' In any event, it is a matter of record that my father and Uncle Dave Godwin were in charge of the Red Cross stores in Biberach. My father was appointed chairman of the Red Cross Committee, possibly because he was a good administrator and constable of his parish, and, probably more importantly, because he was by now fairly fluent in the German language. Uncle Dave was also an unrivalled choice, as he had matchless personal experience of operating and administering a large grocery and wholesale concern on Guernsey.

The Red Cross stores were housed in a large building, formed with heavy iron girders and struts and a high pitched-roof area. It had been constructed on the edge of the camp towards the bottom left-hand corner, and was not far removed from the southwest boundary of the barbed-wire fence. Next door was a cobbler's shop and a washhouse. As far as I can remember, my friend Mike Martel's father ran the cobbler's and he was deeply admired by my father not only for refusing to work for the Germans but also for giving up his free time to help make children's toys in the Red Cross stores.

I think Uncle Dave and my father, apart from doing a difficult job well and efficiently, soon found themselves conveniently insulated from camp politics, rumours and the normal day-to-day pettiness that life exudes in such cramped conditions. They both had such a wonderful sense of humour and went about their work quietly and without banging the drum or blowing their own horn. For them, one of the most important aspects of their work was the thought that they were working for our people and not for the Germans. I think they made their duties appear so very easy and simple, because after the war a number of the deportees who had helped out in the stores started taking personal credit for all this work, which seemed to increase in importance with each telling. My mother became so frustrated and annoyed by this turn of events that she wrote to the various German officials who had been involved with the camp administration and the Red Cross in Biberach and secured a written testament! My father, however, ensured this was never used. He used to say, 'The real people who matter know what we did, and in a thousand years who will care anyway?'

As a matter of record, however, the testament reads:

1945 Testimony

During the time I was looking after the 1,200 British Internees coming from the Channel Islands, I have appointed several men for special work in our camp at Biberach/Riss, South Germany.

Among those was Mr Cecil Matthews, who was in charge of the Red Cross, distributing parcels from the Red Cross in Geneva and the YMCA as well as the YWCA. It was a pleasure to cooperate with Mr Matthews, as he was an outstanding character, absolutely reliable and righteous in his work. He never said a word too much, he remained calm when others got excited and was friendly to everybody.

I appreciated him as a perfect gentleman and wonderful personality, so did Mr Laib, who was the German official in charge of the Red Cross. Also he regarded Mr Matthews as a clever and capable man doing well whatever he was undertaking.

The International Red Cross Representatives from Switzerland and Sweden, who visited the camp regularly, assured me that it was a pleasure for them to converse with Mr Matthews upon many subjects regarding the Red Cross and the camp. He will always be in our minds, remembering the camp at Biberach/ Riss during the war.

Signed: Helen Roschmann
Interpreter and Administrator of Biberach Camp

Once the Red Cross parcels had been issued to the prisoners and the contents decanted, the cardboard and the box cord from the parcels were immediately recycled and used by those people of a more practical bent in the production of a whole wide range of innovative products. The prime movers in these endeavours were Mr and Mrs Makarios, who had been sent to the camp from Greece, where they had previously owned a number of shoe shops. They taught my mother, and many others, how to weave the box cord to make a photograph frame, using the cardboard for the backing, but it was obviously very time-consuming and boring work and she never attempted it again. We still have the photograph frame and even to this day it has never carried a photograph. Inmates also made rope sandals, again under the supervision and teaching of Mr Makarios, but I hated wearing them, as they caused friction burns when I ran and anyway, where a growing boy was concerned, they never really lasted for any great length of time.

Neville and Ralph Godwin and I loved visiting the Red Cross stores and seeing our fathers working there. One spring morning, they showed us a blackbird's nest built high up in the gantry and they had arranged the parcels especially for us, in a series of steps so we could gently and quietly peek over the top into the nest. I can remember the brood nestling down in the warmth of the nest and I could see the thin yellow line around their mouths, showing the gradual formation of their beaks.

Once we had climbed down, we also noticed a small, young kitten drinking from a saucer of watered-down condensed milk. We were very concerned for the welfare of the young birds but our fathers told us the nest was too far away for the cat to reach and, anyway, this was their new worker, who was now being employed to keep the place free from mice. I thought then how very sad that a cat had to look for scraps of food in a concentration camp, itself bereft of any real nourishment. I wanted to take the kitten back to my barrack room each night and promised to bring him back every morning, but my mother would have none of it, so I stated somewhat categorically that, when I went home again to Guernsey, one day I would have a large dog instead.

At the very beginning there were some very snide remarks made about our parents and how they were benefiting from their 'exalted' position to the point that they were receiving more than their just dues from the Red Cross parcel issues. The routine was therefore quickly established whereby we would be the last of the families to receive parcels and these parcels could be delivered only by a recognised official, excluding my father and Uncle Dave, and so eventually these stupid and divisive rumours died away.

When you are starving, Red Cross parcels are an absolute joy and a necessity to receive. On opening one, there always arose a wonderful sweet smell; this luscious, cloying scent still lingers in the memory. The Red Cross boxes were made of strong, heavy-duty cardboard and then tightly bound with box cord. The boxes were oblong in shape and carried the Red Cross symbol and designation, while inside the goodies were protected by small wedges of thin strips of multicoloured cellophane. The contents of the parcels varied from time to time but usually they included jam, a tin of condensed milk, chocolate, a tin of powdered milk called KLIM, and it was not until I was a little older that I found out 'KLIM' was 'MILK' spelled backwards. I loved KLIM because, if you ate a spoonful of the powder, it would stick closely to the roof of your mouth, where it could be licked slowly for quite some time.

There would also be biscuits, a tin of corned beef or Spam, perhaps a tin of sardines, raisins or dried prunes (I hated these), rice pudding, salt and pepper and sometimes a little butter and cheese. There would be a small allowance of cigarettes, which went straight to my father, but for me the worst item of all was a bar of soap. Once the parcels had been distributed and opened, little groups of prisoners congregated alongside various bunks in their barrack rooms, and became vociferously engaged in swapping or bartering those items they didn't want for more welcoming fare.

I have read reports that some of the prisoners in Biberach had interior-sprung mattresses: some hope! We lay on nothing more than sacks stuffed full with straw. I can remember having to go with my thin, cotton-ticking palliasse to a storeroom near the Red Cross stores. This room was piled high with straw and we were given only a short time to empty and refill our mattresses before having to lug them all the way back to our barrack rooms. The whole exercise was most uncomfortable as the storeroom soon became filled with dust to the point that breathing became extremely difficult. This procedure was conducted with the usual Teutonic efficiency, on a barrack-by-barrack, room-by-room basis, but only once a year. So this was going to be our bed for another year. At first you could see the steam rising up from the bunk in the early morning, and the whole thing became very lumpy until you were finally able to wear it down after several weeks' usage. In addition we had no pillows but only a dirty old brown blanket to rest our heads on.

Up to this point the full responsibility for looking after the deportees had fallen to the Wehrmacht, under the command of a camp commandant who held the rank of a lieutenant colonel. He was also responsible for another camp called Ilag VC Wurzach, nineteen miles away from Biberach, which also housed a large number of Channel Islanders. Understandably, the army didn't wish to become embroiled in controlling civilian prisoners, so it subsequently came about in December 1942 that the German Interior Ministry assumed dominion over the camps, with security coming under the aegis of the local police. Although we didn't realise it at first, this was tantamount to divine intervention because the deputy commandant and senior guard was Otto Laib. In fact his name was not Otto but Franz. Otto was a nickname given to him by the prisoners. He had been born in 1888 and by this time he was already fifty-four years of age. My father used to say Herr Laib was ever courteous and concerned for the welfare of prisoners in his care, and he firmly believed civilians could be securely guarded without having to resort to a shouting match. History says Laib came to Biberach after breaking a shoulder that required a short period of convalescence, otherwise he would have been designated to serve on the Russian front, where he would have inevitably been responsible for the liquidation and disposal of Russian prisoners. As a devout Christian gentleman, he could not possibly have acquiesced to these orders, and his fate would have been a swift execution for failing to obey Nazi commands.

Franz Laib was kindly regarded by most of the camp inmates and in time he became a firm friend of our family and of many other families who had also been detained in Biberach. After the war, Franz Laib and his wife visited the islands at our invitation, which gave us all a wonderful opportunity of meeting him again and thanking him for his very many kindnesses extended to us during our enforced stay in Biberach.

The cold winters in Biberach seemed endless and the snow lingered with giant icicles hanging from gutters and roofs. The older boys built themselves igloos against the exterior walls of the Concert Hall and sometimes we small ones were allowed inside to marvel at their beautifully made dens. The barracks were really quite inadequate and desperately cold, and each room had only a bare electric light-bulb hanging from the ceiling. There were washrooms with toilets, basins and cold running water, although in truth these were only concrete troughs fixed along the length of a wall. Being somewhat resourceful, my father devised and made an electric kettle from a Peek Frean & Co. biscuit tin, having first discarded the lid. A thin wooden strip sat across the width of the tin and this held the electricity supply, which was plugged into the light socket. Then, two prongs, probably long nails, acted as the homemade elements and were firmly fixed into the wooden strip. The prongs then hung down into the liquid and heated the water. At this point I am assuming the power supply was of a Continental low-voltage type, because electric shocks were all too prevalent. In spite of continual warnings not to touch any part of the kettle when it was switched on, most people forgot, and Auntie Bobbie, the Polish lady and usually the recipient of more jolts than anyone else, soon christened the kettle 'the Old Devil'.

As time went by, life gradually took on a more orderly routine and a pace of its own. The roll calls continued in the same dysfunctional manner but the new German regime was generally content to let its charges operate the camp more as a self-regulatory body. Some people had brought or acquired gramophones and, as spring approached, music flooded out of various barracks and rooms. This would have been fine and enjoyable if it had not been for the fact that it was nearly always the same selection of music. 'You Are My Sunshine' is for ever locked into my now already seriously depleted memory cells. Even when a record was mercifully broken or damaged, there still appeared to be an inexhaustible supply of the same to keep the song alive and pounding out all over the camp.

The song was a very popular recording hit in 1939 and was declared one of the State Songs of Louisiana in the US. It was composed and written by Jimmie Davis and Charles Mitchell, although some researchers believe the song was actually written by Oliver Hood. One favourite version was sung by the world-renowned crooner Bing Crosby to the words:

> You are my sunshine, my only sunshine;
> You make me happy when skies are grey;
> You'll never know, dear, how much I love you;
> Please don't take my sunshine away.

The song then drones on for a further nine interminable verses, and trying to combat the effects of 'You Are My Sunshine' always coincided with the cacophony produced by the high-pitched, tinny sounds emitted from the German loudspeakers strategically positioned throughout the camp. This was a more draconian form of 'Happy Campers', invariably starting with a fanfare and then going on to extol the continuing virtues and breathtaking victories of the German armed forces against the Allies – or the 'aggressors', as they were frequently termed. This had quite a depressing effect on many people and, although they didn't want to believe these continuous debilitating news bulletins, it is a little like advertising, where, if you hear a message often enough, you are inclined to accept it as being the truth. In any case, there was nothing else available to judge the veracity of these sometimes wild and absurd statements, which was a great pity, especially as the British 8th Army had just secured such a great victory at El Alamein, against Erwin Rommel and the Afrika Corps.

My father's birthday on 20 April came around as usual and with it the celebration for the Führer, Adolf Hitler, born on the same day. Many of the guards arrived at the Red Cross stores to wish my father well; some of them brought him small gifts, and a few even brought German-language books to encourage him to improve his language skills. I think it made a great difference when an inmate could speak German and could therefore relate to and communicate with the German guards. My father, in turn, found his cigarette allowance had virtually disappeared, as he felt he had to return the various favours bestowed on him. What my father found most interesting in talking with the guards was that they couldn't understand why we weren't on the same side this time in fighting with the Russians, who they felt were clearly the ones seeking world domination. After all, they argued, as Anglo-Saxons we all came from the same ancient stock and should therefore stick together.

About this time and just before the arrival of springtime, my health started to deteriorate, mainly brought on, I suspect, by malnutrition and the freezing conditions, compounded by the fact that, as a young boy, my strength and vitality were not keeping up with my growing size thanks to the lack of food. I remember days of feeling listless and being confined to my bunk as I listened to the general hubbub going on all around me in the barrack room, and yet feeling completely detached from all such events. On hearing the details of my illness from my worried father, Herr Laib started to bring in a little fresh milk and occasionally an egg or two. I can recollect my very first egg as this was Easter time, and my father had drawn and then painted a country scene around the circumference of the egg. I was so entranced with this that I caused quite a fuss by not wanting to have the egg cooked and see the delicate picture destroyed, but in the end common sense triumphed and the egg was boiled gently in the 'Old Devil' kettle.

During the time I was *hors de combat*, I had many kind visitors, including Ethel Sophia Cheeswright, a world-famous watercolour artist who had been deported from the feudal island of Sark, where she had an artist's studio. Miss Cheeswright made a great impression on me and started me on the lifelong path of art appreciation. She would perch on the edge of my bunk with a scrap of paper in her hand and a pencil and start making higgledy-piggledy squiggles on the paper. Every now and then she would stop and show me the lines and ask me if I knew what she was drawing – and of course I never knew. Then, with a few final flourishes with the pencil, it seemed to me that the picture would come alive, to be revealed as one of the Seven Dwarfs or of Snow White or Pluto the cartoon dog.

# CHAPTER 9

# SETTLING DOWN

As far as I am concerned, the deputy commandant, Franz Laib, is one of the true heroes of Biberach Camp: he saved my life during those difficult times, and only through his kindness did my health rapidly improve. When I was fit enough to go outside, Laib would sometimes take me on his bicycle out into the countryside accompanied by his Alsatian guard dog, Alex. I know it is much smarter today to call the breed a German Shepherd, but in those days it was an Alsatian and it is what I still call him. Alex was probably about two years old and very fit with a lovely long shiny coat. He would pad happily alongside us, and this was the start of a very special relationship between Alex and me, a warm relationship still lingering in the deep recesses of my mind to the present day.

One day I went off travelling with Herr Laib, sitting in the strong wicker basket that draped over the handlebars of his bicycle, and, as usual, we were accompanied by Alex, who ran effortlessly alongside us. As we passed through the guarded main gates and onto the road outside the camp, we made a right-hand turn. I thought this must mean we were going towards Biberach town, but, after proceeding for only a little way, Herr Laib stopped by the side of some garden allotments. We dismounted and walked over towards a small, black-painted wooden shack, which had a lopsided roof. This was where the allotment holders kept their tools and other miscellaneous horticultural items, and it was possible to see that the padlock and chain normally used to secure the hut at night had been broken. I remember there was part of a sawn-through tree trunk inside and resting on the surface was an array of mouldy, half-eaten old chestnuts. Herr Laib told me a British prisoner of war had tunnelled out from another nearby camp in a bid to make his escape towards the Swiss border. However, if all he could find to eat nearby was a handful of mouldy and rotten chestnuts, then the omens for his successful getaway weren't very great. I felt very sad to hear this, and could only wish the prisoner, whoever he was, good fortune and eventual success.

After much cajoling, bargaining and even pleading on the part of our camp leaders, the Germans finally gave in and started to allow small, escorted walking parties of incarcerated civilians to leave the camp several times a week. Columns of prisoners left with an armed guard and an Alsatian dog at the front, and another armed guard bringing up the rear. There were two favoured routes: the one to the right led towards the castle tower and the town of Biberach, and the one to the left took us out towards the Black Forest. My parents decided that by now I had recovered sufficiently to enjoy the walk and considered that the exercise and the fresh air would do me good. The day started well enough as we all assembled in lines in front of the reservoir by the main gates of the camp. I was near the front of the column, with Herr Laib and Alex, while my parents were just behind us.

As we marched through the gates we turned right and made our way along pathways to the castle tower, which stood on the outskirts of Biberach. Near the tower the area had been paved and there were several stone benches, where we could sit and rest for a few moments. The other guard and his dog joined us, but within minutes, and after much low growling, both dogs suddenly burst into full-scale snarling and began to attack each other. All I could think about was my friend Alex, so I joined the fray and tried to prise these two dogs apart. In the ensuing altercation I was knocked over, with both dogs piling in against me. In the end, I was rescued by my father, who waded in and picked me up while Herr Laib grabbed Alex by his collar and yanked him away. No harm was done, but I think now it must have been a very close-run thing.

After resting for a short time, we continued the walk down towards the town, and on to the riverbank, where the water was rushing along at quite a fast rate after the recent rainstorms. Halfway along the bank was a weir, cordoned off by an extended decking of timber so the water could flow rapidly underneath the wooden planks and down into the weir. My mother told me not to go anywhere near the weir because, once anyone fell in, it would be the end of them because it would be impossible to fish them out. Everyone was chatting together in the sunshine and, being somewhat bored, I walked out onto the wooden planks, making sure I was nowhere near the weir, although the noise from the torrent below was utterly deafening. One more step and suddenly the wooden planking gave way and I dropped down into the fast-moving water. It all happened so quickly that I had no time to shout out and, even if I had, I doubt that anyone would have heard me.

I can still vividly recall looking up through the water and seeing the mottled sunlight streaming in beams through the water one moment, and then, in an instant, the darkness closed in as the planking blotted out the light, since I was being carried quickly downstream towards the weir. At the very moment I disappeared, my father had just looked up and saw me vanish from view. He ran straight out onto the boards, taking care not to place his feet anywhere near rotten wood; moreover, he kept shifting his weight from one foot to the other to reduce the chance of fracturing any of the already-weakened planks. Instead of going to the spot where I had fallen in, he had the stroke of genius to bound to the next available hole a little further on. As I floated past, still under the water, he reached down and grabbed me by my collar, and yanked me clear, only a few yards from the weir. It probably was a miracle I was not hurt in any way and only shocked – and very wet! All my mother could say to me was, 'Well, you're now going to have to walk all the way back to the camp in your wet clothes, and you'll probably catch your death of cold.' I realised then it must have been a very serious situation because no one scolded me, and, all in all, I have to say that this was not one of my better days.

My birthday soon came around again, and there were many presents and birthday cards, but the most memorable present was a signed, hand-coloured drawing on card by Ethel Sophia Cheeswright called *Mickey Mouse in Biberach*, dated 7 June 1943. The card contains a message inside which reads, 'To dear Stephen with love from Auntie Bet'. Auntie Bet was a cousin and she was married to Uncle Alf Pomeroy, who had been a captain of the Marines during the various upheavals in China. Auntie Bet, so I was told, had been a missionary out there and that was how they met. Although I cannot trace Miss Cheeswright's deportation from Sark, she is nonetheless shown on the lists of Channel Island prisoners housed at Compiègne in France. Compiègne was a prison camp built near Paris and to all intents and purposes it was used as a transit camp; here too the environment was very degrading for the victims. Eventually, most of the islanders held in such appalling conditions were transferred to Biberach.

I doubt the transfer to Biberach from Compiègne was much of a closely guarded secret. In all probability my father would have been notified to make arrangements for Red Cross food parcels to be made readily available for the new arrivals, and; knowing German efficiency, there would have been a detailed list of names. It all becomes patently clear when my mother describes her exhilaration:

It is June 1943 and another welcome change and excitement for us. Other barracks had to be opened and prepared for the Guernsey people coming from Compiègne camp, and of course directly I knew this and saw the list, I bagged a room for Auntie Bet Pomeroy, Mrs Chilcott and Mrs Wyatt. We were all at the gates to welcome them and also Auntie Rita Rabey and Mrs Willis, they all looked very tired and under the weather, but it was great to see fresh faces and have new topics of conversation as they had such a lot to tell us.

How Miss Cheeswright produced this birthday card and where she obtained the materials we will probably never know, although fellow prisoners and the International Red Cross did supply her later with some drawing paper and paints. She was already sixty-nine when she made this card, although she was by then in poor health and gradually going blind. Miss Cheeswright was later repatriated to the UK because of her failing health, and, after the war, she returned to Sark, where she died in 1977, aged 103. At the age of 101 she was asked by a newspaper reporter how she felt, and her instant reply was, 'I am just so excruciatingly bored.' Today, some of her paintings still appear for sale from time to time in London at Christie's and Sotheby's.

I can also see that the birthday card she produced is very symbolic. It shows a sanitised image of the barracks together with only part of the barbed-wire fences showing. It reflects, too, the feeling that freedom lay just beyond the wire and away over the delightful rolling green hills. In our repressive environment, totally devoid of anything natural, the flowers, the birds and the animals she drew provided ultimate hope for survival and for the future. Part of this hope for the future also lay in choosing Mickey Mouse, for it surely represented the power of the United States of America. Even in those desperate, terrible days and at such tender years we all knew who Mickey Mouse was. Today, I have several of her paintings, one commissioned by my grandfather well before the war, one from my parents painted just after the war, and two others I bought myself in memory of such a wonderful lady.

Many years later when I had just completed my business training in London, the company employing me sent me to Sark to meet with a very important client of theirs. I had to stop off on Guernsey, and my parents, hearing I was going to Sark and after discussions with various friends, stipulated I should make contact with Ethel Cheeswright, as they were all becoming greatly concerned over her health. I arrived on Sark on a bright and sunny day after a gentle sea crossing, looking very debonair for the occasion. I was wearing a light-grey, three-piece suit made in Savile Row with highly polished black shoes I had bought from a well-known shop in Jermyn Street in London, and of course I was carrying the all-important monogrammed leather briefcase.

At that moment a somewhat dishevelled figure wearing a moth-eaten fur coat detached itself from the waiting crowd assembled on the Sark quayside and in a loud voice shouted up, 'Is there a Stephen Matthews on board?' Taken momentarily by surprise, I shouted back, 'Yes, here,' to which the apparition replied, 'Well, now you've seen me, you can just bugger off back to Guernsey!' Even to this day I can still feel my cheeks flushed with embarrassment. Undaunted, though, I disembarked and followed her up the hill, maintaining a judicial distance behind her, until she finally turned around and said to me, 'Oh, well, you'd better come in for a cup of tea or something else.' And that meeting was the last time I ever saw her. A copy of the birthday card now rests in the Walt Disney Museum in America, where they state this is the only drawing in their possession depicting a Walt Disney character ever to have been produced in a German concentration camp during World War Two.

In Biberach Camp, the evenings, too, came around soon enough, and I, like many others, had to wash in ice-cold water before climbing into bed. Prayers had to be said and I had to make sure I included my brother in Oldham. Then the blanket curtain was lowered, allowing me to drift off to sleep. Early in the morning, as if by magic I would find a small half-square of chocolate lying on the horizontal metal bedframe just above my head, and this would herald the beginning of yet another day in camp. However, I was not allowed to speak until 8 a.m. and any communication with my mother in the top bunk had to be accomplished first by pushing hard against the underside of the bunk and then afterwards by mime. It is only recently, since finding my mother's journals, that I realise she had lost her voice for nearly a year, probably brought about through the trauma and stress coupled with the bitterly cold conditions of these camps.

Summer came in grudgingly, and with it the Hitler Youth members soon appeared on the adjacent hillside alongside the camp, carrying their gliders, which they positioned most carefully at the very top of the hill. The hill was called Lindele, like the camp, because of the long line of linden trees, standing as silent sentinels along the rim of the hill. The Hitler Youth attached long, snaking ropes to the gliders and these were gathered up by lines of youths, who, at a given signal, would start rushing pell–mell downhill until the gliders took to the air and began searching out the necessary thermal currents. Over the course of the next few years this would be a common sight throughout the long hours of summer daylight.

The Hitler Youth camp was fairly near ours but further south and a little lower down on the plateau. Hitler Youth (*Hitlerjugend*) was a paramilitary organisation devised early on by Adolf Hitler to support the Nazi Party. It existed in various forms from 1922 until 1945, and its members, aged thirteen to eighteen, were specially selected in the early years to become Aryan supermen. In 1936 membership stood at some five million. During the war they also helped local fire brigades and rescue teams in the numerous bombed-out German cities.

In 1945, when German military casualties began to mount significantly, Hitler Youth recruitment started to take in candidates from as young as twelve. Their motto was '*Blut und Ehre*' ('Blood and Honour') and for this they led a Spartan existence with dedication and fellowship for Nazi conformity. They were always turned out in immaculate condition with crisp khaki shirts and shorts and with the ever-present Nazi swastika armbands. In Biberach, quite often members of the Hitler Youth would walk around the outside of the barbed-wire fence, shouting and making faces and sticking their tongues out at us inmates; but everyone was just too scared stiff to say or do anything in retaliation.

In camp, the younger prisoners banded together and met socially most days, playing various games, including football, and sometimes with one of my tennis balls. We all became great friends, both boys and girls, and even after the war had ended and we were safely back on Guernsey these strong friendships continued. Later the inimitable Tom Remfrey, himself a young prisoner in Biberach, founded the Guernsey Deportees Association, which still meets regularly and continues to fight the old battles all over again! It is strange, though, for we may have grown older and greyer and suffered the inevitable ravages of time, but I still see these friends as they were then, so energetic and vibrant; young people, who continue to occupy a fixed place in my heart. As children, we didn't bother then about inter-island rivalries and in many cases we didn't even know where our friends came from, nor did we care; when you are young and unworldly, the only thing that really matters is a personal, friendly and trusting relationship.

Even though we detested our German overseers, there were several unsung heroes and heroines among them, who have never received any acknowledgement for the care and consideration given to the prisoners in their charge. One was the Christian German nursing sister called Annie Sigg, who worked in the women's section of the camp hospital, which had been established in Barrack 7. Annie lived outside the camp but came in every day to work alongside Sister Norah Last, the wife of another camp figure, Harry Last. Sister Annie brought in little gifts of food for her patients – including for my mother when she was in the hospital, having fallen down heavily in the snow and ice of a terrible German winter – which Sister Annie paid for out of her own pocket.

Eddie Coll, from the St John Ambulance on Guernsey, also rendered valuable services to the men's section of the hospital in the adjacent Barrack 8. Eddie was tireless in his efforts, and devoted to helping people. Even after the war, when I would meet him at various events such as the numerous Island Agricultural and Horticultural Shows, he would be sure to spend time talking to me and was so keen to know how I was getting on, and always gave me great encouragement.

My mother also points out in her writings, 'We had a Doctor McGlashen who was in charge of the hospitals and also a Doctor Sutherland who had been taken prisoner at Tobruk. He was very young and he always had a surgery full of women!'

One other major figure who played such a prominent part in our lives in Biberach, and who was so loved by the internees, was Helen Roschmann, a young and very attractive Bavarian administrator and interpreter who was attached to the camp's administrative services. Aged just twenty-six, she had the most beautiful, honey-coloured hair, often braided, which soon earned her the name of 'Goldilocks'. During our time in the camp, Goldilocks went out of her way to listen to people's problems and often took our part against the German authorities – no mean feat. All in all, she was a very remarkable woman, who, in the end, did not escape the wrath of her superiors and was eventually moved to the German censorship section, where she could be corralled and kept under strict supervision by one of the brutal SS's senior female administrators in the section.

# THE DAY THE NAZIS CAME

It has been recorded that Goldilocks contracted typhus as a result of handling contaminated British POW letters from outside the camp. However, this seems most unlikely, and I have my doubts as to the veracity of this report, especially as typhus was an ingenious and regular method of 'disposal' used by the SS in order to rid themselves of an inconvenient problem. Nevertheless, Goldilocks miraculously survived and lived on into her nineties. After the war, she married one of the more kind and humane camp guards, who had become a pastor of his church. Like Herr Laib and his wife, Goldilocks and her husband were invited by former prisoners to visit the islands after the war had ended, as a measure of our appreciation for all her endeavours.

We kept in touch with Goldilocks for many years, but unfortunately, as is often the way of the world, I lost contact with her for a little while. However, my good friends Tom and Wendy Remfrey came to the rescue and through them I was able, once again, to start writing to her, although by this time she had become a widow. Her last letter to me, written at the age of ninety-one, talked about her love of languages and how she envied me for living part of the year in France, where the very words of the French language sounded like beautiful and gentle music to her. Shortly afterwards, she died quietly in her sleep and another chapter of my life in Biberach came to a sad but peaceful close.

However, this was far from being the end of her story because, no sooner had the manuscript for this book been completed and sent off to the publishers, than I came across a letter written by Goldilocks, describing part of her life and the manner in which she was sent to Biberach Camp as an interpreter by the Nazis. The letter reveals Goldilocks's enormous and understated courage as a young woman living in Germany at the beginning of World War Two. In her letter she wrote:

I was born in 1918 as the daughter of a Lutheran clergyman of a village in the Black Forest. When I was three years old, my father moved with his family, two boys and myself, to a place near the university of Tübingen (South Germany) in order to enable my two and seven years older brothers to go the 'Gymnasium' (only for boys) to learn Latin, Greek and Hebrew. Later on I went to a similar school, only for girls, to learn what was called 'modern languages' such as English, French etc.

Having passed all ten years of school, I was invited by an English lady to come to England. My younger brother met her on a train in Italy and on her way back to England she paid a visit to our home and liked it so much, that she came every year until the war. On her return she invited my brother to come and see her. But as he could not go, in 1936 I went instead of him, to Horsell-Woking, where she was a music teacher and owner of a boarding-school for girls. After having learned the English language at school for 6 years, I would improve my knowledge by attending a class of 16 years old girls.

After half a year I wanted to learn to know an

English family-life and went as an 'aupair-girl' to a young couple with a 6 months old Baby, whom I had to look after. According to my permit to stay in England, I returned to Germany after one year's stay (altogether) in Great Britain. Having got fond of the English, I decided to study the language at the University of Leipzig in the north of Germany. My first job after my study was to be a secretary of the German consul of Sweden. He possessed the best Travelling Agency in Stuttgart, and when I had some time left I took part in his interesting work. In 1939 the war started and some weeks before many Jews came to buy a ticket to America by Hapag Lloyd. Our office could get many transfer tickets for the boat to America and other parts of the world. This made us all very happy.

Owing to the war it got more and more dangerous to travel, so the Agency lost most of its customers and at last closed it. Also the consul of Sweden closed his office, so I found another job by working for the Social Department of the Ministry. This gave me much satisfaction as I could help poor women who were ashamed to ask for financial help of the Government. However one day a letter arrived from the Army Headquarters, telling me that I had to pass an examination in the English language (at a certain date) in a department of the Army at Stuttgart.

I was examined in writing and verbally and had passed quite well, and as a result got an order by letter to go to Biberach as an interpreter of the Internees Camp.

As I could not oppose the order (nobody could!) I went by train to Biberach, where I had to report at the district office and was sent to the camp officer where I introduced myself as an interpreter and in my heart I prayed to God, that HE may give me the strength and wisdom to be of help for the internees, whom I never regarded as an enemy, only human beings in distress. With this attitude I risked my life, but God has protected me as an answer of my parents' prayers. (When the officer with soldiers left the camp after several months, the 'Gestapo' took over – very dangerous Nazis.)

In spite of receiving the life-saving Red Cross parcels, we were still hungry. This was partly because each parcel had to last a family ten to fourteen days. One lunchtime, my mother gave me a piece of mouldy ersatz bread but, wonder of wonders, it was liberally smothered with something called strawberry jam. I had absolutely no idea what strawberries were and I was entranced by her explanation. She pointed to one of the two red lumps on the bread, which she said were real strawberries, and then shooed me outside as she wanted to get on with cleaning her section of the barrack room. I sat outside on the kerb near the concrete washing troughs and contemplated my bread and strawberry jam. First, I gently nibbled one edge and tasted a little of the jam, and the taste just seemed to explode on my tongue, with its sweet and fruity sensation.

Just then, one of the young Guernseymen who were passing by stopped and asked me what I was doing. I told him I was eating real strawberry jam made with real strawberries. 'No,' he said, 'I just can't believe that.' So I showed him the bread and pointed out the strawberries. He took the bread from my hand as if to examine it further and then started to eat it. The whole piece was entirely consumed in an instant and all I could think of was to tell him he had just stolen it. He looked at me for some time and then said, 'Well, it's your word against mine, and I know who people will believe.' And, with that, he just strode away.

I was absolutely stunned and horrified. I rushed off to the Red Cross stores to tell my father, who, although looking very angry, told me it would indeed come down to my word against that of the thief – but I shouldn't worry, as he would fetch me another piece of bread and jam.

Like most things in a concentration camp, rumour and news spread like wildfire, and it wasn't long before everyone appeared to know what had happened. This was compounded the very next day by my mother, who waited until the young man was sitting with friends in the small converted canteen, and marched in and slammed a small pot of jam down on the table in front of him. She told him in no uncertain manner that she was giving him the jam so he wouldn't need to steal food from poor and starving little children any more. She said afterwards that at least the man's friends had the decency to get up and leave the table.

This was the day, though, when I first came across a really effective and marvellous new weapon, which was my sullen and silent confrontational approach. I followed this man wherever he went around the camp. I kept a short distance away, although always remaining visible, so every time he looked up he would see me glaring back at him. This lasted continuously for several days until he could stand it no longer and went to see my father to apologise for his actions and to ask him to call me off. In retrospect now, I feel so sorry for him, not only because abject hunger is such a diabolical state to be in, but also because his one hasty action brought down unending misery on his head. Even years afterwards on Guernsey, I would sometimes see him coming down the High Street in St Peter Port and, when he saw me, he would quickly scuttle across the cobblestones into a nearby shop and wait for me to pass on by.

As time flew by, we younger ones thought the older boys were having a much better time and a lot more fun than we were. They seemed so well organised. So we decided to ask them if we could join their 'gang' and be part of their group. After much discussion, it was agreed we could join, provided we passed their initiation test. The test consisted of making a paste from crushed brick and lime dust, with a little added spittle from each of the gang members. Each of us younger ones was then expected to eat a portion of the paste, after which we would be specially admitted to the ranks of their society. After much deliberation and mature reflection – and the thoughts expressed by Robin Bartlett, who had recently arrived from Compiègne prison camp – that the concoction might be poisonous, we regretfully, although perhaps wisely, declined the offer of gang membership.

Another friend, called John, had recently arrived in Biberach with his family and we became very firm friends. I can remember his mother, who had appeared in the camp wearing her expensive fur coat that she had somehow managed to smuggle in with most of her jewellery sewn into its linings. Most people thought she was just silly but by the next severe winter I think the majority of them had changed their minds about it. John said to me once, 'I know people think my mother's silly, but she's the only mother I have.'

Soon, we had a little nucleus of friends, both girls and boys from Guernsey, such as Mike Martel, Jill Chubb, Neville and Ralph Godwin, John Benham and Robin Bartlett; then there were my friend John, Gordon Buchan and Peter Cardnell from Jersey. We would meet regularly and play together, often visiting each other's quarters because we were very territorial youngsters and inclined to spend most of our time near our own particular barrack room.

The day for the final dress rehearsal for the camp concert arrived and I had reluctantly agreed to play the part of a fairy in this production, complete with transparent wings, fixed with string to my shoulders. I had to wear sandals, which I loathed, and my pyjamas, which I detested, and all of this combined to make me feel very self-conscious. I believe I was chosen only because I had blond hair and could look quite angelic on occasions.

The dress rehearsal started well enough, when the curtains were drawn back and the assembled crowd applauded the players and the colourful scenery. Seated in the front row alongside Herr Franz (Otto) Laib were the twins Neville and Ralph Godwin. When I strode onto the stage, Neville's face took on a look of shocked horror when he saw me, but Ralph was a far different matter. Ralph, like his father, has a very keen sense of humour, and just occasionally, if you can capture the right moment, you can make him laugh and laugh until the tears run down his cheeks – and this was just what happened on this day.

I am afraid I brought the whole production to a grinding halt as I refused to go on any further until Ralph stopped laughing. The producer was summoned to the edge of the stage and tried to talk to him, but this proved nigh impossible. Ralph was still chortling away with his head buried in his outstretched arms. In answer to the producer's call if he would stop laughing, Ralph acknowledged this by a quick nod of the head, but by now the cause was well and truly lost.

I abandoned the performance and left the stage, withdrawing completely, and on the way back to our barrack room my mother used the words I would continue to hear at regular intervals throughout my formative years: 'I am mortified, utterly mortified, and I just don't know what people will think of us.' I think my father, who usually adopted a very low profile in such circumstances, was probably eternally grateful for the peaceful seclusion of the nearby Red Cross stores.

It was not that I disliked concerts. Far from it: Freddie Williams was a theatrical producer of immense talent and energy and did much to lift the spirits of the inmates; the YMCA and YWCA were kind enough to supply various musical instruments; and a good orchestra was formed to play at dances, concerts and musical shows. The finale of each event was unfailingly the playing and singing of the forbidden British national anthem. Freddie Williams was always extremely active organising and preparing shows. Most of the plays were far too sophisticated for me to understand, but I revelled in some of the shows put on by Len Teel and, even more than seventy-two years after one particular show, I still cannot get some of the ludicrous lyrics out of my mind. 'Sandy, he belongs to the mill / And the mill belongs to Sandy still.'

But the shows were bright and effervescent and people were able to forget their dire circumstances, even if only for a few precious hours. Tommy Mees was also a great favourite of mine, and he seemed to be everywhere at once, playing in the orchestra and then organising various theatrical productions. The main thing about all these people was they spared their valuable time to talk with the young children and they went out of their way to make sure we young ones were all kept happy and well entertained.

It was quite normal for me to saunter into the theatre and secure a front-row seat. However, on one occasion the camp police decided I couldn't be allowed in without a ticket. I went back to my barrack room in high dudgeon and told my mother I was going to make my own ticket. I don't think she believed me but later on, when she found I was missing, she hurried to the theatre, only to find me happily engrossed in the concert from my usual prime seat of honour in the front row.

There was also one great sporting event, when a football team selected from Jersey inmates played against a team from Guernsey, this being rather reminiscent of the peacetime inter-island rivalry. The excitement was contagious and the shouting and cheering could be heard all over the camp. Jersey scored a goal in the first half, but Guernsey came back at them and gained an equaliser about ten minutes before the end. Some weeks later with the camp band playing happily on the sidelines, Guernsey won the replay match 6–1.

A few months after that, the YMCA, through the auspices of the Red Cross in Geneva, provided the camp inmates with cricket equipment and a match was subsequently arranged to take place on the parade ground using a woven rush mat for the crease and real wooden stumps on a stand with bails. I was more than a little proud to know my father was going to play, especially as the match was between Guernsey and Jersey. My father's team won the toss and elected to bat, and I was overjoyed to see my father was one of the opening batsmen.

On a lovely sunny afternoon, all went well and the score steadily mounted. I walked backwards and forwards among the spectators, luxuriating in their genuine comments on my father's playing abilities: 'What a good shot!'; 'You can see he's played this game before'; 'I think he could easily reach his hundred.' My father's score reached twenty-seven runs when disaster struck. He hit a ball just a little on the offside and shouted 'No' to his partner as an indication they shouldn't attempt a run. To everyone's amazement, the other player shouted 'Yes' and began to scamper down the pitch. Eventually, my father was run out. I was simply devastated.

After the game, and although Guernsey had scored eighty-nine runs to Jersey's twenty-five all out, I still felt humiliated. Bearing in mind my previous success with my silent stalking routine, I started following the itinerant batsman throughout the camp; whenever he turned round, there I was glaring at him. This continued for several days until, in desperation, he too spoke with my father, who in turn talked to me about sportsmanship and how it was essential to be a good loser. Another valuable lesson learned.

At this same juncture we saw the beginning of the Allied bombing raids on a German city lying only some forty miles away from Biberach. This soon became a regular performance on the part of the Royal Air Force and the American Eighth Air Force. At night we could see lights in the sky as the planes overflew the camp, and during the day we marvelled at the long vapour trails of the B-17s and B-24 Flying Fortresses and their fighter escorts. Although we didn't know it at the time, the target was the V-2 Rocket production facility inside the Zeppelin works. Allied aircraft generally flew at a height of 21,000 feet and their missions, emanating from England, usually lasted more than nine hours. Sometimes we could see the blood-red glow in the sky in the direction of Friedrichshafen, so we knew just how efficient the Allied bombing could be in starting such massive fires.

One side effect of the visible passage of the thousand-bomber raids overhead was the uplifted spirits of the prisoners, and it gave the lie to the shrill loudspeaker announcements of continuing German military victories. Now, each German announcement was met with hoots of derision and ribald comments, until the point was reached where the loudspeakers were finally turned off and silence reigned throughout the camp.

# CHAPTER 10

# MY FOUR-LEAF CLOVER

I have to say our family have always been most regular in the conduct of their daily ablutions. Normally, I would wake at an early hour, before anyone else was up and about, and, as usual, I would find a small half-square of chocolate on the horizontal metal bar that acted as a hard and uncomfortable headboard. Once I had consumed the chocolate, I would take my German-issue aluminium mug and slip out quietly to fetch a cup of water.

On this particular morning I was approaching the concrete washing troughs, perhaps a little bleary-eyed, when a ghostly female apparition with long pendulous breasts suddenly sat up right in front of me. Well, I yelled – I mean, I really yelled – and at the same time I dropped my aluminium mug, leaving it echoing loudly as it bounced around on the stone floor, and then I hightailed it back to our barrack room.

I immediately jumped into my bunk and covered my head

under the old blanket, while my mother, becoming a little alarmed, asked me what the matter was: all I could say in reply was I had just seen a ghost. My mother was out of her top bunk in a trice and careered down the passageway to confront the ghost, and I soon heard loud voices raised in anger. It turned out that one of the women deportees, finding the atmosphere in her barrack room to be too hot and stuffy, had decided to cool off by lying down in a narrow trough of cold water, thinking no one would be about so early in the morning. After this contretemps and such a fierce exchange of words, the matter appeared settled and forgotten – well, almost.

I am afraid to say I don't recall very much about schooldays in Biberach. I can easily recollect the kindness of the headmaster, Mr Foote, and I know Auntie Joy Godwin was a teacher, as was the lovely Miss Gwen Barnet. I can also remember where the school was housed in Barrack 23 near the Red Cross stores, which suited me extremely well because it meant I could easily visit my father after school.

I believe we didn't spend all day in school but went along most afternoons for just about two hours. Still, I do recall one important lesson, which was all about good manners. Our teacher stressed the importance of good manners in our daily lives and how it behoved us to wish all and sundry a hearty good morning, or afternoon, whenever we met them, and more especially to do so with those people we knew well. Moreover, we were told we would be astonished by the immediate and kind responses, besides the cheerful reactions, from those people we greeted, so I decided to give it a try. As far as reactions were concerned, the teacher was absolutely correct, as the response was really amazing: people beamed and were much friendlier than before. So I resolved to develop this new-found tactic, albeit, as it turned out, it would prove to my serious detriment.

I continued my new approach to good manners with some vigour the very next morning while I was sitting in one of the toilet cubicles, with the door firmly shut. As each person came along to the other cubicles, they were greeted in turn by me with a personal 'good morning' and their name, and, although I have to say I was slightly disappointed by the response, which usually generated only a few low grunts, I still vowed to disregard this setback and to continue with my new-found means of communication.

Several days later I was summoned into our barrack room, seemingly full to overflowing with people, to face the first of what I came to know as a kangaroo court. It was obvious to me that my mother was greatly distressed, and it turned out that Uncle Arthur Langmead, who was a senior member of the civilian police in the camp, had received a complaint from the 'ghost' lady to the effect I had been looking at her while she was sitting on the toilet – otherwise how would I know who she was and how would I be able to call her and greet her by name? She had also press-ganged some of the other early-morning performers to join in, and as a group they were all demanding a special hearing and seeking eventual satisfaction.

Uncle Arthur Langmead was a Guernsey policeman, besides being a friend of the family. He had arrived in Biberach after most of the others, having been first sent to other camps, but now he was here he could, in a professional capacity, represent the camp authority. However, he was both fair and thorough and in this case had made a detailed examination of the toilets beforehand, finding it was totally impossible to look under the doors. This may have been a little disconcerting at first for the old biddy, but she soon came back on the attack and suggested I must have been looking through the keyhole. As Uncle Arthur said, the problem with that theory was there were no keyholes. In desperation, the old biddy insinuated I must have climbed up on top of the partition and had seen everyone from a high vantage point. Uncle Arthur was by now becoming a little tired with the case and stated it was 'most unlikely, unless Stephen had changed his name to Harry Houdini'. However, even I knew the matter had to be resolved somehow.

The old shrew went straight back onto the offensive by saying, 'I may not know how he did it but he did, and he deserves a damn good hiding.' Although I wasn't sure what all this was about, I was becoming somewhat concerned for my own personal safety at this juncture, because I had no real idea why I was there. Uncle Arthur then explained carefully to me what the fuss was all about and asked me to explain the whole mystery from my standpoint.

I explained all about my new code of good manners, and that the whole affair was really quite simple: the old lady wheezed continuously, so it was easy to identify her as she came along; another of the women from another barrack room walked with the aid of a stick, which had lost the rubber ferrule, so it made a clicking sound on the stone floor that you could hear miles away, each time she took a step; then there was one person who had a deep smoker's cough; and someone else who had a limp; so it was very easy to identify them all by their various characteristics. To be fair to Uncle Arthur, he just burst out laughing, as did most other people in the room, and it took quite a few minutes for the brouhaha to subside.

But, when it did, Uncle Arthur turned furiously on the old woman. He accused her of being spiteful and vindictive and, more importantly, of wasting police time. If she wasted police time again she would find herself in the 'cooler' for a short spell. When he left and everything quietened down, I decided it would be much better if I stopped being so polite to people in future, and more especially so in the toilets. But on this note an interesting point was made in one of the International Red Cross inspectors' reports, which stated in regard to some of the deportees from the Channel Islands, 'They are generally untidy and seem to take pleasure in upkeeping a quarrelsome spirit, which leads to trivial, petty gossiping the whole day long.' But oh! How very, very true!

There was, however, one life-changing moment that occurred at school which is indelibly imprinted on my mind. On a lovely sunny day all the schoolchildren were congregated together in the theatre hut, where the headmaster, Mr Foote, announced we were each going to receive a book, courtesy of the YMCA in Geneva, Switzerland. Even now I can see the raised stage with Mr Foote and Miss Gwen Barnett standing in front of a large table, piled high with new volumes. One by one we were all called up to receive one, and when it was my turn Mr Foote shook me by the hand and gave me a hardback book called *Friendly Village* – one of the 'Alice and Jerry' educational series. The inside cover bore the handwritten message, 'To Stephen Matthews, in memory of school-days spent in Biberach', and it is signed by both Mr Foote and Miss Barnett. The same page also bore the green stamp of the YWCA 'War Prisoner Aid World's Committee' together with a black stamp of the German censor – number 10598 – and also the rubber stamp of the German Biberach Camp Administration. *Friendly Village* was printed by Row, Peterson and Company, who apparently had offices in New York City, Evanston in Illinois, and San Francisco. It was most gently and beautifully illustrated by Florence and Margaret Hoopes, and through this combination I could not only live a make-believe life outside the confines of the camp but I also developed a lifelong thirst for knowledge, especially for other countries and peoples and their cultures.

The beauty of the book lay in the fact that the heroes of the moment were two children, sister and brother Alice and Jerry, and they both appeared to be about the same age as I was. I could see the world through their eyes and easily imagine I was enjoying and taking part in their adventures. There was one particular chapter in the book headed 'Cowboys and Indians', and here I learned about the Great Plains of America, with rolling countryside and happy cowboys rounding up large herds of cattle. There was exciting information about living on a cattle ranch and about the cookhouse and the cowboys. Then came the piece about the Indians, who lived in the great outdoors in tents called tepees, and they all had wonderful names such as Silver Cloud and Snapping Turtle.

As I read, I made myself a promise that one day I would go to America and visit a ranch, riding the range with cowboys and living in a tepee with the Indians – or Native Americans, as we would say these days. In reality, it was some fifty-five years before I could fulfil this promise, when I arrived hopefully and then left reluctantly several days later by helicopter.

*Friendly Village* also contained an episode about a goat pulling a bright yellow cart, and I thought perhaps one day I too could have a goat with a cart so I could put all my books in it and go off to school. Later, this notion was to get me into more trouble again, as we will see in one of the following chapters.

Schooldays – or, rather, afternoons – weren't always trouble-free. I loved English lessons and learning new words, but one day during an English test I was given only six out of ten marks for some of the words we had just learned. I couldn't believe this and asked to see the 'book' to check for myself. Naturally, this was refused and the whole affair made me quite cross. Back in our barrack room my ire continued to erupt and, in the midst of it, I was stunned to hear my mother saying to one of our fellow-occupants, 'I don't know what's the matter with Stephen, but he has the seven little devils inside him today.' I didn't know what she meant, but it sounded quite serious, so I went back to the teacher and told her I was sorry about my behaviour but it was only because I had the seven little devils inside me and didn't know how to get rid of them.

Sometimes on those wonderful hot afternoons, while most of the older people were resting in their barrack rooms, my mother and I would take a short walk along the perimeter fence of the camp, eventually ending up at the Red Cross stores. Here we would stop off for a chat and cup of bramble-leaf tea (which put me off tea for the remainder of my life) with my father and Uncle Dave Godwin. Once on the way back to our barrack room I was mumbling to my mother about how green the grass was on the banks, and she told me it wasn't grass at all, but something called clover.

I had never heard of clover before, so I picked some stalks and closely examined the three attached oval leaves on each. My mother told me a story, explaining that, if one could only find a stem with four clover leaves instead of the normal three, this would be very lucky indeed. She said the fairies and elves, who were known as leprechauns, from a country far across the sea called Ireland, would come and grant you a wish for whatever your heart desired, and that wish would always come true. This struck me as a really neat idea and I asked my mother, if she had a wish, what she would want most in the entire world. She replied that her greatest dream was we would all be back together again as a complete family, with my brother, and living quietly on Guernsey; however, she added that a four-leaf clover was very, very difficult, in fact almost impossible, to find.

It appeared to me then that there was an awful lot of clover about and, as I was going nowhere, and also had a great deal of time to spare, the rewards could easily outweigh the drudgery involved. I could see I would have to explore endless clumps of clover, so I decided to keep the operation a total secret from inquisitive and perhaps interfering parents. If I should be lucky enough to find this elusive four-leaf clover, I would turn it into a big surprise so we could all sit up together and wait for the leprechauns to grant our wish and transport us all back to Guernsey.

I started the next afternoon; with people resting, it was a very quiet time. I tried to be systematic – well, as much as a young boy ever could be – and I commenced at one end of a grassy bank and gradually moved along from top to bottom until I reached the far end. In an attempt to make sure I knew exactly where I had last finished looking, I found a wooden peg lying about, and used this as my guide by pushing it into the earth whenever I had to stop searching for any reason. The days passed by happily enough, as I worked on this new project of mine only when the weather was fine.

I soon realised this wasn't going to be an easy job, and from time to time various friends came and sat with me for a while. They didn't seem to find my actions strange in any way but, all in all, this was really painstaking and boring work. Sometimes the true monotony of the long afternoons was broken only by seeing platoons of busy ants at work or watching large black beetles or even the occasional green crickets. This was the time when my stubborn nature manifested itself and I couldn't contemplate being beaten.

Soon, the days turned into weeks, and I moved from the sloping banks of the parade ground onto the grassy plots in front of some of the barracks. Then, on one fine afternoon, the miracle came to pass and I came across a four-leaf clover.

I could hardly believe it and I rushed back as quickly as my legs would carry me to our barrack room, in a state of high excitement. I felt absolutely sure from my knowledge of all the fairy stories about elves, goblins and leprechauns that they would soon be visiting us, and, with the wave of a magic wand, we would be out of this horrid place and off back to Guernsey.

I presented the four-leaf clover to my mother with a somewhat theatrical gesture, but wasn't prepared for her reaction. 'Is this what you've been wasting your time doing these last few weeks?' she demanded. I replied, 'Yes, because the leprechauns will soon be here and grant our wish to go back to Guernsey and I can see my cat Dinky again.' Her reply to this was, 'You would have been much better employed studying your schoolwork and not wasting your time on such silly things.'

My mother's reaction took me some time to absorb, but as children we well knew that parents often forgot about important things such as leprechauns, or they suddenly changed their minds about such things, so it really didn't matter all that much, although I was really sorry I wouldn't see any elves.

So the matter was put to rest and then forgotten. But many, many years later, after my mother's death, I was going through some of her personal papers when I found her old German identity card (*Ausweis*) and there, securely pinned inside, was my preserved four-leaf clover: by no means forgotten. Perhaps the wish for a united family back on Guernsey had eventually come true after all.

So my Plan A had come to nothing but, being somewhat positive by nature, I resolved to develop Plan B, which revolved around the recommissioning of the old escape tunnel in my father's room in Barrack 6. The problem with this strategy was that I would have to wait an eternity until I was seven years old, so the matter was put on hold for a little while. Seventy-two years later, when I was attending an anniversary in Biberach to celebrate the liberation of the camp, heavy machinery being used to landscape a roadway near the old camp unearthed the remains of the tunnel that had been built by POW Lieutenant Colonel Michael Duncan MC and his twenty-five colleagues, allowing them to escape.

Even though in the midst of winter temperatures could fall to about minus 20 degrees centigrade, leaving the camp deep in snow, the inmates still had to take their once-a-week cold shower. Our barrack occupants had to go along to the bath house each Thursday at 1.30 p.m., with the exception of the children, who went in separately. In her jottings my mother says:

> We only were allowed two minutes each to shower, therefore we had to be ready to dive in, as time was so very precious but my problem was that some of the dear old ladies wanted me to wash their backs and several times I got left behind but at least I got wet! On one Thursday bath day, it was extra cold and the two Germans in charge had difficulty in getting the showers going, so Mrs Stuart organised a game of 'follow my leader'. Just imagine how funny we all

looked with only out hats on. I had Steve's Skipper-Sardines hat on and it is extremely difficult to envisage bathing like this with 85 other people.

There were clearly some happy, even hilarious, moments of camp life, interspersed among the pain and suffering. I can recall one time when Billy Walker must have had a serious disagreement with his wife, who I think was called Alice. This state of animosity had lasted for many days and there didn't seem much chance of a reconciliation. The Walkers had an amazing party trick, almost like a circus act, whereby Mr Walker would stand on a table, and then dive off with his arms outstretched, and his wife would deftly catch him in mid-flight. We must have all been sitting in the canteen with several of the tables butting up to one another, and, as usual, the Walkers weren't on speaking terms.

After a little while, Mrs Walker got up to leave and, by the time she was near the door, Billy Walker suddenly sprang up onto the table and shouted out, 'Look out, I'm coming, Alice!' With that he started to bound along the tabletops, with enamel plates and bowls flying in all directions. Mrs Walker quickly bent down to adopt the position ready to catch him as he launched himself into the air. At that precise moment she calmly stood up and let her hands drop to her sides, and we watched poor old Billy hit the floor and slide up against the far wall in a crumpled heap.

People were just astounded but I thought it a marvellous performance and we were all so pleased when, immediately after this exhibition, they patched up their disagreement.

After the war, the Walkers went back to their onion-pickling factory on Guernsey and produced what I believe were the best pickled onions I have ever tasted. We used to visit them at their workplace and buy them by the bottle, as the perfect accompaniment to some of Mr Gardener's famous mature Cheddar cheese, which he dispensed from Lipton's grocery shop in the Arcade, right in the heart of St Peter Port.

In Biberach, the outside-walks scheme had started originally to benefit priests, hospital staff and Red Cross workers (although my father and Uncle Dave very rarely ventured out). However, these walks were usually of a very short duration and the walkers themselves were of course escorted at all times by armed guards and their dogs. The German reluctance to allow prisoners to roam outside the perimeter wire was motivated by the thought of possible mass escapes by large groups of prisoners. However, they soon came to the right conclusion: with families and children to contend with, this was unlikely ever to happen, and they fully realised the value of these hikes. After much cajoling by the camp officials, the German authorities eventually capitulated and allowed all of the prisoners to participate.

The best walk for me was when we turned to the left on leaving the camp, as this took us out into the open countryside, along hedgerows and through dark, green forests. In many ways it represented storybook magic, because we would often pass by charming wooden chalet buildings and large red toadstools that might have come straight out of one of Grimms' fairytales. These country strolls gave all of us a chance to scavenge for acorns, which we could roast and then grind down to make the most appalling coffee, or to pick bramble leaves that we would grill and shred into tea leaves. Best of all, though, were the games involved in collecting wood for the black pot-bellied stove in our barrack room.

During all these various activities, my mother, in company with many others, would start the process of negotiating and bartering with local German villagers, looking to exchange some of our chocolate ration and tins of sardines for fresh eggs and vegetables. In all these transactions the villagers were kind and helpful, though it was soon apparent they too were suffering great hardships. The main difficulty in bartering lay in the fact that there were too many prisoners and not enough villagers, so, inevitably, the deals were generally settled in favour of the villagers.

One promenade, though, turned out to be one of the saddest days of my young life. This time when we set out, the procession turned to the right outside the camp and I was at the head of the assembly with Herr Laib and his dog Alex. After walking along for some time, we came to a clear open space and it was decided we would rest here for a short period. I sat down alongside Alex, and stroked his long shiny coat and scratched just behind his ears, which I knew he loved, when one of the guards came up and roughly pulled me out of the way. Alex immediately flew to my defence and bit hard into the guard's arm, breaking it, and it took quite some time before Herr Laib could persuade Alex to let go.

It was totally unheard of for a German guard dog to bite one of the *Herrenvolk*, or 'Master Race', while defending an enemy prisoner of the Reich, so poor old Alex was sent away to be retrained and I never saw him again, although he retains a very special place in my heart to this day. At least, for many decades I thought Alex had been sent away for retraining, but in my father's 1944 notebook, discovered among photographs as late as 2015, I found in the entry dated 7 September 1944 that Alex had been put down. I suppose everyone wanted to save me the grief of finding out the truth; but I can only think now that Franz Laib must have been completely devastated by the loss of his companion.

Many years later, as an inspector in the Northern Rhodesia Colonial Police Force, I had a very exceptional Doberman dog I called Alex in his memory, and this Alex turned out to be one of the greatest dogs anyone could have – a dog that saved my life more than once and protected my family in those difficult times in far-off Central Africa. This latter Alex was a true friend, having the distinction of being regarded as a witchdoctor by the local African tribes, and he was surely a dog deserving of his own book.

Perhaps one day.

At another time, we were all assembled by the front gates of the camp with the White House directly behind us, ready for our next jaunt. In front of us was a reservoir filled with water and, in the usual confusion with the Germans trying to agree numbers, one of the camp's youngsters fell in. Instinctively, several of the men in the party made a move forward to rescue him, but one of the guards panicked, produced his rifle and threatened to shoot anyone who moved. I can visualise the German idiot's face even now, contorted and purple with anger and full of hatred. The men still moved forward and the guard continued shouting, but mercifully the young lad reached the side of the reservoir on his own and was able to climb out unaided. This episode stayed with me as a prime example of how one small act of crass stupidity and thoughtless action can precipitate a cataclysmic result.

There was certainly no love lost between the Polish and Russian prisoners. 'Auntie Bobbie', who was Polish by birth, used to tell me horrendous tales of how the Russians inflicted barbaric acts of cruelty upon the Polish nation, and she always finished her stories by warning all of us young ones to stay away from the Russian prisoners, 'As they eat children for breakfast.'

During this period, from time to time Russian prisoners of war appeared outside the barbed-wire fence of the camp, having been forcibly brought in by the Germans to help cultivate the adjacent ploughed fields. On this particular occasion, one of the prisoners, who was dressed in a filthy, long, khaki greatcoat, gradually edged ever nearer to the camp's barbed-wire fence. As I passed by along the inside track he tentatively waved for me to stop. Bearing in mind Auntie Bobbie's dire warnings, I was understandably nervous and wary – but he seemed friendly enough and I still had the security of the barbed-wire fence between us. We were standing at the midway point between the two German observation towers when he took out a small, flat, enamelled, coloured cigarette tin from his greatcoat and threw it to me through the barbed wire.

I opened the tin and clearly remember looking at a creased, dog-eared, faded black-and-white photograph, which had almost become sepia in colour through age. It depicted a splendidly attired soldier in full military dress uniform, complete with sword, sitting on a high-backed chair. The soldier had a baby on one knee and alongside him stood a lady in a long white dress. On the right-hand side there was an oak table with a tall aspidistra in the middle. As he pointed to his chest I gathered from his gesticulations he was the soldier in the photo and this was his family. He then made a movement of his hands towards his mouth and I understood he was asking for food. Not having any, I spent some time thinking about it, then had the idea of perhaps using the putrid waste scraps from the communal kitchen, so I indicated to the Russian that I would return, and I set off straight away.

If our own food at this time was awful, just imagine what the waste scraps and the pig's swill were like. There was no one about, and I soon filled one of the dustbin lids with rotten potato peelings, stalks and stinking cabbage leaves. Having finished my task, I set off back to the Russian, who in the interim had been joined by several more Russian prisoners. I threw handfuls of the garbage through the wire and the Russian prisoners fell on it like a pack of ravenous wolves. After some time my new Russian friend stood up, tore one of the brass buttons from his greatcoat and threw it high over the barbed-wire fence to land at my feet, which I took to be some form of payment or gift.

I met my Russian again the next day and once more filled a dustbin lid with the same sort of revolting garbage, which was nevertheless greatly appreciated. However, the third day didn't go along quite as planned, because, having made sure my Russian was standing by the barbed-wire fence, I set off once more and had half-filled the dustbin lid when disaster struck. During the operation, I suddenly heard footsteps approaching and I ducked down out of sight, behind some of the metal dustbins, hoping against hope I wouldn't be caught. It was a German guard on patrol and, on seeing a half-filled lid, he picked it up and slammed it down hard on top of the dustbin. Unfortunately I had stupidly kept my hand on the rim, and the force of the descending lid broke two of my fingers. The pain was excruciating and seemed to flow upwards, and blood was streaming from the damaged fingers, yet I couldn't cry out. I prefer to believe this was a pure accident and the guard didn't do this on purpose; however, I have always been worried in case the Russian prisoners may have thought I had abandoned them, because I never saw them again.

There had been much excitement and bustling activity throughout the camp until, finally, the long-awaited sports day arrived. There were field and track events scheduled and the contestants were kitted out in all sorts of homemade ensembles. The older residents became spectators and played their part in encouraging the younger contenders. The marshals and judges strutted about full of their own importance, and there was an air of expectation throughout the whole camp. Some of the proceedings took place on the parade ground but other events were scheduled on the flat areas between some of the barracks. To say the sports day was memorable is probably a gross understatement, not because of the prowess or determination of the contestants but mainly for one isolated incident that had me smiling then and still does so even to this day.

It was decreed the shot-put event would take place alongside our own barrack, and I revelled in the excited noise and exhibitionist poses of the competitors. The proceedings were just about to commence when a startling figure emerged from behind the barracks and immediately reduced the spectators to absolute silence. It was my old *bête noire*, Can Can, whom we met earlier in the story. He was dressed in a swirling Scottish kilt and sporran, topped off by a bedraggled tam-o'-shanter, with his bent and knobbly knees hideously accentuated by his large hobnailed boots.

He began by going through his loosening-up exercises, doing a series of knee-bending, arm-waving and shoulder manipulations. Then, on being invited to take his place, he even produced some chalk powder from one of his pockets and started to dust his hand with it. By now, the crowd were certainly expecting great things as he placed the shot securely under his chin, and then he was off. Unfortunately, during the actual launch, he tripped over one of his loose bootlaces, so his feet went one way and his body went the other, leaving the shot to fall to the ground virtually where his feet had been originally, whereupon he picked himself up and withdrew hurriedly from the field. The crowd erupted into spontaneous convulsions of laughter until the tears were running down many a cheek; and I for one certainly felt a great deal better. It has to be said, though, that not all these events were as happy as that one.

On one such occasion, my father and a team of helpers had made a selection of toys in the Red Cross stores and these were augmented by the Red Cross, who had also sent presents for the children, and they were all handed out by one of the camp dignitaries. I received a long, narrow gift wrapped up in glossy red paper. Some of my 'elders and betters' were of the opinion my parcel was a popgun, and certainly the outline of the parcel looked like a rifle. I was so thrilled as I rushed back to my barrack room, placed the present on the bunk and hurriedly proceeded to rip the paper off, only to find it contained a number of wooden struts and a ball of string. I was devastated as the accompanying instructions showed a picture of a kite, not a gun, and, to make matters worse, there was a notice printed on the inside of the paper that read, 'Please keep the paper to cover the kite.'

On 4 April 1943 my mother wrote a postcard, in pencil, to my brother in Oldham, which he eventually received in spite of the German censors. The card reads:

Dearest Alan and Aunties,

What a thrill to receive your letter of the 28 February 1943 and in your own handwriting. We are so pleased to see how well you are getting on. You have such kind aunties to make life enjoyable and buy such beautiful presents. We can see how happy you are and what a grand home you are in and we love your aunties dearly and long to meet them. It is very good of you to send us parcels and we will let you know when they arrive. Some have already arrived in camp. Our address is the same as on this letter, and cannot think what other address you have received. I would like Wellington boots for Stephen size 11 and brown shoes size 10 as we cannot get any repaired here. Hair-grips, elastic, brown shoe polish and, talcum powder.

We wish we could be with you before this is sent. We have had some glorious walks, about 200 go out at a time with guards. Stephen was thrilled last week to go for a walk, you will love him, always up to some mischief, but I shall be glad to get him in a decent school and away from some of the crowd we are forced to mix with. He is doing well at school. The few teachers who are with us have a difficult job as they lack equipment.

We long for your letters and aunties'. We haven't heard from Auntie Leila for a long time. Tell Auntie Alice that Auntie Bet and Uncle Alf Pomeroy are in some other camp and hope to join us soon. Stanley's dad is also somewhere near, I am playing a lot of netball and feeling very fit. Daddy is just the same and longing for his boy. Longing for snaps of aunties and will try and send snaps taken of us in 1941.

Cheerio Darlings Yours – Lovingly Mum and Dad and Stephen.

There were two types of communication allowed by the Germans. One was a postcard, or '*Interniertenpost Postkarte*', and the other was a letter just called '*Interniertenpost*'. Once these were written they were posted in the camp and then directed to the German camp censors. If it passed their careful scrutiny, the letter was rubber-stamped and then routed, presumably to the Red Cross in Switzerland. Afterwards, and having been delivered to UK authorities, the letter was again reviewed by the British censors and rubber-stamped 'Passed'. Usually these letters took about six weeks to reach their destination.

# CHAPTER 11

# THE LONG,
# WINDING ROAD

On most fine days, my mother had started walking around the inside-perimeter wire fence, usually at mid-morning, mainly for exercise but most probably to obtain some relief from the closeness and oppression of everyone living on top of one another in the small and overcrowded barrack room. As was customary, I was dragged along as well on the basis that, 'More fresh air and exercise will do you good.'

A few days into this routine, we were joined by a Mrs Pittard, who had been deported from the previously idyllic Channel Island of Sark. Mrs Pittard seemed a very quiet and reserved person, and it took a few more days before she felt able to confide in my mother. On this one particular day she asked my mother if she could keep a secret (they both appeared to ignore the fact that I was there), and without waiting for a reply Mrs Pittard launched into her exciting story.

She explained that, on one particular night, she was in her home on Sark when she thought she heard a noise outside. She put the hall light on and immediately heard a British voice loudly exclaim, 'Put that bloody light out.' I knew this was going to be a very exciting story because I was never allowed to use the 'B' word. She continued by saying that, when she switched off the light and opened the front door, she was confronted by a party of British Commandos who had landed on the island some time previously. The Commandos all piled inside the house and their commander told Mrs Pittard they had been sent by submarine to Sark to carry out a raid and that they had accomplished their mission on the island, but in doing so they had unfortunately killed two German soldiers. After resting for some little time, the Commandos all left and only just managed to get away from Sark unscathed.

The next day German interrogators arrived at the house and started to question Mrs Pittard about her involvement with the Commandos. Although they were convinced of her complicity, they were unable to prove her guilt, so, after several days of questioning, she was sent to Germany and prison 'out of spite', and subsequently fetched up in Biberach. As she said, 'If the Germans really knew I had sheltered the Commandos, I would have been shot out of hand there and then.' In retrospect Mrs Pittard was surely a courageous British patriot and another of our unsung Channel Island heroines.

I was so very intrigued with this story that when the walk ended I rushed off to see my father in the Red Cross stores and told him this fascinating tale. He warned me not to say anything to anyone about it, as it was all such a great secret. He said Mrs Pittard must be a very brave and clever woman for, although the Germans thought she was guilty, they couldn't prove it. I didn't know then who or what Commandos were until Dad explained they were soldiers who often landed on enemy shores at night, wearing dark uniforms and with their faces smeared black, often by using mud, and they sometimes arrived as if by magic in a speedboat or even by submarine. I was captivated by all this, especially the piece about Commandos having black faces and not having to wash, so I stated straight away that I wanted to be a Commando when I grew up.

On a wonderful day in May 1944, the circus came to Biberach town. I know this because I have the original postcard featuring my favourite acrobatic act of the day, known as 'the Three Steys'. In all probability it should have been 'the Four Steys' but the male lead was no doubt off somewhere fighting for Hitler and the Fatherland.

The act comprised a lithe female figure, who was certainly the mother of the other two participants, a girl and a boy not much older than I. The fact that we were taken by the Germans, for the cost of one German mark each, to see the circus in the town centre of Biberach at the height of a major war the Germans were losing has never ceased to amaze me. One moment we were being starved and denied our basic human rights and the next we were happily positioned in seats in the very midst of our German enemies, surrounded by their swastika-covered banners and flags. As we watched the circus and the performers together with such an enthusiastic German audience, this was to be one of the most surreal and bizarre moments of the entire conflict.

There were many acts, but the only one I can really remember clearly was the Three Steys, and I was so impressed that, once their act had finished, I went up to them and shook hands with the young boy, who gave me their advertising postcard, which I have kept safe ever since.

Within a period of a few short months, the elegant cobbled streets and ancient timbered buildings of Biberach would lie in ruins, brought about by Allied bombing, and many of the German audience would lie dead or wounded in the rubble.

Shortly before Christmas 1943 I lost my German-issue aluminium mug. I know it was difficult to use, but at least it was mine. It had a thin black handle and a fairly sharp rim and you had to be careful not to cut your lips. Its other major fault lay in the conductivity of the aluminium. In the bleak freezing winters I had to be watchful, otherwise there was the likelihood my lips would become stuck on the frozen rim of the mug. On the other hand, if anything really hot was ladled into the mug, there was the distinct possibility of receiving severe mouth burns from the scalding metal. On the plus side, the mug was fairly large, being 9.5 centimetres tall with a diameter also of 9.5 centimetres, which meant I could, if very fortunate, receive more than my fair share of the putrid, greasy, watery cabbage soup.

I looked everywhere for my mug and visited all the places I usually called on during the course of my normal day, but without success. My mother certainly didn't scold me but furnished me with a much smaller, but adequate, enamel cup. Christmas Day dawned and among the presents was my own precious mug, not only returned but this time polished and engraved. My parents had surreptitiously removed the mug and taken it to a Mr Byll Balcombe, one of the Guernsey prisoners, who had then hand-engraved it in a rather naïve fashion. The inscription reads: 'Xmas 1943 – Stephen Matthews from Mum and Dad'. There are also several religious texts and the number 25, which was my prison-camp registration number. Byll Balcombe had served in World War One as well, and in moments of extreme boredom had learned the art of trench engraving; and he did this by working on old, expended brass artillery shells. My parents told me Byll engraved these mugs by using only a nail and part of a steel knitting needle. The mug has been with me ever since and now stands in a place of honour in my study.

In our barrack room, Auntie Bobbie, the dynamic and loyal Polish lady who hated the Germans only slightly more than she hated the Russians, would, as we sat around the barrack-room table, endlessly tell us how she had managed to save her husband's life in Poland and was able to catch the very last train leaving Warsaw. The story goes they were both taking refuge from enemy bombardment by seeking the protection afforded by various underground shelters, when a detachment of German SS troops came in and started dragging the male occupants outside. The idea was to use at least fifty Poles as human shields against their own people, and force them to walk in front of the German tanks in the forlorn hope the Polish patriots wouldn't open fire on them.

When they reached Bobbie's husband Gabriel, one soldier grabbed him by the lapels and pushed him towards the exit, when Bobbie shouted, 'Leave him alone. He is an American.' For some obscure reason the soldiers halted and then pushed him back against the wall of the shelter and left.

On a sunny and crisp late afternoon the belated walkers from the camp outing had returned from the countryside with their spoils. Young Gordon Buchan, from my own barrack room, was at the concrete washstand just outside our barracks, while a few of us played together in the near vicinity. Gordon had just surfaced from his obligatory afternoon rest, and was now washing a few of the vegetables his mother had bartered or bought from some of the returning walkers. During his washing exertions, one of the vegetable pods fell onto the concrete and, as Gordon stepped onto it, produced a loud popping sound, which in turn made everyone laugh. Fired up by this funny situation, Gordon then dropped a few more pods and started jumping up and down, squashing the vegetables flat as he went. While all this high-spirited fun and jubilation was taking place, his mother suddenly appeared in our midst and, when she saw what was happening to her precious vegetables, she demanded in her most strident voice to know what had been going on. Poor Gordon, overcome with remorse and in total fright, merely pointed at me (I being the nearest person standing alongside) and said, 'He did it.' Like the Wicked Witch of the North, one minute she was there and the next minute she had disappeared, finally to materialise once again in front of us, although this time she had my mother in tow.

My mother grabbed me by the shirt and without warning started to lay into me by striking me on the head and shoulders. I was really upset and kept protesting my innocence, but all to no avail. I was certainly no saint but if I did anything wrong, which was fairly often, I always owned up. Finally, in desperation I turned and twisted first one way then another until I eventually broke free from my mother's grip, and ran off in order to escape further punishment. I was followed by a few friends, including John Benham, who could see I was really upset and who took me to his own barrack room, where he explained my predicament to his mother.

John's mother sat us both down on wooden stools and made us a hot cup of cocoa with condensed milk. There was no way I was going back into a hateful environment and I think Mrs Benham could see how determined I was, so it was agreed I would stay with them at least one night. John and I shared his bed, sleeping top to toe, and the next morning I was up early and sitting outside the barrack wondering how I was going to manage for breakfast when my father passed by, as if by accident. All he said was, 'You must be really hungry after all that excitement. You'd better come with me to the Red Cross stores and have something to eat.'

I spent the morning at the Red Cross stores with my father, and I made myself as inconspicuous as I could. At about our normal lunchtime my father said, 'Your mother's probably worrying about us now, so we'd better go and see.' I wasn't so sure and hung back a little, but nevertheless I went along with it. It was something of a dreamlike experience to enter my own barrack room. No one said anything but everyone looked embarrassed and averted their eyes. It soon transpired Gordon had confessed he was the one who had stamped all over the vegetables, although nobody apologised to me, and in fact no one ever referred to this incident again. However, my mother and I continued to eye each other in a warring state for several days, until eventually more pressing events occurred, refocusing everyone's mind, and pushed this particular incident into the dim and distant past.

I met Gordon again many years later in Jersey, and we had quite a laugh about this episode, although, sadly, I believe he died prematurely a little while later. When I was much older I would often talk about these times with my father, who once said I must have been the only person imprisoned in a German concentration camp who ever ran away from home.

About this time a strange event took place in Biberach, which in turn created a family riddle I have managed only partially to solve after sixty-six or so years. There had always been an old family story concerning the rumoured distant connection with the titled Slade family from Somerset. On a late-autumn morning in the camp, my mother was standing in a queue of women, probably alongside the canteen. I say that because, according to my mother's oft-repeated story, she saw my father coming towards us across the parade ground from the general direction of the Red Cross stores. As he came nearer and waved happily to us, one of the foreign women standing several places behind my mother started to cry out in Italian and began gesticulating wildly towards my father.

After quite some time she quietened down a little and, since she had only a few words of English, someone in the crowd translated her story. She said she had received a tremendous shock in seeing the ghost of her dead husband walking across the parade ground towards her. It transpired her name was Marie Slade, although my mother referred to her as 'Mary'. She was born into an Italian family but on marriage to an Englishman from Somerset she had obtained a British passport, which caused her eventual downfall, as she was later deported from Italy by the Germans. During the same night in Biberach she was apparently notified of her imminent transfer to another prison camp, but before leaving she gently slipped a card containing a handwritten message under my mother's pillow as she lay fast asleep.

This was the last time any of our family heard from her or about her. For some years I had tried to trace the Italian side of the Slade family without success. However, I recently came across Marie Slade's postcard, written in Italian, which had been hidden by my mother (once again) in the old family Bible. This spurred me on to try to solve the riddle and eventually, by spending many long hours trawling the Internet, I found part of the answer.

Her name had been Marie Perruche from Puglia in Italy, and she was certainly Italian by birth. On 2 May 1914 she married Lieutenant Commander Frederick William Slade, who had been born on 19 January 1892 in England, and was part of the titled Slade family from Somerset. The couple continued to live in Italy, and Frederick Slade fought in the Dardanelles campaign, being involved in submarine warfare, and was later awarded the Military Cross for his actions. However, Marie survived her incarceration in various German concentration camps, and when the war ended she returned once again to Italy.

In November 1944, 149 Libyan Jews arrived in Biberach, having been sent there from various other camps in Germany, and the camp inhabitants soon gave them the name of 'Benghazis'. I don't remember their arrival; it just seemed that one day there was nothing and the next day a teeming mass of half-starved humanity. Unquestionably, they were in a terrible condition and appeared to be wearing only rags, and very few of them even had shoes. The camp residents soon rallied around and many gave up their hard-won clothing, shoes and food, while the Red Cross, YMCA and YWCA provided additional clothing and other materials.

Nevertheless, the Benghazis were all totally disruptive, unmanageable and unruly, and we soon realised that, unless valuable articles in our own barrack rooms were virtually nailed down, they would soon mysteriously disappear. It was certainly a case of biting the hands that feed you, and their divisive attitude soon affected everyone in the camp. I have often wondered how a group of people, embroiled in such a terrible condition, could turn on those who had saved them from certain death, and repay them in such a detrimental way.

The Benghazis were housed in two adjacent barrack blocks, facing a cleared and flat area of land where we younger children often played football together, usually using one of my tennis balls. These Arabs were fenced off from the rest of us by thin strands of wire stretched across concrete posts designed to keep them contained within their own compound. However, it was just too easy for the Benghazis to squeeze under the sagging strands of wire and gain entry into various sections of the camp.

On this particular day, we children were playing together, enjoying the afternoon sunshine and involved in a game of football, with jumpers placed on the ground to represent the goalposts. The game had been in progress for only a little while when suddenly one of the younger and taller Arabs sneaked under the wire, burst through our number and kicked my tennis ball back towards the Arab compound, where it was soon picked up by another youth, who quickly disappeared with it into the confines of the Arab territory. This was a bitter blow for all of us but more especially for me, as this was the very last of the tennis balls brought from Guernsey. It wasn't just the loss of my tennis ball that hurt, although that was serious enough; it was the way all the Arabs lined up along the wire fence, jeering and waving their arms jubilantly at us, that caused the most anguish.

Soon, some of the older Guernsey boys heard what had happened and came along to see if they could do anything to help, and one of them did have a very bright idea. He organised a barrack-by-barrack collection of very old socks, preferably woollen bed-socks, and these were fashioned into two identical pink footballs. In one of the balls, we embedded a large and heavy round stone while the other was left as a normal kickabout ball. We devised a plan whereby we would play football initially with the good woollen ball until we felt sure we had the Benghazis' full and undivided attention, and then we would surreptitiously change it for the sock containing the round stone.

So this was exactly what we did. It wasn't long before a large crowd of Arabs had gathered at their wire fence, where they watched the game progress in rapt fascination. Then, at a signal from one of the older boys in our group, we all went into a mêlée, where the ball with the large stone was substituted for the good ball. After a little mock-tackling and barging about, we moved slowly away as if to rest from our endeavours, leaving the ball lying there as temptingly available bait.

Sure enough, within seconds the bait was taken, because the same lanky Arab scrambled through the wire strands, and with a few long strides he ran up to the ball and gave it one mighty kick. The result was immediate: first of all, the ball didn't move very far, and at the same time the kicker gave a thunderous yell, jumped high in the air, then settled down and hobbled off back to the Arab zone, moaning loudly as he went. He was accompanied on his way by jeers and chants of derision on the part of our group, and peace reigned once again, if only for a short time.

By way of comparison, there were several Greek families who had been transferred into our camp and, although they couldn't speak a great deal of English and we couldn't speak Greek, they were just simply marvellous people. They loved children of all nationalities and were kindness itself, exercising enormous patience with us as we struggled to learn Greek nursery rhymes. In particular there were Mr and Mrs Makarios, and I have only the greatest admiration for their stoicism and love of family life. They taught us to say a rhyme in Greek along the lines of:

> Eeny, meeny, miny, moe,
> Catch the Krauts by the toe,
> If they holler let them go,
> Eeny, meeny, miny, moe!

Their impact on camp life cannot be overstated, as Mrs Makarios was a wonderful dressmaker and Mr Makarios taught the prisoners how to make shoes and various artefacts with cardboard and string from the Red Cross parcels.

There was even a Greek wedding that took place in our camp, which I think was opposite us in Barrack 14, and I can remember people donating scraps of candles, which were subsequently lit and placed all around the main entrance to the barracks, to shine brightly in the late evening. Thankfully, the happy pair and their friends didn't engage in the Greek tradition of smashing the crockery. The atmosphere was wonderful, with people dancing in the open air and clapping their hands to the Greek music, and it all seemed to create a perfect ambience in the mind of a young boy. Even as young as we were then, we could see this marriage was created out of hope against adversity.

But there was another side to some of the foreign deportees in Biberach. There were, for instance, seven Norwegian ladies who had skied from Norway with the intention of avoiding the German occupation of their country. In all, six married couples and a daughter set out, but almost instantly they were enveloped in a thick fog, which lasted for three days. After three long days and nights of skiing, they realised they had taken a wrong turning, for as the fog cleared they found themselves trapped in a small German seaside town and were soon captured. The wives and the daughter were sent to Biberach but their husbands were rerouted to various death camps, where they finally all perished.

During the latter days, conditions in Biberach Camp significantly deteriorated once again, for, as the Allies penetrated deeper into Germany, so did the intensity of their airborne bombing raids. Red Cross parcels took much longer to reach us because of these disruptions, but it has to be stated that the Germans never purloined, stole or requisitioned any of the parcels for their own use. However, as the German people started to run out of essential commodities themselves, they did gain some small respite by denuding all the fuel stocks held within the confines of their concentration camps. In Biberach I was unwittingly one of the first to stumble across this gross violation.

I was walking down the steep slope towards the camp's coal store when I came across a sizeable two-wheeled cart with high wooden sides, being drawn by one of the large draught horses famous throughout Bavaria. It was obvious, even to me, that the cart was heavily overloaded with coal, surreptitiously requisitioned by the Germans from our own fuel stocks. The driver was a rather intimidating and filthy figure covered in coal dust and with a coal-stained sack covering his head and shoulders. As the poor horse valiantly struggled to move the cart, the driver started to beat him unmercifully with a whip. This was more than I could stand, so I shouted at the man and pulled at his arm, only to receive a sharp blow to the side of my head, which sent me flying into some of the nearby metal dustbins.

The driver continued to beat the poor horse and the sweat began to cascade down the animal's flanks as he desperately tried but failed to move the cart. I got up and rushed at the driver, kicking him hard on his shins, and once again I received another slap on the side of my head. At this juncture a German guard came out of the store and, on seeing what was going on, started to rebuke the driver in no uncertain terms, and insisted that some of the cargo be offloaded. When this had been done, the guard then collected quite a few of the young prisoners who had been playing football on the parade ground and together they helped push the cart up the steep incline. The end result was twofold: the camp soon ran out of hot water and heating and I had to explain to my mother how I had received another black eye in the fracas.

On one of the daylight bombing raids, when the RAF aircraft were just passing over the camp, one of the Sark women ran out of a nearby barrack and started waving a white towel violently in the air. On being restrained by a German guard, she hit him several times across the face and shoulders, until she was unceremoniously carted off to the prison cooler for quite some time.

However, all was not sweetness and light within the camp itself. I can remember a day of violent arguments and shouting in the Red Cross stores, of angry men and red faces, although I had no idea what it was all about. Many years later, I discovered in an old briefcase belonging to my father several typed sheets on carbon copy paper headed 'Police Headquarters Bar 16' dated 7 April 1945. The papers hold the original signature of an 'Inspector A. J. Langmead', who had eventually been transferred to Biberach from Compiègne. 'Uncle Arthur' had been an officer in the Guernsey Police Force and had been deported by the Germans. The document was addressed to 'The Camp Captain, Biberach Camp', and has a sub-heading: 'Alleged Fraudulent Conversion by Baillie'. The document continues:

> 'I beg to report that at the request of Mr C. Matthews, Camp Chairman of the Red Cross Committee, I made an inquiry into the above allegation and I find that the facts are as follows and that a case as above could be made out.'

The substance of the case was that the leader of Barrack 12 housing the Benghazis had been given a roll of grey flannel material in order to make shorts for the Arab boys and skirts for the girls, who had arrived in such a pitiable state from Tripoli. The order comprised eighteen yards of grey flannel and six yards of a yellow lining. Normally the work would have been carried out by other camp sources. However, the barracks leader said he had his own tailors in his barracks and could arrange for the work to be done there. This was agreed to.

In essence, my father found out that the barrack leader had misappropriated the clothing order and then commissioned his own tailor to make two pairs of trousers, one for himself and one for his deputy (another deportee). The pages continue to detail several witness statements, which corroborated the evidence, and, although the barrack leader was found guilty, I have no indication as to the final action or discipline handed down by the authorities.

My mother has also given a very graphic account of a mysterious occurrence that took place in the camp, which I have never heard of before. She wrote:

> Apparently unknown to me at this time, agents had been put into the camp. As new arrivals they had to go to the Red Cross stores for food parcels. Naturally Cecil would ask them where they came from and this one man said he had come from 'Woolwich.' After asking several innocuous questions about Woolwich, Cecil soon realised the man didn't know anything about Woolwich. When the-powers-that-be came to see Cecil, they showed him a photograph of the man they were looking for. Cecil said 'He's here' and the man was never seen again.

There is no indication, incidentally, from my mother's notes of who exactly the 'powers-that-be' were. Were they Germans or, more likely, our own British administration? If it was the

British, then how would they have obtained a photograph? It is surely all very strange, but coincidence is often someone's undoing and in this case Woolwich was the key, as my father had been stationed there for a little while with an artillery regiment during World War One. Strangely enough, my mother continued, 'Cecil had many such experiences.'

There were many deaths in Biberach and, as part of his duties as chairman of the Red Cross Committee, my father used to attend each funeral and burial held outside the camp, generally accompanying Herr Laib, the deputy camp commandant. Afterwards, they would adjourn to Laib's nearby quarters for a cup of tea or coffee, and it was here that Laib would indicate a cupboard in the dining room. On opening the cupboard, my father would find a concealed German radio set already tuned in to a BBC station. Laib would then leave my father to listen to the English news on his own, while he went outside to tend to the vegetables on his allotment. Bear in mind that, had they been discovered by the Nazis, instant execution would have awaited them both.

The difficulties experienced in bartering with the German villagers on our roaming walks soon came to a head with the realisation that the canny German civilians were playing the prisoners off against each other, and it was also crystal clear they were gaining the upper hand in most of the negotiations. This was mainly because there were too many deportees trying to barter and all at the same time. It was my father who came up with the solution, as he felt I was growing older and becoming more responsible, besides which my German-language skills had also dramatically improved. It was his idea that I should leave the organised party at some point during the walk and then head off towards outlying farms and smallholdings in the far distance to engage in bartering activities, but return in time to rejoin the column at the same place as it eventually returned to camp.

On that basis he worked out that I would have approximately an hour and a half to get there and back. So, with my mother's tacit agreement, the plot was hatched and scheduled for the next week, by which time I would be kitted out with a homemade haversack. My father had preselected a spot on the walk where, at a sharp bend in the road, I couldn't be seen by the guards either at the front or rear of the column. At just the right moment, my father pushed me through the hedge and then I was off running through the long grass.

It all worked out like a dream, as I easily reached the outlying villages and soon my haversack was filled to the brim with carrots, potatoes, lettuce and, best of all, fresh farm eggs. I returned to my appointed spot by the hedge and waited for the long trail of prisoners to return, when, just at the appropriate moment, I would thrust through the hedge and rejoin the group. I was pleased and excited by this adventure, not just because I was the family hero of the hour but, rather, I had really enjoyed the utter freedom to roam at will through the beautiful German countryside.

However, I was soon to meet my nemesis. On one of our regular outings I had set off as usual and soon reached a farmstead I hadn't seen before. There was a young German boy about my age playing with his sister in the farmyard, and in the corner stood a huge pile of steaming horse manure. The children's mother presently arrived and welcomed the idea of tinned sardines and real chocolate, and in return she said she would give me something really special – apples – as these were very scarce and much more beneficial than mere eggs and vegetables, and so naturally everyone really wanted them. I fell for her story, hook, line and sinker, as I had heard about apples but not actually ever seen or eaten any.

I returned to the trudging ranks with my bag filled to overflowing with apples and feeling very pleased with myself, and waited for the expected hearty congratulations. What I received instead was a sharp intake of breath from my mother, who then went on to explain gently that apples, although very good and nourishing, weren't what we should be looking for. Once again my father saved the day, by saying, 'We must remember that he's never, ever seen an apple before.' And so our disappointed party tramped on back to camp in complete silence and, although no more was ever said about it, I could see for myself the day had been a complete disaster.

Nevertheless I harboured a deep-seated grievance about the incident and I vowed to exact revenge the moment a good opportunity arose. The chance came the following week. By then all was forgiven and forgotten in the family. The group of us set off once again on the afternoon's walk and, thankfully, took the same road to the left, and in my normal manner, the moment we reached the same bend in the road, I was away again on my adventures.

I cautiously approached the infamous farmhouse and, seeing nobody about, slipped into the wooden barn standing a little way away from the main house. I soon found a large wooden bin and helped myself to a good portion of potatoes, then I came across some cabbages, and finally I saw in the corner the chickens' nesting boxes, devoid of chickens but still holding five or six fresh eggs. Once again, I was soon fully laden, and so far this hadn't cost me anything. As I left the barn I could hear the voices of the children playing in the farmyard.

I very gently laid my precious bag down on the ground and slowly crept up on the children without being noticed until, with one bound, I rushed at the boy and pushed him full length into the steaming pile of horse manure. I then exited the scene as quickly as I could, picking up the bag as I went, and legged it back to the hedgerows as fast as I could go. As I ran off, I could hear the brewing furore behind me but I just didn't care, for as far as I was concerned justice had finally prevailed.

Once I had reached the comparative safety of the hedgerows, I needed to catch my breath, so I settled down for a few minutes and enjoyed several squares of my free chocolate bar while I contemplated the fact that honour had at last been restored. After a while I decided to see if there was any sign of the returning column of prisoners, so I stepped through the hedge onto the roadway, and in doing so inadvertently stumbled across three Hitler Youth members who were also resting by the side of the road. I think at first they believed I was German, probably on account of my blond hair, so initially they were quite polite. I noticed one of them had a remarkable carved blackthorn walking stick and so, feeling fairly confident after my recent success, I offered some of my chocolate in a fair exchange for his walking stick. This boy was much older and taller than I was and his hair was a golden colour with reddish strands running through, and he looked so very smart in his pressed khaki short-sleeved shirt, and with his strident Nazi armband and his clean, short trousers. He readily agreed to the transaction and I handed over the chocolate without a quibble, which he began to share out with his other companions. When I held out my hand for the walking stick, he suddenly spat at me. I stood there dumbfounded and humiliated as the spittle traced a path down my face. The three of them marched away across the fields laughing and, although I didn't know it then, I would meet the ringleader again in the near future, but in far less pleasant circumstances.

The civilian camp leader was a Garfield Garland, himself a deportee from the islands, who had been elected *Lagerführer* (camp leader) by the prisoners themselves while in Dorsten camp. On moving to Biberach he retained his title and position as the civilian representative because the Germans had made it abundantly clear they wished to deal with only one man. My mother's journal expounded on this a little by saying, 'Unfortunately, Mr Garland was not very popular especially as he unceremoniously left our camp to live outside in the White House, with the Germans, where he was free to come and go as he pleased!'

This is the first time I have ever heard of this bizarre arrangement; I don't remember its being disclosed in any book or article before now. Even though he has been described as a very able administrator and at times cajoled the Germans into giving the camp increased favours, I have wondered what reasons persuaded Garland to do this. I recently brought this subject up with my friend – and local historian – Reinhold Adler in Biberach, who told me the Germans regarded Garland as the SBO (Senior British Officer) of the camp and there were many cases where senior British POWs lived outside the main camp.

Still, I think this was a poor decision on Garland's part and one that clearly rankled with a number of people, including my father. At one time, when my father was meeting with some of the high-ranking Red Cross officials from Geneva, they were apparently very pleasantly surprised to find he was located in Barrack 6 and not occupying a privileged place in the White House with Mr Garland. According to my mother's journal, my father told these officials, 'If you live in Buckingham Palace or the Dorchester Hotel in London, how will you personally know about the suffering of your fellow men, who, in this camp, are surely the very salt of the earth?'

## CHAPTER 12

# THE BEGINNING OF THE END

On 20 July 1944, there was a serious assassination attempt on Adolf Hitler right inside his heavily guarded 'Wolf's Lair' in Rastenburg, East Prussia. This was the third attempt on Hitler's life and represented the culmination of much planning and scheming by a number of German resistance groups. It was followed by a fatally flawed military coup d'état. A bomb had been planted in the main conference room by Claus von Stauffenberg, using a pencil detonator and a one-kilogram block of plastic explosive. Although a number of people attending the conference were killed or seriously injured, Hitler lived on to fight another day, and consequently more than seven thousand Germans were arrested by the Gestapo and more than five thousand of them were summarily executed.

In all probability this event could have been foretold after three failed attempts, and also because Hitler had developed an overriding preoccupation with survival. During his time in the Wolf's Lair a German citizen, Margot Woelk, and a team of other German nationals were forced to taste all the food Hitler and his lover Eva Braun would consume each day. The food was assembled between 11 a.m. and 12 noon and each member of the team had to taste the ingredients for traces of poison. Throughout this period the food nearly always consisted of fresh fruit and vegetables and never meat or fish. Although Margot Woelk survived, the remainder of the tasting team were killed during the Russian advance on Rastenburg.

Those outrageous events gave rise to another frequent example of history impinging itself on modern-day life. On 7 June 1962, I was leading a small, armed police patrol up on the border between Northern Rhodesia (now Zambia) and the breakaway state of Katanga. The day was my birthday and I was anxious to return to our base in Chingola, on the Copperbelt, to enjoy a birthday celebration in the police club with my wife and friends. En route, and as a matter of our routine procedure, we stopped off at one of the border farms to ensure the occupants were secure and untroubled, where I met the young owner and couldn't help noticing he had a slight foreign accent. Inside the farmhouse, I saw a few birthday cards and it transpired it was the farmer's birthday, the same day as mine. I also observed a framed print of a German family coat of arms. Not only was this both our birthdays but we were the same age, and I could see from the picture he had originated from Bavaria.

During our discussions he asked me what I had been doing on 7 June 1944 and I told him I had been incarcerated in the Biberach concentration camp, on the edge of the Black Forest, although I had received some homemade birthday cards on that day. He told me his father had been a general in the Wehrmacht, and was home on leave, having been wounded in the fighting on the Russian front. The family had a picturesque hotel not far from Biberach and his birthday too had been a wonderful family occasion. Still, some seven or eight weeks later, a large convoy of Mercedes staff cars manned by members of the Gestapo arrived at the hotel, and, after brief introductions, they took his father down into the hotel basement and there hanged him from one of the ceiling beams with piano wire, for his alleged complicity in the conspiracy to assassinate Hitler.

But let us return to Biberach, where, on 24 July 1944, the air-raid sirens sounded in the camp, and shortly afterwards a number of Allied planes flew very low over the camp towards Biberach town. We could hear the ensuing sound of gunfire and a little later we learned the fighter aircraft had attacked a train standing in the railway station at Biberach and had killed the train driver outright.

Some weeks later, 13 September, it was a balmy late-autumn day. I recall the date not because I have a very good memory but rather because it is now a matter of official German record. I was playing football outside our Barrack 15 with the twins Neville and Ralph Godwin. There was an area of cleared ground on the northeast side, towards the main gates of the camp, and it was here we were strenuously engaged in our game. After some time we heard an aircraft engine and soon spotted a German fighter plane flying high in the sky just above the camp. The plane was twisting and turning and we could see the sun glinting on the silver wings and body of the plane as the pilot put the fighter through its paces.

A little while later, as the aircraft went into a controlled roll, there was a distinct and loud cracking noise and we saw the tail fin fall away and start spinning down to earth, rather like a leaf falling from a sycamore tree. The aeroplane turned over and began to plummet down towards us. People all around started to shout and scream and began running backwards and forwards in total, blind panic. We three acted as one, dropping to the ground without a sound, and, lying out flat on our tummies, burying our heads in our arms. We could hear the high-pitched engine screaming and straining as it plunged towards us. Just when it seemed the noise was right on top of us and enveloping us, there was a great whooshing sound as it passed over our heads, only to be followed seconds later by an earth-shattering explosion as the fighter aircraft plunged into the ground and blew up alongside Barrack 13 just opposite us. The three of us immediately rolled over in the dirt to see what had happened, but all we could see was a huge plume of smoke and debris rising into the air from the crash site, and we realised then what a narrow escape we had just had.

The camp rumour pronounced that this was a new prototype fighter from nearby Mengen airfield and was being extensively tested before the production models would mount a direct challenge to the Allies in mortal combat over the skies of Germany. The authorised German report is that the aircraft was one of four Messerschmitt Me 109 G-6s belonging to the Fighter Squadron 3/I/Jg 106. They were all on a practice flight and operating from the nearby Reichenbach military airfield when one of them crashed.

The pilot in question was named as *Fahnenjunker* (Officer Cadet) Hans Paddanberg, who was unfortunately killed instantly. Apart from a few pieces of aluminium casing, nothing was left of the aircraft as it was completely buried deep in the ground, and to this day it is officially stated that neither the pilot's body nor the plane itself has ever been recovered. I like to believe eyewitness accounts of the event, which said the pilot struggled valiantly to ensure his plane didn't come down on top of us, but only in the final moments was he able to lift the fighter just high enough to miss us and the barbed-wire fences.

During our late-autumn walks, as we often passed by the crash site, I always felt sad to realise the pilot had died trying to save us, and in the following spring when the tree-lined road was full of pink blossom my mother said it was because the body of the pilot was lying slumbering under the ground, but he could feel no hurt as he was now in heaven. After the passing of so many years, isn't this a good time to reclaim what remains of his body and give him a decent hero's funeral with full military honours?

Another postcard was written in pencil by my mother and sent to my brother in Oldham on 14 September 1944, the very next day after the air crash, and it began to chronicle a significant change in our circumstances in Biberach. She specifically noted that a number of the sick and elderly were beginning to be repatriated back to England. She wrote:

My Dearest Alan,

I suppose by now you have heard from several people about us, and it was quite an exciting day to see all the sick leave the camp, but it also made us feel very homesick and we hope with all our hearts our turn will soon come, but I suspect it will not be until the war has ended. We are all keeping fit and tell Auntie Phyllis and Norah we are still longing for roast potatoes and Yorkshire pudding. Stephen is quite a case and always up to some mischief. At the moment he is trying to barter with a boy. He is offering his chrysalis for a toy banjo – what a scream but needless to say it didn't come off.

Well darling always thinking of you and of happy days in store. Love to all

Lovingly Mum, Dad and Stephen.

However, I do find it strange that no mention was ever made about the aircraft crash and my near miss with death, but I suppose that, even if she had written about it, the sentences would have been deleted by the vigilant German censors.

Because of the continual disruption brought about by Allied bombing, the German camp administration soon decided dental patients who would normally be due for serious treatment outside the camp would no longer be sent to Ulm for care but would be redirected to a local German dentist in the nearby town of Biberach. The Germans also thought it would be a good idea if my father went along with the prospective patients so he could act as an interpreter, as the local dentist was unable to speak English.

One very early morning a small party of men set off down the hill from the camp into the town accompanied by my father and an armed guard. The group assembled in the dental waiting room with the guard, while my father was settled comfortably in the surgery with the dentist and translated the various patients' problems and symptoms as they came in one by one for examination and treatment.

At the end of the session, when everyone had been taken care of, the dentist invited my father to sit in the chair and have a free dental inspection. As the dentist bent down, he inclined his head just a little and lifted one of the lapels of his white jacket to reveal a badge denoting the hammer-and-sickle emblem of the Communist Party. He told my father in rather hushed tones he knew there were many men imprisoned in the camp and he could personally obtain guns and ammunition for everyone if they were prepared to mount an armed insurrection against the German guards, as soon as the Allied troops drew nearer to Biberach. In this way the camp could be liberated and, with the assistance of Communist elements from Biberach, hold out until relieved by the Allies.

My father forcefully pointed out to the dentist that the camp was primarily occupied by many of the old and infirm, besides umpteen women and children, and their safety must not be jeopardised in this way. The dentist urged my father to reconsider the proposal and, if he did have a change of heart, he should make a further dental appointment when the whole concept could be taken a stage further.

Back in the camp Red Cross stores, after what had turned out to be quite an eventful morning, my father discussed the situation with Dave Godwin, and they both reached the same conclusion: the whole affair should be totally ignored. They also realised that, while the dentist might well be genuine and probably was, he might also be acting as a German *agent provocateur* as part of an ingenious German plan to uncover malcontents and subversive elements within the camp prisoner fraternity. In the end no further action was either contemplated or taken in the hope that, in the confusion of war, the matter would come to nothing, which was exactly what happened.

Repatriation! I'm not sure I knew what the word meant back then, but it transpired a number of our old or sick prisoners were being allowed to go home and would travel by train across most of Germany to the Swedish port of Gothenburg and then on to Britain. Early one September morning, my good friend John came to see me and explained that he and his family were going back home, as his mother hadn't been very well.

We were both upset at the prospect of his going and we vowed that, as real, best friends, we would never forget each other. We also promised that after the war we would do everything we could to find each other again. In the time-honoured way as embellished in the best chronicles of ancient pirates, we agreed we would give each other our most prized possession, which would be used as our treasure trove and buried there in Biberach Camp, so that one day we would return and dig it up. We obtained a shallow metal tin, and John put in his favourite penknife while I added two of my best watercolour paintbrushes.

We stood by the central concrete washstands positioned just outside my barrack and, as all good pirates would, measured out the required steps. Take ten paces to the north, then turn and take five paces to the east, turn once again and take a further six paces to the south. We took some time digging a hole of the required depth as the ground was so hard and had generally been formed by builders' rubble. Eventually we were finished and the tin was safely buried. We scattered loose earth over the spot, then washed it all in with water from the washstand, so that, after an hour or so, no one would ever know real treasure had been buried under their very feet. Then John and his family were gone and the world would never seem quite the same again.

Over the intervening years I tried to find John at every opportunity. I cycled all over Guernsey, calling on families who had the same or similar names as John's family, but all to no avail. In the mid-1980s I went to live in Jersey for a period and once there I decided on impulse to place an advertisement in the *Jersey Evening Post*. I received a charming letter from a previous internee, who told me I had spelled John's family name incorrectly and that he and his family had moved to Britain soon after the war, but nevertheless she included his present telephone number. All this was exactly forty years since our pledge of total loyalty.

It was with a great sense of apprehension I telephoned John. He answered the telephone call personally. Perhaps my approach wasn't exactly one of the best: 'John, this is Steve Matthews. Some forty years ago in Biberach Camp we said goodbye and promised we would never forget each other – and here we are once again speaking to each other after all those years.'

The reply, when it came after a short pause, wasn't the one I expected. John said, in somewhat stilted tones, 'I have to say that my time in Biberach was extremely difficult and traumatic and I have no wish to remember those horrific and difficult times. Therefore I would be obliged if you wouldn't bother me again.' And at that point the telephone handset was replaced. Although initially stunned, I could eventually see it didn't really matter. What really mattered was that I had personally kept a promise and satisfactorily fulfilled my end of a bargain, irrespective of the time it had taken.

In relation to some of those times in the camp my mother described a few of the frightening events that happened. In her manuscript she states:

> We certainly had many frights, such as the time when Freddie Williams got a small wireless set, goodness only knows how. After they used it nightly they would carefully remove the aerial and the set was then hidden away. But what exactly happened I don't

really know, only that the German loudspeaker on the square suddenly blazed out 'This is the B.B.C. calling, and here is the 1 o'clock news with so and so reading it!' Imagine the panic and we were all punished of course by the Germans because of our cheering, as people in Biberach town could hear the racket within our camp.

Not for the first time her impeccable notations raise more questions than answers. Where did Freddie Williams, doyen of stage management in Biberach, obtain the radio? How was it used and were news bulletins ever issued to the inmates? Did Freddie deliberately sabotage the goons' loudspeaker system and what punishments were meted out to the inmates?

One of the last walks of the year in Biberach took place shortly before the bad weather set in and the snow flurries arrived. It was not a significant day and nothing much happened until we returned to the camp and approached the main gates. There, parked in front of the White House, was a magnificent official German officers' staff car. It was gleaming black with enormous chrome headlights and the canvas hood was down. Sitting in the back of the car was a sleek black-and-tan dog that appeared to match the very colours of the paintwork and the leather interior. I had never seen such a beautiful animal before and, on asking, I was told by one of our throng it was a German guard dog called a Doberman Pinscher, and this breed was well-known for its intelligence, courage and ferocity. I resolved there and then that one day

I would have such an animal – and one day, although it was seventeen years later, I did have such an animal and I called him Alex in memory of Herr Laib's very special guard dog.

From this one encounter the serious camp rumours started to spread, stating that the car belonged to Field Marshal Wilhelm Keitel, who – as the Allies were moving ever closer towards the German borders – was visiting the camp in order to discuss ways of eliminating and disposing of us, the inmates. Apparently, there were two preferred methods. One revolved around the inmates being shot to death and the other was that the Nazis would place high explosives in all the barracks, which would be activated once the Allied armies came within shelling range of Biberach. I thought even then, as a young child, that Keitel probably had more trouble on his hands dealing with the deteriorating war situation, without bothering about us!

Of course, nothing came of these wild rumours, and life continued along the same lines as before, although I now believe we were very lucky indeed because, the very next day, Franz Laib visited the Red Cross stores and asked to speak to my father in complete confidence. They took a stroll around the perimeter fence and Herr Laib told my father that Hitler had indeed decreed that all concentration camps as well as some German municipal buildings were to be mined with heavy explosives in exactly the same manner as had been done in Poland; hence the visit of some high-ranking Nazi officers to the White House. After the Nazis had left, it was resolved by all the camp's senior officers that the German forces in Biberach would do nothing of the sort, as they were forcibly aware the Allies were already dangerously close to Biberach and moving nearer to the camp all the time. In any event, Keitel was eventually tried in Nuremberg, convicted and hanged as a war criminal after the war.

There was an undeniable rapport existing between Franz Laib and my father, based on mutual trust, and from this a strong friendship developed. I sense that in the boiling cauldron of fear and uncertainty Laib had no one he could talk to in order to unburden his tortured soul, because it is abundantly clear from my father's notebook of 1941 that Franz desperately feared for the safety and lives of his family in nearby Ulm. There was, however, much more to this story than at first thought, for, because of continuous day and night bombing, Franz Laib had no information as to whether his home near Ulm had been destroyed or, indeed, if any of his family had been killed or injured. On or about 17 December 1944 an RAF raid on Ulm had left 25,000 residents homeless and killed many of its local inhabitants. It was estimated that 81 per cent of all buildings in the city were destroyed, although the great cathedral was left completely untouched. In all, the raid lasted only twenty-five minutes and in that time the RAF dropped 1,450 tons of bombs.

Whether they hatched a plan together is pure conjecture, although I like to think this was the case, because not long afterwards my father, as chairman of the camp's Red Cross Committee, was detailed by the German administration to accompany Franz Laib to the city of Ulm, where a number of the camp inmates were receiving medical attention in one of the local hospitals. The intention was to make sure they were all right and hadn't come to any harm through Allied bombing raids. The prime RAF targets had been two lorry factories and several German army barracks. Nonetheless, a number of civilian and military hospitals were also destroyed in the confusion.

Franz Laib and my father set off together initially by train from Biberach station to Ulm thirty-one miles away. There were frequent stops on the way as bombing debris was still in the process of being moved away from railway tracks or urgent repairs were being made to the overworked German rail system. Before reaching Ulm, Franz asked my father if he could trust him not to escape and would he give him his word in this matter? My father agreed, not knowing what this was all about – but, then, he had nowhere else to go, especially with his own family back in the camp.

Franz said his home was on the outskirts of Ulm and he was now becoming increasingly worried about the lack of news concerning his own family, so would my father accompany him to his home? However, whatever happened, he must say nothing to the German authorities. My father agreed again, although with some trepidation, as he was warned not to speak to any Germans or give away the fact he was British, as anti-British feeling was running exceedingly high in Ulm following the recent Allied bombing raids.

Although the devastation was great, large swathes of the outskirts had been left untouched and, happily, Franz Laib's home was still intact. There was an embarrassing but happy reunion between husband and wife and then Franz and my father set off once again for Ulm. What my father didn't know and what I have only just discovered was that Laib was desperately worried about his heavily pregnant daughter, Maria. It had been agreed that Maria would be moved away from the constant bombing raids over Ulm into the safer realms of the countryside, and there, on 30 December 1944, she gave birth in an isolated and inaccessible hut to a daughter called Christa.

After walking along several deserted and damaged streets piled high with rubble, they eventually caught a tramcar, which bumped and rattled along at a very slow pace. The nearer they approached the city centre, the greater the damage appeared. The few occupants of the tram looked totally demoralised and tired, and my father noticed one woman eyeing him somewhat suspiciously. After a little while she moved seats until she was sitting directly opposite him and then said in well-modulated English voice, 'Fee, Fi, Fo, Fum, I smell the blood of an Englishman!' My father often said that this clearly pronounced sentence nearly gave him a massive heart attack; happily, it turned out the lady was originally British, living in Ulm, and had married a German soldier shortly after the 1914–18 conflict.

My father told her about all the British subjects from the camp who were in a hospital in Ulm. She had been unaware there were any British civilian prisoners being treated in local hospitals, but she promised to find out and visit them on a regular basis. My mother concludes by writing, 'She was absolutely marvellous, visiting them all and always taking them a few luxury items.' But who was she? I suppose we shall never know now.

Once Franz Laib and my father had found the various hospitals and established that the patients were well and being treated as well as local conditions would allow – although they were scared out of their wits – the two of them left to return to camp. On the way back to the railway station, Franz suggested they visit one of the few coffee-shops still open, again advising my father not to say anything to give away the fact he was British.

Sitting in the café and facing the street, he could see through the broken panes of the café windows that the damage was just simply horrifying. More importantly, he was able to listen to the conversations at adjoining tables, whispered gossip about factories having been bombed out of existence, of a population knowing the end was near, and it was becoming increasingly difficult for the German people to continue, and so perhaps they should give up now. Sitting at the next table was a young man in an officer's uniform with his mother. He was telling her about the terrible air-raids on Berlin and how the Germans were losing the war. My father wished he could somehow ensure this information reached the Allies, but he had the frustration of knowing that was just an impossible dream.

Some time afterwards, on 4 March 1945, the Americans using 223 of their B-17 Flying Fortress aircraft bombed Ulm once more, going for the marshalling yards, aircraft factories and ammunition dumps. In the attack it was significant that the US Air Force suffered no losses during this specific and successful raid. Daylight bombing raids became a normal feature of our day-to-day routine as they overflew the camp en route to bomb Friedrichshafen.

However, this time there was a major disruption to their plans because, unbeknown to anyone, the Germans had recently installed an anti-aircraft gun battery just outside the town. The guns opened fire, and suddenly we saw that one of the bombers had been hit, with smoke pouring out behind the aircraft. Gradually, the bomber began to lose height until, at long last, we saw several objects fall from the plane. A general sigh of relief swelled from the watching prisoners as we saw the parachutes open, and then they started counting out the numbers and assured everyone the whole crew had managed to bail out.

While all this was going on, the air armada had continued on its way, except for one solitary fighter, which detached itself from the bomber group and circled back over the site. After making several runs, it returned towards the fast-disappearing planes, but we could see several of the bombers peel off and start coming back towards us.

In the meantime, the aircrew had landed in a broad swathe with several of them coming down right in the middle of the ploughed fields alongside the camp, where soon they were rounded up by armed German soldiers. Within minutes the bombers were over the distant gun battery and plastered the whole area with a number of well-aimed high-explosive bombs.

Days later, rumours started to fly around the camp to the effect that the battery had been totally destroyed with many dead and wounded, but, more worryingly, the Free French aircrew had been lined up and shot soon after landing. During this whole episode the Germans said nothing and, at the time of writing, I have been unable to elicit any definite information about this particular incident.

On 2 January 1945 young Rex Wearing, the son of Rose and Ruben Wearing, died in Biberach Camp at the age of only four. The Wearings were all good friends of our family and Rex's premature death caused great shock and dismay among all the prisoners. It turned out that he had contracted one of the diseases brought into the camp by foreign prisoners, and I think it is true to say Rose and Ruben never quite got over their son's tragic death. It came as quite a shock to me because young Rex would sometimes join our party near our barracks; but once again my mother explained to me he was far better off now and safe in the arms of Jesus. That was fine as far as it went, but still no one appeared able to explain to me why, if Jesus was so good and kind, nobody ever came back to talk about it.

A little later my friends and I noticed that Robin Bartlett, one of our little gang, hadn't been seen for some time. I asked my mother about it and she told me Robin was very poorly, having caught some awful disease. I worried about this for some time and then decided to go off and see him myself. I was met at his barrack-room door by his mother, Auntie Lilly, and I asked her about Robin and if I could see him. She gently told me he was very ill and shouldn't be disturbed just at the moment, but in answer to my next question, as to whether he was going off to see Jesus, she just seemed to go a very funny colour and swell up in size, until at last she burst out into a frenzied bout of shouting and screaming that had me running all the way back to my barrack room just as fast as I could go. In the following years, when I sometimes used to go and play at Robin's house, I made sure I kept as far away as possible from Auntie Lilly Bartlett.

25 January 1945 started off fairly happily, but it would mark the beginning a span of days that would culminate as some of the most distressing and traumatic I have ever known. My father came to my barrack room to collect me and to take me to the camp hospital to see my mother, who was a patient there, as she had fallen down heavily on the ice and badly injured herself. This was the day before her birthday and, after a quick visit, my father and I went to the Red Cross stores, where I was soon busily engaged in drawing a special birthday card for my mother for the following day.

Four days later, on the morning of the 29th, Franz Laib, the deputy camp commandant, came to see my father to say that by late afternoon he needed a work party of prisoners to meet a train at Biberach station. The train would be carrying a new batch of prisoners from another camp, including men, women and children, and it was deemed a good idea to take a number of handcarts down to the station to help the new arrivals with their luggage. The stores soon became a hive of anxious activity as people came and went, orders were issued and administration matters arranged, until finally, by late afternoon, the party set off for the station. I followed on with a few friends and Herr Laib, together with a party of armed guards, and I remember it was quite an excited crowd, wending its way down the long, winding hill to Biberach railway station, in spite of the bitterly cold weather.

After a long wait and in the gloom of a late winter's afternoon, the train steamed into the station and everyone, including the German guards, was horrified to see the pathetic and bedraggled mass of humanity alighting from the carriages. I saw ill-clothed walking skeletons, and a nearby German guard was being violently sick by the side of the railway tracks as he witnessed the appalling state of these people. After some urgent consultation with the railway officials, Herr Laib told my father these prisoners were Dutch Jews holding Paraguayan passports and had until recently been incarcerated in the infamous death camp at Bergen-Belsen. They were part of an original party of 301 Jews who were being sent to Switzerland on 21 January that year to be exchanged for German nationals being held in various Allied countries. However, after several days 130 of them had been removed from the train and placed on another transport train to be rerouted through to Biberach.

Showers and delousing stations had already been set up and I can remember dark-green sacking screens that covered wooden struts leading to the changing rooms. The way in was dimly lit by naked, blue, electric light-bulbs and I can vividly recall looking at the bulbs and thinking the tiny chips in the blue paint looked like the bright stars in the night sky. In the men's changing room my father told everyone to strip off and leave their belongings, such as they were, in a neat pile on the floor. Even I could see their belongings were heart-rending and pathetic: a small piece of soap here, a broken sliver of comb there, or a shattered fragment of mirror. All I could see was their skin, the colour of old parchment, tightly stretched across protruding bones, and then they were gone. At that moment my father began to worry whether, on their return, there would be chaos and trouble over ownership of the various piles of clothing; yet, when they did get back, everyone went quietly to their own pile of wretched belongings and stood waiting patiently for their next orders.

As the Jews stood around, my father told them that once they had dressed they would be taken to Biberach Camp to be fed and housed. At this juncture he thought he was standing on someone's clothes and, on turning around, he was horrified to see he had been standing on the bare toes of one of the prisoners. The man had been so used to violent ill-treatment in Bergen–Belsen that he had been too frightened to say anything or indeed to move. It was the first time I had ever seen my father cry and it was this more than anything else that was the precursor of the worst day of my life. Eventually, the party started to struggle the several kilometres up the hill towards the camp, and the handcarts became essential in helping those unable to walk so far.

I walked along with my father and some of the camp inmates, who were pushing and pulling the carts now being filled with adults and children too weak to continue walking. On our cart I noticed one man hadn't moved for a long time and I told my father, who seemed to have noticed it as well. There were three young girls trying to comfort the old man but he just didn't appear to be aware of them. At the camp, everyone managed to get off the cart, albeit with some difficulty, except the man, and I said to my father, 'I think he's just gone to see Jesus.' My father went to shake the man's shoulder, all to no avail, and he came back and said to me, 'Yes, Stephen, I'm afraid you're right: he *has* gone to see Jesus.'

The next day my father called for me early in the morning and we went straight to the hospital to wish my mother a happy birthday, even though I hadn't been able to finish her card. She pointed to a young Jewish girl in a nearby bed, and suggested I should go and talk to her. I found out she was called Rachel and she was nearly ten years old. This girl made a great impression on me and I could see she was very ill, with translucent skin like bone china. The next day my mother left the hospital and came back to our own barrack room and life returned to some form of normality, but after several more days I decided to call in at the hospital to see how Rachel was making out.

The German nurse, Sister Annie, who had worked tirelessly to nurse and help her sick Jewish patients, took me to the now empty bed with its neatly folded army blankets, the sun streaming through the windows and highlighting the floating dust particles in the air. Sister Annie was crying and gave me to understand Rachel had now 'departed', and I took this to mean that Rachel had died, and I too was so very sad. I had a passing thought: if the Germans hated the Jews so much, why was Sister Annie crying like this?

Over the years I wondered if Rachel had really died or whether this was a normal problem with language interpretation and comprehension. So, in the intervening years, I took every opportunity to try to trace either Rachel or her family. One rabbi once told me in Amsterdam, 'Look, we lost well over six million of our Jewish nation in that war, and how many do you think were called Rachel?' I visited Holland several times and I tried various Jewish associations, but all to no avail.

Finally, after sixty-five years, I found a marvellous caring man in Professor Henry Joshua of New York, who had been on that very train in Biberach in 1945. Even today I find it amazing that, among the maelstrom of humanity on Biberach station, we probably passed each other on the darkened platform, and I cannot, even with my own knowledge of the time, imagine what despair he must have felt. Only days before leaving that monstrosity of a hellhole called Bergen-Belsen with his mother, brother and sister, his father had died in the camp from the after-effects of typhus and malnutrition. Today, Henry talks about his first meal in Biberach as being one of boiled potatoes, 'which were so very precious that they all saved some for the next day'.

As part of my father's strategy as chairman of the Red Cross Committee, he had created a reserve stock of parcels, mainly because the Allied bombing raids had disrupted normal distribution and with it the movement of Red Cross parcels to the camp. This was called 'saving it all for a rainy day'. Still, a special issue was made to the Jews on my father's own initiative, although no one demurred, even though this was part of the camp's precious and important food stocks.

At last, in 2010, through Henry Joshua's supreme efforts, he finally traced Rachel to Amsterdam. It transpired her name was actually Rahel and not Rachel, and we had all misheard it in Biberach. The whole Jewish episode left such an indelible mark on the character of my mother, a deeply Christian lady, who wrote a special passage about these events, with which I'd like to end this chapter:

It was a great experience living with the Jews in 1945, when the Germans realised they were losing the war. I just couldn't believe what we were seeing, just skeletons of people. Our camp doctors very carefully prepared diets for them, starting first of all with milk and water. There were three dear little girls who had 'lost' their mother on the train, and whose father died on Cecil's truck bringing them up the hill to the camp. It was a dreadful sight as they were also so dirty and full of lice and so very weak – they were all just skin and bone.

I had fallen on the ice and was in the camp hospital and one night Sister Last came into the ward and said, 'Who would like to cuddle this little girl?' and then added 'There is no fear as she is quite clean.' I said that I would love to have her in my bed as I thought Sister Last was carrying a small child until I saw her long but thin legs, however Doctor Sutherland was quite marvellous.

They were also wired off from the rest of us because of the threat of contagious diseases. No one can ever understand the state these poor people were in through the behaviour and torture of the people responsible for their plight. They were almost dumb with fear, however, when they were thoroughly clean we were then allowed to mix with them, and of course we shared all our clothes with them. However Doctor Sutherland said that many of the children would never walk properly again as they had developed flat and deformed feet. In no time at all Mrs Bradshaw had a team of workers making soft toys for the children with materials provided by the Red Cross and also the Makarios Greek family had another team of people who were diligently plaiting box-cord retrieved from the Red Cross parcels and then weaving sandals, otherwise many of the Jewish children would have been without shoes.

## CHAPTER 13

# LIBERATION

There was, however, one sequel of a happier nature concerning the arrival of the Jews, and this involved a recognised champion Jewish bridge-player who gave full-time lessons in the camp. My mother was a regular student. I found the main drawback to all of this was that, in later life, I learned not to play cards with my mother, as she had been taught to memorise the sequence of cards and likely possibilities during any type of card game.

It was early April 1945, and the air-raid sirens sounded once more, to the point that it was fast becoming a ritual. Allied fighter aircraft overflew the camp and this time tragically dived onto a Red Cross train carrying wounded German soldiers on the outskirts of Biberach railway station. In the ensuing mêlée thirteen injured soldiers were killed and many more suffered further additional serious injuries. My mother wrote of these times:

# THE DAY THE NAZIS CAME

The raids went on day and night and one dinner time, all of a sudden the beautiful clear blue sky looked like glittering stars as masses of wide strips of bright silver paper were dropped from the aircraft, and as the planes got nearer and nearer we realised it was our planes. It was oh so marvellous to watch the aircraft returning and the leader going backwards and forwards to encourage those planes that were very badly damaged to get back home. Others were shot down and I think this was the only time I really cried to see our boys having to bail out.

It was 12 April 1945, and I suppose this day had started as so many others had done before. However, it wasn't very long before the air-aid warnings sounded once again and, as usual, the adults emerged from their various barrack rooms and started shuffling us all along the corridor towards a large storeroom. I could feel the panic and the sense of urgency in their voices and through their general demeanour, which became even more heightened as we heard the droning sound of the approaching aircraft engines. People started to cry and shout and, when it was my turn to enter the storeroom, I could see it was filled with a number of metal buckets, mops and brushes and all the sundry but bulky paraphernalia necessary to clean the barracks. I reckoned then it would be more dangerous to be inside the storeroom than outside, for one unlucky shot could create serious carnage in there with flying debris and shrapnel. So I opted out and ran outside towards the concrete washstands nearby and settled down underneath, with my back placed firmly against one of the large and substantial concrete buttresses, where I felt completely safe.

The flotilla of American planes swept low over the camp and flew onwards towards the town of Biberach, and within seconds came the crump of detonations as their bombs started to fall on the ancient town. The violent explosions seemed to disturb the very ground I was sitting on and their vibrations moved ferociously up and down my body, so that everything felt like it was shaking all around me and I began to lose my equilibrium.

It has been officially stated that the bombing of Biberach was a deadly error brought about by units of the United States Ninth Air Force stationed at Beaumont in France as part of the 386th Bomber Group. Fourteen bombers had been instructed to bomb Kaufbeuren, also in Bavaria, but some forty miles (around sixty-five kilometres) away from Biberach the weather and visibility that day was not of the best. According to the authorities, Kaufbeuren wasn't bombed at all, and it has been assumed that the US aircrews thought they were over the right area when in fact they were directly over Biberach.

The fourteen bombers were Douglas A-26 Invaders and each aircraft could carry 10.5 tons of bombs. Biberach was hit by forty-two bombs of Type 500GP, each weighing 226.8 kilograms. The official history of the United States Army Air Forces doesn't mention Biberach at all, but still names Kaufbeuren as being the target for the day.

The air-raid alarm had only just sounded when the bombs

began to fall. The people of Biberach hadn't expected that a raid such as this would ever take place. Many of them had miraculous escapes, such as the aunt of Reinhold Adler, who was wending her way home with her three daughters and was lucky enough to survive by taking shelter under a large doorway; although, when they all finally emerged, they found their home had been completely obliterated, together with thirty-seven neighbouring houses. All in all, in a matter of only a few minutes 139 houses had been destroyed or badly damaged; 55 people had lost their lives, with a further 14 being seriously injured.

Several days later I was taken with Herr Laib and my father to see the actual debris of collapsed buildings in and around the *Obstmarkt* (fruit market) with rubble lying in the streets; we saw lopsided houses with large sections of tiles missing from their roofs, as homeowners struggled to clamber over the debris to rescue some of their personal belongings. A few days later in a combined fighter-and-bombing attack on Biberach railway station, two more innocent civilian women and their two children were killed.

It was a time of bustle and activity, and an air of nervous energy and anticipation permeated the camp. Rumour followed hard upon rumour, each one feeding on the other, but they all echoed the familiar pattern: 'Did you know the Germans have made plans to get rid of us all?'

We were, apparently, going to be exterminated just like the Jews. My father used to say it always seemed so very strange to him that nearly every rumour started with the words 'I have it on the highest authority': 'I have it on the highest authority that the Germans are going to fill the barracks up with explosives and blow us all to Kingdom Come.'

All the same, for us children, life continued in very much the same vein as before and all this upheaval generally passed us by, leaving us in a kind of quiet oasis where we were left to our own devices. It wasn't because we didn't notice what was going on all around us, for we did. We could see Allied planes had total control of the skies and could pass overhead at will. We could also see the deep-red glow in the night skies as nearby German towns blazed following their raids, and we could hear the crump of artillery shells each day as the Allies crept ever nearer. There was also the thin trickle of German soldiers moving silently along the top road and shambling in retreat alongside the camp's barbed-wire fences, some on crutches and many others who had been wounded being pulled along on handcarts by their comrades.

However, on this one afternoon while our elders and betters were settling down to their regular afternoon nap, a small group of us were sitting by the side of the internal road leading down to the camp's coal depot. I think my friend Robin Bartlett was there, as was probably John Benham. I know my other great friend John and his family had been repatriated some time earlier, as had Mike Martel. However, I am equally certain the twins, Neville and Ralph Godwin, weren't there because they would never have allowed themselves to be excluded from what was about to follow.

Our group were sitting right opposite the White House and alongside a ten-foot-high, single-strand barbed-wire fence. Between the fence and the main building lay a plot of very tall grass, which must have been somewhere near twenty feet wide and forty feet long. One of our number was resting partly against the wooden supporting post and partly against the barbed wire, when a portion of the wire fence gave way and gently swung inwards.

It appeared as though a small wire door had just been opened in the fence, as if by magic. The opening wasn't square or rectangular but cruciform in shape and we all realised an unknown soldier from a previous incarceration must have made it. The breaks in the wire had been neatly concealed by weaving in a very thin strand of wire, so it was almost impossible to observe the deception unless you knew exactly where the breaks had been made.

As far as we were concerned, we were on the verge of a new and exciting world waiting to be discovered. Like a beckoning beacon, the top of either a wooden hutch or kennel could just be seen rising above the tall grass in the middle of the compound. So, in the hope of seeing some real, live animals, it was decided two of us would go through the hole in the barbed wire to investigate while the others would carefully close the wire behind us and stand guard.

To my eternal shame, I don't recall who came with me on that day, and this lapse of memory I can only put down to the passing years and the frailty of creeping old age! Moving quickly along through the long grass on our hands and knees, we soon discovered the rabbit hutch, for that was what it was, completely deserted. In the midst of this anticlimax we came to realise that just above us one of the ground-floor sash windows of the White House had been left wide open: in an instant, even though we knew we were trespassing in strictly forbidden territory, we decided to just go and have a quick look.

Soon we were peering in at a deserted storeroom of narrow and long dimensions. Without hesitation, we scrambled over the windowsill and dropped down what felt like a very long way to land next to a high wooden skirting board. In hindsight I suppose the drop wasn't too long but only seemed so because we were so young. Anyway, we found ourselves standing on a polished, honey-coloured parquet floor. There were two long wooden tables side by side and covered by German army blankets, which hung down over the table legs. There were a large number of small khaki-coloured metal boxes lying in heaps on the tables, and each of the tins had yellow German writing on it.

The tins must have been about sixteen centimetres long, nine to ten centimetres wide and only five centimetres deep, and when I opened one of them I found it contained a selection of medical instruments such as scissors, a scalpel, syringe and tweezers. I took a pair of scissors out and put them in my pocket, carefully closing the lid of the tin box and replacing it on the table. No sooner had I done that than we heard footsteps marching along an outside corridor, so we immediately ducked down under the tables and backed up against the far wall as best we could. Within seconds we could hear the door being opened and then closed, and the steps came towards the table. Horror of horrors! We were now looking down at the highly polished toecaps of a pair of black German-army jackboots.

Over the course of the next few minutes the boots came and went into and out of view; backwards and forwards they moved, until at last they receded and we heard the door once again open, then close, and finally, with some relief, we heard the key firmly slide the lock back into place. We waited just a few more minutes to make sure there would be no return visit by the unknown German officer, then we hightailed it out of the place as quickly as our legs could carry us.

Later that afternoon I handed the scissors over to my mother, who, far from being pleased by my efforts, gave me a stern lecture on the possible dangers involved and whether God would regard this act as stealing (although I have to say that, at the time, I was pretty convinced God would be on my side). The next morning we had an early visit from the Methodist minister, the Reverend Flint, and once again I was invited to go over the previous day's activities. The scissors were produced and everyone admired the quality and workmanship involved in their manufacture. Soon, though, I was allowed out to play and put the whole incident out of my mind.

It was only an hour or so into our games that I received a summons to return to my barrack room. I found yet another group of petulant people waiting for me, who would go to make up the second kangaroo court I would have to face in Biberach. Reverend Flint gave a brief but fairly accurate summation of the events, and then the diatribe broke out, with everyone trying to speak at the same time. Didn't I realise this was stealing? Didn't I realise that to purloin German military equipment was punishable by death? This continued for quite some time until I began to lose interest. Reverend Flint nevertheless took my part and told the assembly in his loud preaching voice that this hadn't been stealing, but I had merely liberated and taken possession of a very valuable asset that could be used only for all our general welfare.

The heated discussion moved backwards and forwards, but the end result confirmed my suspicions that adults were often prone to vacillation, as my conspirator and I were invited to go back and acquire a further selection of scissors on behalf of the whole camp. The wire trapdoor was sprung once again and we were through, moving quickly forward on hands and knees between the tall grasses. It was with great fear and trepidation that we hoisted ourselves up onto the windowsill, only to find the room was now completely empty and devoid even of tables.

The scissors remained in our family for many long years and served to remind us of times past. After the war had ended, Reverend Flint would often preach at our chapel on Guernsey, and, although his sermons were inclined to drag on a little for a young boy, there was always one part I loved. He had an exceptionally loud, one might even say booming, voice and he would use this to great effect in bringing down hellfire and damnation upon a subdued and wilting congregation. His voice at the outset would be soft and appealing and the members of the congregation would visibly relax until they were almost anaesthetised; then suddenly, with a loud shout, he would bring his hand crashing down hard on the Bible with such a loud bang, shaking everyone out of their self-induced lethargy.

# THE DAY THE NAZIS CAME

In early April 1945, Hitler moved his headquarters to the specially constructed *Führerbunker* that had been built directly under the Chancellery building in Berlin. This task had been undertaken because of the accurate and effective bombing raids carried out by the Allies. The bunker was a vast underground communication complex, created on two floors and incorporating more than thirty rooms.

On 15 April, Bergen-Belsen, one of the worst death camps of World War Two, had been liberated by British troops, who were confronted by the appalling sight of thousands of Jewish corpses lying sprawled among both the living and the dying throughout the camp. Illness and disease raged through Bergen-Belsen, with typhus being the main culprit, although there were other serious outbreaks of typhoid fever, cholera and dysentery claiming many lives, even well after the prisoners' liberation.

My Aunt Annette, the Guernsey nurse who had written letters home from the deserts of the Middle East, knowing they could never actually be posted, had by now been transferred to the European theatre of war and, as a captain, she was included in the first party of medical personnel allowed to enter the camp to assist and treat both the living and the dying. Not only was she devastated and horrified by this view of hell on earth, but she also became fearful for our own family's safety in Biberach.

At this critical point, another human tragedy was played out in her life. During her travels she had formed a very close and personal attachment to one of the young British army doctors in the company. Within a very short space of time this doctor too contracted typhus in Bergen-Belsen and died a little while later. After a period of bereavement, Annette never married but went on to be a respected matron of a number of major United Kingdom hospitals.

Up to this point there had been only a mere trickle of forlorn German soldiers retreating along the road passing in front of the main camp gates. We could also hear the deep, far-off boom of heavy-artillery fire, sounding at times like a distant summer thunderstorm. American fighter aircraft often flew overhead, doing what they could to harry the fleeing Germans, and I began to spend more and more time huddled under my substantial concrete washstand. My father also heard from the German guards that the Allied forces had finally entered the outskirts of Ulm and the city was now suffering under a heavy and continuous bombardment.

As the days followed quickly one upon another, so the trickle of German soldiers became a grey flood. One thing I learned then was that there is nothing more distressing than seeing a broken army in full retreat. Shambling, wounded men in their stained and shabby field-grey uniforms intermingled with a mélange of cars, lorries, horse-drawn wagons and ambulances. This line of depressed and suffering humanity continued to pass by our camp every hour of every day and night.

Some of the retreating rabble continued to cause mayhem in their wake, as there were frequent cases of sniper fire directed at the camp and its inmates. Generally, the culprits were members of the hated SS divisions and, although no one was reported wounded, there were many near misses. The situation became so bad that Herr Laib, in his official capacity as deputy commandant, went out into the fields under a flag of truce and told the recalcitrant militants he was under the direct orders of the Führer to protect the camp occupants, and, unless they desisted in their behaviour, he would order his machine-gun towers to open fire on them. And that was the end of the matter for the time being.

My father's birthday, and Hitler's, came round again on 20 April. Although on previous occasions there had been great celebration and jubilation, on this occasion in 1945 the camp guards chose to ignore it. I made a special card for my father, and I think overall he fared much better than Hitler did. As a gesture to some of the guards for their many kindnesses, my father gave them several small squares of chocolate from his ration and a few cigarettes. The deputy camp commandant visited my father later in the morning and told him it would now be only a matter of hours before the Allies arrived to liberate the camp.

Not knowing what the final outcome would be, and in remembrance of their friendship over these extremely difficult times, he gave my father a watercolour painting of an old traditional German farmhouse. By and by, my father found a small parcel on his table in the Red Cross stores containing a few German war medals, a forage cap and a Nazi armband, all donated by some of the guards.

It may have been Hitler's fifty-sixth birthday but his birthday luncheon in the bunker was a very solemn and depressing affair. It was attended by Göring and Himmler, who then fled immediately from Berlin once the meal was over and they had passed on their heartfelt and loyal congratulations to Hitler. Hitler was stooped and trembling, his uniform was stained with food, and his hands were shaking and palsied by the onset of Parkinson's disease. As he consumed his meagre lunch in Berlin, some distance away in Biberach his beaten troops were gradually emerging from the forests and roadways below the camp and trudging through the mud of the ploughed fields to pass along the camp's barbed-wire fences; in the meantime, throughout this historic period, the noise of the Allied artillery was growing louder and louder.

While all this was going on, I was standing by the barbed-wire fence watching the demoralised rabble shuffle by when one of the soldiers stopped and started shouting at me. It was some time before I realised this wounded and bandaged apparition was one of the Hitler Youth I had encountered on a country walk, who had stolen my chocolate and then spat all over me. I could see he still carried his carved walking stick, as it was just poking out of the top of his sullied uniform jacket. He stood in front of the fence and indicated by hand movements he wanted something to eat, most likely chocolate. In return he would offer me ownership of the coveted walking stick. I, too, signalled by hand movements he should wait there, and then I hared off to purloin the necessary goods. Not wishing to be taken in again, I took a bar of chocolate from my mother's secret cache and carefully removed half of the contents, and then added some silver paper to make it look like a full bar again.

On my return to the barbed wire, we agreed we would throw our individual packages over the fence at the same time. One, two, three, the chocolate bar flew over the barbed wire one way, and the walking stick travelled the other. On retrieving our respective spoils, the Hitler Youth member soon realised he had received only half a bar of chocolate, and I found that the bottom half of the walking stick, previously partly hidden under his uniform jacket, had been smashed and shredded, probably during a previous engagement with Allied forces. Suddenly, we both started to laugh and, with a final wave of a bandaged hand, he turned away and trudged off towards the top road. I would never see him again but I wished him well and could only hope he would survive the next onslaught.

On 22 April the number of retreating German soldiers had been reduced once more to a mere trickle and the tension in the camp began to build again, because it appeared evident the Allies were moving ever closer. On this very same day, Hitler in Berlin held a three-hour military conference during which he suddenly went berserk and let loose a hysterical and shrieking tirade against his army and universal treason, lies and corruption within his own regime.

Meanwhile, the Allies were gearing up for their final assault on the Biberach sector. In discussions held between the Free French military, commanded by General Philippe Leclerc, and the US military command, it was tacitly agreed that US forces would take the lead in the forthcoming battle. In the event, it was the French who moved first, much to the Americans' surprise and puzzlement, although in reality there should be no puzzlement over the French actions: the first Battle of Biberach had taken place on 2 October 1796, when French forces under the command of General Moreau launched a devastating and successful counterattack against the Austrian army. I have no doubt some French student of military history saw the similarity in the two situations and decided to pre-empt the attack. General Leclerc was the respected commander of the French Second Armoured Division. Although his real name was Philippe François Marie Leclerc de Hauteclocque, he used his Resistance *nom de guerre* in order to protect his family, who were all still living in France.

The first sign of the emerging Allied forces occurred during the late morning of 23 April, which was St George's Day. From the road in the far distance, down across the ploughed fields below the camp, I saw two tanks slowly move onto open ground from the shelter of the forest edge as the Germans started lobbing shells over the fence in their direction from various defensive positions to the rear of our camp. There have been several written accounts of prisoners hanging white flags and bedsheets from the barbed-wire fences, but, although this may well be true, I certainly didn't see any. What I do know from my own observations and mother's penning is the following:

Cecil came into our barrack room and then sure enough at 1 pm the battle was on, tanks and more tanks, it was so strange to watch. Also on top of the hill behind the camp was a German tank, banging away over our heads and therefore we were all in a very dangerous position. Actually it was thought that the big White House had been turned into a hospital as some of the wounded were arriving. Herr Laib hoisted a huge white sheet whilst coming under heavy fire and he was really very brave and respected by everybody in the camp. Afterwards we realised that the Hitler Youth camp below us had been hit and had just vanished.

Most people took their stools and stayed with the children in the barrack corridors where the walls were quite thick, but Cecil and I and Stephen wanted to see for ourselves what was happening, never for one moment thinking we would come out of it alive and that is when we both experienced a wonderful stillness and we knew all would be well. During this long time of waiting, Cecil and I just held hands, and it was a strange calming feeling and we knew that all would be well. It was as if we were not alone.

We spent minutes just looking at each other before we spoke because the experience was so tremendous. We just wanted to be together, holding hands although the guns were banging away and everything was black with smoke around us – but we were not afraid.

There was much consternation among the occupants of the camp as the tanks, one after another, seemed to be hit by accurate enemy shelling and caught fire. In response, the German gunners naturally shifted targets but, after a while, I could see one of the burning French tanks, imperceptibly at first, begin to inch forward once more. It was subsequently revealed that the French had fixed oil drums onto the rear of the tanks, which they lit to simulate a direct hit, and, at the same time, they tied strips of red-and-orange canvas onto the turrets to look like flames. Machine-gun bullets thumped into buildings and whined overhead; luckily, no one was hit, although it was rumoured one tank shell passed through an open barrack window and ploughed into a wooden bed bunk but failed to explode. Soon, the Germans were running about in all directions and the battle finally ended by six o'clock in the evening. So this was our liberation day on 23 April 1945 – and we were all free at last.

My mother continued:

> Just after 6 pm when things began calming down, one of the French commanders came into the camp and was absolutely astounded to see nappies on the lines and see that women and children had been in the line of fire. He explained that we still needed to be very careful as many snipers were still around.
>
> We also had the pleasure of seeing all the SS being rounded up, thousand upon thousand, as they had been hiding in the Black Forest. They were all put into a huge field with French tanks at each corner. There was lots of activity and gradually we were feeling much safer at night, especially as we could now receive the BBC News.

At the time we were enduring the short-lived battle of Biberach, Russian troops reached the outskirts of

Berlin, while in the *Führerbunker* Hitler had received a telegram from Hermann Göring. Hitler, in one of his now frequent rages, termed the contents 'high treason' and he immediately removed Göring from his various positions of power within the military and also the Nazi Party – which included commander-in-chief of the Luftwaffe – and as Reichsmarschall. The telegram had been received in the isolated bunker by radio and it asked Hitler to confirm that he (Göring) was to take over 'total leadership of the German Reich'. He added that, if he did not hear from Hitler by 10 p.m., he would infer Hitler was incapacitated and he would then assume full leadership of the Reich.

Once the initial euphoria of our liberation waned, it soon became apparent there were some serious problems to be faced, with special regard to communication with our liberators. Prior to liberation there had been a small party of French soldiers imprisoned in Biberach. They were led by a man I knew as Captain Christian, whom I remember as tall and upright, with a charming manner and disposition. I heard later he had been made mayor or head of the administration in Biberach, as he well knew not only who the good Germans were but could also identify the misfits and the bullies, and I thought then this was a really clever move. I have a feeling many of the camp residents forgot that, although they had been liberated and were free to move around, the war was still going on and even now there were significant dangers lurking for Allied soldiers.

The greatest of the camp grievances were directed towards

the tough and often brutal French Moroccan troops, who obviously spoke no English. The Moroccans had greatly suffered at the hands of the German enemy throughout this campaign and they were in no mood to appear conciliatory. Whenever we left the camp it was prudent for us to wear little Union Flags on the lapels of our coats for quick and positive identification and to ensure our self-preservation. However, to their credit, the French immediately set about supplementing our meagre diet of ersatz bread and rotten meat and they increased the milk allowance for all the camp children. Nonetheless, in spite of all this effort, chaos and confusion continued to reign. Even so, I liked the Moroccan troops enormously, particularly their broad white smiles as they passed by in their vehicles, and they always enthusiastically acknowledged my waves.

The warning about SS snipers was soon to be proved all too true, for the following morning after our liberation, when my father and I were walking back to our room from the Red Cross stores, he suddenly felt something brush by his hair just before a bullet ploughed into a nearby supporting fencepost, sending a splinter of wood high into the air. We both ran helter-skelter for the nearest barrack doors; our approach was so forceful that I saw the heavy-duty wired-glass panel shatter as we barged our way through.

My father was well aware the American lines weren't too far away, and I feel reasonably sure that, because he could speak fluent German, the prisoners' committee agreed he should try to reach them and describe to them some of our prevailing and more pressing difficulties. So, early one morning, my father 'liberated' two bicycles and he and my mother, together with me riding pillion, set off towards the American zone, with strict instructions not to speak to any Germans we might encounter on the journey, so that our British nationality wouldn't be revealed. (Much later, in reading through Mum's personal notes, I find that the cycles were kindly donated by two of my German heroes, Nursing Sister Annie Sigg from the camp hospital, for my mother and Deputy Commandant Franz Laib's own cycle for my father.)

We left by the camp main gates and turned left towards the forest. The trees by the side of the road were still displaying their spring colours, and perhaps it was my imagination but they appeared to be more colourful in the place where the German fighter aircraft had previously crashed.

After about half an hour, we came across a grey German military truck by the side of the road with a buckled front wheel. The driver's door was wide open and some of the vehicle's contents, such as black army boots, papers and clothing, were strewn all over the road. There was no sign of the driver and, as my mother said she could do with a little rest, she sat down by the side of the road and I wandered off on my own to investigate my new surroundings.

From the edge of the road and looking into the woods, I could see a little stream wending its way just below, and I climbed down a rough-hewn pathway towards the gurgling water. On the way I saw some short, red spikes with triangular pieces of cloth hanging from them, but it didn't mean anything to me at that time, so I just ignored them. After moving on for about fifty yards, I was suddenly confronted by a single, bloody jackboot with a piece of human leg still inside and only a white piece of bone poking out of the top of it, then I noticed a red tide of blood and ripped clothing covering the grassy slope.

I can tell you it certainly stopped me right in my tracks and I started shouting out as loud as I could for my father. As soon as he started climbing down the pathway towards me he realised the stakes marked out the boundary of a German minefield, so he shouted to me not to move a muscle but to keep very, very still. Looking at the bloody boot in front of me, I can assure you I didn't move a muscle but remained rooted to the very spot. My father inched forward towards me very slowly and lifted me high up onto his shoulders, then he gradually moved backwards one step at a time until we were well clear of the danger. I always wondered why he put me up on his shoulders: in later years, during my paramilitary training, I realised it was to try to protect me from any exploding mine.

Our journey towards the Americans continued and by now I was sitting on the handlebars of my father's bicycle. Occasionally we could see movements in the dark forest and every now and again we caught a glimpse of men in field-grey uniforms. My father explained these people were all probably the 'grey wolves' who were lost German soldiers or guerrillas hiding out in the woods. I suppose to the grey wolves we must have looked like normal German peasants, especially having me in tow with my blond, Aryan-looking hair.

After a few more miles we reached a small market town and, while my parents were parking their cycles and making them secure, I sauntered off to see an African American army sergeant reprimanding a forlorn uniformed German soldier who was securely bound by thick rope to a lamppost. As I stood there the sergeant suddenly spotted me and, taking off his forage cap, he came at me in a threatening manner and shouted, 'Just get the hell outta here, you lousy Kraut.'

According to my parents, I just stood there and, placing hands on hips and with legs slightly apart, said in reply, 'Excuse me, but I'll have you know I'm British,' whereupon the sergeant swooped down to pick me up and started dancing me around the lamppost. Within minutes a Jeep arrived on the scene and we were all ushered on board, and, with our cycles hanging off the side, we sped off to the US army headquarters.

Well, did the Americans make a fuss of us! At this point it is much better if my mother explains what happened in her own words:

We went to the American command base and it was so exciting to walk up the steps of what was once an old farmhouse and say to them 'How lovely to see you all,' and then watch their faces. They just could not believe that there was a British camp in Biberach. Then the telephones started ringing and a General rang the local Burgomaster to order six more chickens and after hearing his reply said 'Look, if the chickens are not here within the hour we will hold new mayoral elections.' Then we were taken along the road to the cook-house; however when D.

Company returned for their meal they played games with Stephen who then asked if he could have his meal with them, while we went on to eat in the Officers Mess.

As it was nearing lunchtime, my parents were escorted to the officers' mess, while I elected to stay with the sergeants, who were all African Americans. In their mess I had the best meal I have ever had in my whole life, and one I can clearly recall even to this day. In my now fairly long life I have eaten in many world-class restaurants and hotels, but I would say without fear of contradiction this really was the best – the very best food and amidst the very best company. The meal started with chicken Maryland, served with lashings of gravy and wonderful creamed, mashed potatoes. This was followed by tinned fruit and delicious ice cream, all washed down with iced lemon tea. All the sergeants were so genuinely kind and considerate towards me, and I believe this one event acted as a catalyst for my subsequent Colonial service in Central Africa in later years.

After that gargantuan and incredible meal we were introduced to a young American infantry lieutenant called Tip Tippet, who was just kindness itself. He gave me his own infantry badge and a Swiss Army knife, as well as giving my parents his own service holdall. Then he took us back to Biberach Camp in his Jeep, but with another Jeep as escort, and one sporting a heavy machine-gun in the rear. It was great fun sitting in the front of the Jeep with the windscreen down and I couldn't help noticing two serrated stanchions fixed to both sides of the bonnet. When I asked Tip, he nonchalantly replied that some of the German soldiers were still lurking in the forest, and sometimes they stretched thin wire across the road at head height in an attempt to decapitate the oncoming passengers. However, the stanchions cut the wire so everyone would remain safe.

As my mother puts it, 'We soon realised that the Americans were taking a great risk in taking us back to camp as only the day before a General and his men were killed by the S.S. who were still hiding out in the Black Forest.'

When I heard that, I crouched down a little lower in my seat. Afterwards, Tip and many other US servicemen visited Biberach Camp, bringing sweets and chocolates and giving children rides around the camp in their Jeeps and lorries, and in the interim conditions certainly improved.

After some time Tip came to see us and said he was being transferred down south, which meant Italy, and then later we were told there had been a serious train crash on his journey and he had been critically injured in the accident. Before he left he had come to our barrack room to have a cup of tea with my parents, and when I say tea I mean that this was purely roasted bramble leaves. The twins Neville and Ralph Godwin were there as well and one of them asked to see Tip's automatic handgun. Tip took it out and placed it on the table, and I can still see the shiny metal finish of this .45 automatic pistol.

Over the years I have tried to find the whereabouts of Tip's family in the US but, sadly, to no avail.

# LIBERATION

At this point, an aside: the manuscript for the book was already nearing completion when I came across a single piece of paper written in my mother's inimitable handwriting. I cannot recall having seen this chilling document before, nor had I even heard mention of it earlier, but the scant words and implications made a great impact on me. In the days that followed I tried to blot it out – after all, the book was well on the way to being prepared for publication – but somehow the story kept creeping back and impinging on my mind. It was as if I could hear the victims mentioned in the narrative clamouring for their voices to be heard, in search of understanding and perhaps retribution, even after such a long period of time.

In the midst of the great and overwhelming upheaval brought about by the battle for Biberach and our concentration camp, and in the days of chaos and confusion that inevitably ensued, my mother had written the following harrowing and haunting account:

> The battle had ended but the scares remained. We were no longer locked in at 9pm. We did open the Barrack doors for the sheer joy of being free, and as Patsy Flynn opened the door several shots rang out – we were really scared; but it was incredible to see the shell cases littered everywhere and yet we were safe. The nasty Hitler Youth Camp just below us had simply vanished. It was fantastic to watch this war!
>
> A Red Cross ambulance, driven by two girls, came into our camp during the days we were not allowed

to go out and our camp Doctor wanted to go out and help them but they refused him as it was far too dangerous. He couldn't get over that, however they insisted that he was not allowed to go. Two days later the ambulance was found but the two girls had been killed.

Research from afar is too difficult and after so much time has elapsed extremely challenging, if not impossible, to verify. One thing I am sure about is this is not just hearsay, mainly because of the stated involvement of other people mentioned in the notes, and the fact that part of the camp administration building known colloquially as the 'White House' had been turned into a makeshift hospital; but in spite of all this, there will be unimaginable obstacles to overcome in order to verify such events. At the time, I think we believed that because the battle of Biberach was over and the camp liberated, then all was well, and in our euphoria we were inclined to forget the war was still being desperately waged outside. The killing and maiming continued with soldiers on both sides mown down or blown up in action, and with many needing urgent medical assistance.

Regrettably there were many instances of German civilians and soldiers put to death by liberated forced labourers, and of course the retreating Nazis continued their reign of terror on all groups as they withdrew. It is a matter of record that no Americans were among the battling Allies in Biberach, as they were all French soldiers. The American Army fought only beyond the river Iller, which marks the border with

Bavaria, although not too far from Biberach. Perhaps the girls went in this direction towards the nearby Alps, which was where all the retreating German units were aiming for. This atrocity is most likely to have occurred several days after the liberation of the camp on 23 April 1945, which would indicate a time somewhere after 27 April 1945.

The notes give rise, though, to more questions than answers. For instance, who were these brave paramedics, what nationality were they, and where are they buried? More importantly, how did they die, what records exist of these events, and who were the actual perpetrators? I have the feeling this will be an unending quest, but perhaps in the years to come someone will stumble across a crumpled and fading criminal record, lying somewhere in a dim and dusty storeroom, that will lead to the truth being established. I sincerely hope so.

At around midnight on 28–29 April 1945, Adolf Hitler married his long-term mistress Eva Braun, and, at a wedding breakfast, dictated his last will and testament, in which he blamed the Jews for everything that had happened to Germany. On 30 April, and with Russian shock troops only a block away from his bunker, Hitler shot himself, and Eva Braun took a fatal dose of poison.

It was almost the end of May 1945 and, although the Channel Islands had finally been liberated on the 9th of the month, their overseas citizens were still not able to return home because of the damage caused to their houses by the German occupation. At long last, in Biberach, after a delay of nearly five weeks, we were finally advised to pack our belongings and be ready to move out at a moment's notice. I was distraught by this news because I wanted to move into my father's barrack room on my seventh birthday, which was only a few days away. I approached a number of people, including Reverend Flint and Uncle Arthur Langmead, who was in charge of the camp police, but really they only humoured me. I thought the matter was so serious that I eventually made overtures to the camp leader, the rather imposing and forbidding Mr Garland, and asked him if it wouldn't be at all possible to keep the war going for just a few more days so I could move in with my father in Barrack 6. As an almost-seven-year-old, I certainly didn't understand his expletive-ridden reply!

# CHAPTER 14

# GOING HOME

E ventually, a convoy of covered French army lorries arrived to take us to the US Air Force base at Mengen; as we boarded the transport, my father said to me, 'In years to come we should ensure that honest people will never again be imprisoned in such a place as this.' Yet, within eighteen years, I would be placed under close arrest and threatened with a court martial for refusing to incarcerate ethnic tribesmen in a replica concentration camp that had been built by the British in Central Africa – but that is another story.

When we reached the US airbase at Mengen, there were the usual administrative confusion and delays, but finally we were loaded onto Dakota aircraft, without any seats but with heavy canvas belts to strap us all in as we sat on the metal floor-plates of the aircraft. We were then flown to England, landing at Hendon Aerodrome many hours later. I have very little memory of the journey, except to say it was achingly tedious and extremely uncomfortable, although no one on board this Dakota flight appeared to mind. There was a tremendous rousing cheer when it was announced by one of the crew on the loudspeaker system that we had just crossed the English Channel and would soon be landing.

I do, however, remember leaving the aeroplane at Hendon Aerodrome and seeing a magnificent tethered billy goat near the arrival huts. The animal stood very tall and had enormous curved horns, which set off his beautiful long beard. He looked so strong and wonderful that I momentarily forgot all about dogs. I was so astonished by his perfect physique and condition that I immediately started to pester my parents to look into the feasibility of buying him and shipping him home to Guernsey. It says much for my parents that, rather than giving me a put-down, they seemed to consider my request seriously and actually made enquiries with the airfield staff, although I am now sure there must have been many winks and hints and 'hidden' meanings given during these discussions.

Within a very short space of time a diminutive but extremely smart and bemedalled RAF sergeant arrived: the first thing I noticed was his gleaming and highly polished boots. He explained to me that this beautiful billy goat was a regimental mascot and marched at the head of the regiment on parades and during ceremonial occasions. The problem would be very serious if he wasn't there because most likely the soldiers wouldn't be able to find their way home. The sergeant also told me the King and Queen always took a great interest in the goat and they would be very disappointed and upset if he could no longer appear on parades with the regiment.

I could see some of the difficulties involved and certainly didn't want to incur Their Majesties' displeasure, so I decided to drop the idea there and then. The sergeant then left us, saying how gratified he was by my appreciation of his goat and wishing us all well in the future. We were then taken to a reception centre at Stanmore in Middlesex, and here once again we were deloused, but this time at least we had soft beds and gorgeous white sheets. The very next morning we were given one pound each and taken on to Victoria Railway Station. As regards all the difficult delays involved in a long and tiring rail journey to Portsmouth to see Grandma Matthews, it all just remains a complete and total blank in my mind.

I realise now that my parents developed a philosophy of life tempered in the crucible of their precarious existence in Germany. It was based on a strong love and a total, loyal commitment to each other, sustained by an unshakeable faith in their God. It seems to me their lives were cocooned within a supreme sense of humour allied to an entirely positive attitude.

I can still remember old Grandma Matthews, slightly stooped and dressed all in black from top to toe, but she had a kind, welcoming smile and twinkling eyes. She showed me a photograph and a letter sent to her by the captain of Uncle Alf's ship, stationed in China. In the letter the captain extended both his own and the ship's company's sympathy on

Alfred's untimely death in Hong Kong, and the photograph showed a picture of the graveside with the headstone.

Then, decisions were being taken for us to undertake a long and tiring train journey, first of all to Rickmansworth in order to visit my mother's sister, Auntie Leila, who was married to Uncle George de Garis. At the outset of war Auntie Leila had decided to leave Guernsey with her son Malcolm, and she had taken a position as housekeeper to a wealthy landowner. The idea was for us to rest there in the estate's quiet and wonderful surroundings for several days until we were refreshed and strong enough to undertake the short journey to Oldham in order to collect my brother Alan.

I vividly remember Portsmouth Station with its various dirty platforms and the steam locomotives bustling to and fro. In particular, I can still see this large, dark-green metal-box affair purporting to give out chocolate bars if a penny were inserted into the slot. I begged a penny from my father and then put the coin in the appropriate slot and pulled the handle. Nothing happened, except I heard the coin fall into the tray beneath. I rocked the box, I pushed the box and then I kicked the damn box, but again nothing happened.

An old lady who had been watching my antics came up to my parents and told them she couldn't understand why they had allowed me to put money in the machine, when everyone knew these coin-operated devices had been closed down since the beginning of the war. Once my parents had explained we had only just been released from a German concentration camp, the old lady started to cry and pressed a penny into my hand – which was just fine by me. Then my

270

mother took me outside the railway station and into a small corner shop selling chocolates and sweets. As she explained later in her reminiscences:

> I shall never forget how we joined a queue and then selected some gorgeous sweets. Then at the counter the person asked me for coupons. I said 'What do you mean?' and the other people in the queue started to laugh, until one dear soul said, 'You can all laugh but have you looked at their faces – I don't need to ask them where they have come from with their yellow faces.' In the end I accepted a few sweets for Stephen.

Personally, I thought it was actually quite a good day, as I had been given a penny followed by a sumptuous free issue of delicious sweets.

One thing that remains in my mind to this day was the wonderful train journey to visit Auntie Leila, as it was all just simply thrilling. Looking out of the carriage window across green fields in the late springtime, I could see it showed off England at its very best, with cattle grazing on luxuriant green pastures along with horses and sheep, and not a sign of heavy barbed-wire fences or machine-gun posts anywhere. I had a great time roaming through the spacious grounds of the estate, and we were accommodated in the guest bedrooms, beautifully decorated with green and primrose colours. The main problem was that the beds were all too comfortable and soft: after our recent hardships with hard and lumpy bunks, we couldn't manage to sleep on them. It was then decided we would be far better off sleeping on the floor, which caused my parents infinite amusement.

The estate gardener, although very old in my eyes, was still really active and took pleasure in showing me where badgers lived and where the rabbits had their warren. The next morning I came down to breakfast only to hear loud voices raised in anger. There was a terrible row in progress between the owner of the estate and the gardener, which culminated in the gardener stomping off back to his little shed in the garden. I found him there some time later, still muttering to himself while he brewed a welcome cup of tea. He told me he had just about had enough of being ordered about like a lackey (whatever that was), but after a few minutes he brightened up and, taking down a .22 rifle, asked me if I wanted to play cowboys and Indians with it. My goodness, did I! Before handing me the rifle, he made sure it wasn't loaded and said, for a bit of a laugh, I should go inside the house and tell everyone to 'stick 'em up'. I found the landowner sitting in his study reading the newspaper and, when I pointed the gun at him and said the magic words 'stick 'em up', you would have thought he had died on the very spot.

When the landowner had finally recovered and the story had been unravelled, the gardener was sacked, but he said on leaving that it had been more than worth it just to see the look of fear and consternation on his employer's face. My father took the opportunity to calmly point out to me the inherent dangers in pointing guns at anyone, and this was one lesson I learned straight away and the matter was laid to rest.

After that débâcle, we set off for Oldham the very next day, although this was an entirely different and depressing picture and all I can really recollect was the grime and dirt that seemed to cover everything in Oldham. I presume now this was the effect of coal dust being blown in from the nearby coal mines. First of all we met Alan's 'foster parents', Phyllis and Norah Bennett, two spinster sisters who were kindness itself, and who had looked after Alan so conscientiously and devotedly all these past years; and then we walked to the corner of the road, where a group of young boys were playing football on a piece of bombed-out land that had been later levelled and covered with cinders.

It was difficult to judge which of the boys was my brother. However, this was soon resolved as one of the group detached himself and ran over to us. So this was Alan. We eyed each other somewhat cautiously, and I'm not sure either of us was very enamoured by what we saw in each other.

Tea with the Bennetts started out well enough and then deteriorated, mainly, I suspect, because of my table manners or, rather, the lack of them. At one stage my brother said in a fairly loud voice while pointing towards me, 'Mother, you really must teach him how to eat properly at table.' I think this symbolised the difference between us then, as I had been used to eating on the hoof, or finding food anywhere I could, whereas Alan had the most perfect table etiquette brought about by living with two old maiden-teachers. I was really embarrassed and left Oldham in a state of high dudgeon, and I don't recollect anything of the return rail journey to Portsmouth.

Guernsey was in a terrible mess. The Germans had destroyed and ruined buildings, demolishing many of them to make way for their massive ferroconcrete fortifications or just to widen roads to facilitate the passage of their large military vehicles. At this time there was approximately one German soldier for every civilian, and I am sure the civil government of the island had a hard enough job trying to take care of the existing population without allowing any more evacuees to flood back into Guernsey. So we realised we had to wait until conditions improved. But, all the same, soon after 13 June 1945, my father in Portsmouth received a rather formal letter from Great-Uncle Walter Rabey on Guernsey, which read:

Dear Cecil,

I am so delighted to learn that you and family are now in England. You have no doubt been informed by now of the death of our dear Alfred [Rabey] who died rather unexpectedly last November, that meant that the Managing Director of our firm, J. and S. Rabey Limited, building contractors died and with yourself the other Director away. That left the firm with only Uncle John [the other director] who is in his 77th year and is far too old to take any responsibility without anyone of the managing board to carry on.

Therefore, I am appealing to you to take every step possible open to you, to hasten on your early return to the island and to your business. The occupying military authorities are using any of our men available and are appealing for more men. The civil authorities too are clamouring for men in order to prepare homes and make them fit for the evacuees return.

You are therefore very urgently needed in your business over here and I trust that facilities will soon be accorded you for your return home.

I remain,
Yours Truly
W. Rabey (Acting Manager)

PS.
We now occupy the position of the largest private firm of builders on the island and are expected by the authorities to take our fair share of the work.

I know these were the exact words, as I recently found the letter, which had been kept and placed at the back of my mother's diary.

With my father being required back on Guernsey by the government as a matter of some urgency, it wasn't too long before we all received our authorised travel documents, and, after saying farewell to family and friends in Portsmouth, we caught the very first returning midnight mail-boat from Portsmouth to Guernsey. The clearest memory I have of the voyage is of standing on the deck of the boat early the next morning and watching the sun begin to rise in the east; as we steamed up the Russell between Herm and Guernsey, we could see the whole of St Peter Port harbour bathed in sunlight, and it has to be said that this must surely be one of the most beautiful views in the world. Once the mail-boat had tied up at the quayside and the gangplank lowered, we were then allowed to disembark. There was a large black taxi with huge chrome headlights waiting at the bottom of the gangplank, with the driver holding up a clipboard with the word 'Matthews' written on it. So we all clambered into the taxi, luggage and all, and soon we were off home to Dallington.

On the way, my mother asked the driver to take us along the seafront and to turn up the high street, just for old times' sake, which he did. At that point my mother started to cry, although I was assured by my father that it was purely through happiness. We then drove up Smith Street and around the war memorial, and at length turned up the Grange and on towards our home in St Martin and my cat Dinky.

We pulled up outside our old house, Dallington, in the Rue Maze. The green front gate had lost most of its paint and was hanging lopsidedly on just one hinge. To make matters worse, there were actually people sitting in our front room having a meal. While the luggage was being unloaded I ran around to the back of the house to see Dinky, but without success, even though I called his name, loudly, quite a few times. Returning to the front, I found my mother knocking on the front door. She had to knock for quite some time before a woman opened it, and, before my mother could say anything, the woman said, 'We are living here now and you can't come in.' My mother replied, 'But this is our house and you are sitting on our chairs eating at our table and using our plates.' I could sense the belligerent tone of the discussion so I chipped in with my own most pressing enquiry, which was about my cat, Dinky. The reply left me stunned as she said, 'We haven't seen your cat and most probably the Germans have eaten him.' And with that she shut the door in our faces.

So there we were, just back from imprisonment in a foreign country, trying to gain possession of our own home, but now finding ourselves apparently homeless and destitute. My father had returned at the express wish and command of the local authorities and yet we had nowhere to live. The people occupying the house later denied the goods and chattels in it were ours and my mother wrote of this episode, 'We were just far too weary and exhausted to argue.'

Quite a homecoming welcome from your own people! But soon some of our family and cousins arrived on the scene and we were ushered off to stay with them for several weeks. After what seemed an inordinate length of time, the occupants of our house were rehoused somewhere else and we finally gained access. My mother, though, was in a terrible mood. She smashed all the crockery the previous occupants had used and tore up all the sheets they had left behind, and stated flatly that she no longer wished or intended to remain in Dallington any longer. As regards some of the smashed crockery, she invited one of the brothers from the De La Salle Catholic religious order to come and collect her offerings. They were building 'The Little Chapel', soon to be hailed as the smallest chapel in the world, out of glass and pieces of crockery, and I often wonder where our smashed plates ended up in the scheme of things.

# THE DAY THE NAZIS CAME

Before the war, my father had looked after five or six houses in St Martin for a certain Mrs Cooper, who had then gone to live in Canada for the duration of the war. She had somehow heard of our plight and invited my father to select one of her houses, any one, then fix a fair price and pay her when he could. Mrs Cooper, whom I never met, must have been an extraordinary woman, because within a very short period of time the house Mum and Dad chose, which was called White Wings, had been professionally valued, a generous price agreed in our favour and payment speedily made, even though we had already moved in with all our household effects and belongings. My parents continued corresponding with Mrs Cooper until her death many years later in Toronto, Canada.

So the die was cast and we soon moved away from the Rue Maze to White Wings in Les Camps du Moulin, although the house was still in the parish of St Martin. The house had been occupied by German officers and was in a reasonable condition for the times we were living in. However, the garden was a jungle and had a concrete German pillbox in the front garden and several slit trenches in the back. I had great fun riding on the horse-drawn cart with our building firm's driver, George Baudains, and we all worked hard for several days, moving the furniture and effects into our new family home. (George was an extremely loyal servant any company would have been proud to have employed, and he was married to 'Auntie Queenie', who had cared for my grandfather and nursed him through his final illness.)

However, before that, we had to clear out a great deal

of German paraphernalia from the house. I saw a chest of drawers in one of the rooms and, on opening the top drawer, I found a German Luger pistol and a Nazi-style dress dagger; needless to say, in spite of all my pleadings, I wasn't allowed to keep them.

During their sojourn in the house, the Germans had seen fit to rip out the fireplaces, replacing the one in the dining room with a cast-iron potbellied stove together with a massive metal flue, which passed through a large hole in the wall, breaching the original brick chimney. Some of the doors had been ripped off their hinges and there were many other holes gouged out of the wall plaster. There were no carpets, but my father soon found some squares of linoleum, which, when laid, left a border of floorboards, but these were soon stained and varnished, and all in all we were very happy and comfortable with our new surroundings.

Lastly, my father obtained some masonry paint for the walls called 'distemper': as he said to my mother, this was available on the basis that you can have any colour you like as long as it's either green or cream! Soon, our home was sparkling-bright and warm. We then turned our full attention towards the garden. Overgrown trees were cut, bushes trimmed, and wooden fences repaired as well as we could without all the proper materials – but thank goodness we hadn't as yet filled in the German slit trenches, as I will explain.

While my father, my brother and I worked on the trees and shrubs, my mother was busily engaged in raking up years of decaying leaves and weeds. Dad started a huge bonfire, and soon we had it blazing away; my mother, who had been working in the front garden alongside the German pillbox, regularly appeared with full barrowloads of rubbish, which she unceremoniously dumped on top of the bonfire.

Billowing smoke soon gave way to rampant flames. However, as we all stood together resting from our endeavours, there was a series of loud explosions, then from the centre of the bonfire bits of wood and leaves were hurled high into the air, followed by the odd whining sound of ricocheting bullets, so we all skedaddled and jumped down into the slit trenches, with my brother and me in one and Mum and Dad in the other. It later transpired my mother had inadvertently gathered up large amounts of discarded rifle and machine-gun ammunition the Germans had left lying about since their surrender, and the bullets had exploded in the extreme heat of the bonfire.

We stayed in our trenches for quite some time until at last Alan and I could hear my parents laughing uproariously over and above the noise of the explosions. As the detonations gradually abated, Alan and I slowly and cautiously emerged from our slit trench and waited for the bonfire to die out. Alan sidled over to my parents' trench and I heard him say to them, 'It's no good you just sitting there laughing. It's quite a serious matter. We could have all been killed.' The only acknowledgement he received was a wave of a hand followed by more gales of uncontrollable laughter.

One thing that was very apparent, even to me at the great old age of seven going on eight, was that no one on Guernsey seemed to want to talk about life in a German concentration camp. If they did, it was purely out of politeness, but their eyes soon glazed over with boredom. The thought of the day was that it was all a very unfortunate circumstance that should be forgotten as soon as possible and the whole affair should be firmly put out of one's mind. The war was over, the Germans had finally departed and everything was getting back to normal, so we shouldn't start raking it all up again.

The older generation of great-aunts and cousins, who visited us for afternoon tea, kept making the point that our family weren't the only ones to have suffered, not by a long chalk. 'We really starved as well,' they would say. 'Many of us died through hunger. While you had the comfort of Red Cross parcels, we didn't receive any until the very end of the war, when we were really starving.'

I am sure they were right and we just didn't understand that the naval and air blockades imposed by the Allies after D-Day had in turn created enormous hardships not only for the hard-pressed civilian population but also for the German occupying forces. All the same, I believe that, psychologically, we desperately needed someone to talk to who would understand and commiserate with us.

So, in the end, the deportees found some comfort in each other's company. When we visited shops, fairs or other social events on the island, we would seek each other out, mainly because we had been through the camps together. Each one of us had a different story to share, but we were all united as one by our gruelling experiences.

Not long afterwards, my father was persuaded to stand for election to the Douzaine of St Martin's Parish (the local council) and thus continue his service to both parish and island, so rudely interrupted by the outbreak of war. The family assumed that the election of my father, with the full power of the Rabey clan behind him and his previous service as constable, would make this event a foregone conclusion and only the formalities would remain to be settled.

As prescribed, we all gathered at St Martin's Parish Hall one evening to hear from those seeking election, and my father eventually made his way to the rostrum to give his own election speech. It was well received and, on its completion, the audience were asked if they had any questions they wanted to put to the speaker. One man who lived not very far from our new home rose to his feet and asked: by what right did my father have to represent the parish, being another 'bloody foreigner' and apparently interfering in local affairs?

By now my mum was on her feet and laid into the man by saying my father was of local descent and his parents had been Guernsey-born and, furthermore, his father had served his country in the services. She pointed out that my father had already served as constable of the parish, and, furthermore, she added that we had been living here since before the war, and had then been deported to Germany.

The man smiled and said, 'That's my very point: if you weren't bloody foreigners, then you wouldn't have been deported.' Looking back now over the years, I can see this unworthy jibe greatly affected my mother, especially as there turned out to be some in the audience who would agree with the agitator. In the final analysis, my father was elected with a large majority and went on to serve his parish for nearly thirty years.

# GOING HOME

Several weeks later I was given a humorous lesson in my father's maxim, which seemed to be 'Don't get angry: just get even.' We were both doing some work in the front garden – well, my father was doing the work and I was carting the rubbish around to the back – ready for another bonfire, when a wonderful and imposing Sikh gentleman appeared at the gate. He was resplendent with turban and large grey whiskers, and he had an enormous leather suitcase on wheels with him. On seeing my father, he launched into his sales spiel, extolling the virtues of the household wares contained in his suitcase.

However, before he could open it up to show us, my father said to him, 'Look, there's no money here. I am only the poor gardener, and you can see by the state of my old clothes we're all very wretched.' He continued, 'Now, I think I can possibly help you, as there's a particular house just up the road where the owner is really rich but always pleads poverty. Don't be put off by all this, as I believe you could make a really good sale.'

Father marched the Sikh out of the garden into the roadway and gave him lengthy and explicit directions. This was, of course, the way to the house of the very man who had made such inflammatory remarks about my father at the Parish Hall. Some time later the Indian reappeared at the gateway and told my father he had sold virtually his entire suitcase's stock at the house. He then gave my father a clothes brush as a reward for helping him, and the brush was used by the family for many a long year.

# THE DAY THE NAZIS CAME

I think perhaps we should have seen it coming, although maybe my father had an inkling, because he had already covered all his German-language books in the house with plain brown paper. It all started one day with my mother saying she no longer wanted us to speak German in the house and she made it plain that on no account were my brother and I going to learn German at school. Then, one afternoon, my father came home to find my mother having a large bonfire in the garden, where she was using his books and anything else with German connections to fuel the flames. He gently stopped the conflagration and rescued many of the pictures and documents I have today, but the books had gone up in flames, as well as Tip Tippet's US service holdall containing his US army serial number and many other artefacts. Today, we would probably have called this post-traumatic stress, but I think this was the beginning of the realisation that perchance we didn't belong here and we weren't really wanted, even by our own people.

One item saved from the bonfire was the German Blaupunkt radio we had found in the house, which had originally belonged to the German officers. Although initially it didn't work, my father tinkered with it for some time and eventually had it in good working order. The only stipulation my mother made was that all the German radio stations shown on the tuning dial had to be covered over so there would be no Radio Berlin. However, Radio Hilversum, the Dutch station, was allowed to remain. As we gradually located the BBC stations, more stickers were added, but the radio did its job and lasted for quite some time.

In those days, we were also confronted by strict rationing

and had to register for our ration books, which contained our coupons. The coupons covered most foodstuffs – including sugar, meat, bacon, ham and sausages – normally consumed on a weekly basis, but, in addition, items such as soap were also rationed. Extra coupons were given for children. Coupons had to be handed in to the shopkeepers together with the money before the produce could be released. The ration-book system lasted for several years, with sweets not being removed from the scheme until 1953, and meat being the last to finish in 1954.

So, as a family, we went into the chicken-rearing business, with twenty-five chickens that regularly kept us in eggs until they reached a more mature age and ended up as a superb Sunday roast dinner. My father built a portable chicken run and cage, and from time to time we would move it around the vegetable garden, thus fertilising the ground. This lasted for quite some while until one day my mother went into the hen coop to collect the eggs and was confronted by a large and lively rat. After the rat encounter, she was adamant that the chickens had to go.

Our closest neighbours on one side were Harold and Eva Bartlett, who had been in Germany with us, and on the other side were Mr and Mrs Collins. The Collins family owned a large sweetshop and factory in St Peter Port and manufactured the traditional mixture of Guernsey sweets – alas, no longer available today. They were a very private couple, but sometimes when I was playing in the garden a small brown paper bag of these succulent Guernsey sweets would come flying over the wooden fence.

# THE DAY THE NAZIS CAME

In later years the tradition continued with my three young children, except that this time we had the Doberman called Alex, who hankered after the peppermint assortment. I have this enduring vision of my three children, together with their dog, sitting on the lawn in a circle and sharing out the bag of sweets, with a patient Alex being included, although he received only a few of the peppermint ones. Once he was told he could 'eat', he would gently place one of his claws on one end of a selected sweet and by using his teeth carefully unravel the paper until he could get at the confection itself. Happy and precious days indeed!

Here is a poem discovered in my father's 1944 notebook:

> I believe in immortality
> I believe in God as a great spirit, guiding us all
> by a single call of hope and song
> That lingers on with sunsets and the stars.
> I believe that friendship outlives death
> I believe my love outlives breath
> I believe that beauty is a part of God.

# CHAPTER 15

# AFTERWARDS

The war may well have ended, but throughout this critical period Guernsey still lay in chaos and absolute ruin. Many German POWs remained on the island, entangled in clearing out their stores, bunkers and deep tunnels containing all their military hardware. I can remember lorries of smart-looking British soldiers with a multitude of depressed and bedraggled German soldiers passing to and fro along our busy roads, the Germans still displaying the ravaged signs of their starvation brought about by the Allies' blockade of the islands. All the panoply of war was collected together, including guns, chemicals and explosive munitions, ready for disposal. At the time it seemed that defeated German POWs were everywhere, and it made me realise just how many of them had actually been involved in securing the island for Hitler's personal benefit.

Nevertheless, we were still not allowed to visit Guernsey's

beaches or run along golden sands, as the British Royal Engineers were carrying out a monumental operation to remove the thousands of buried landmines, booby traps and roll bombs laid down by our adversaries. The bomb-disposal operation was under the command of Lieutenant Henry Beckingham, a very experienced officer of the Royal Engineers, who utilised the services of some 1,780 German POWs and 300 civilians. The island community was always concerned for the safety of the British members of this expedition but, when the occasional mine exploded and killed or injured a German soldier, the islanders showed very little sympathy. The expressed thought was, 'They put the damn things there, so it's only right they should pick them up.' My father spoke with many of these young Germans and found most of them to be charming and greatly relieved they had been stationed on Guernsey and hadn't been sent to the Russian front.

There had been some tragic accidents, too, whereby young island children had been seriously maimed or killed while playing with live ordnance left behind in some of the bunkers. So my father, knowing I would be unstoppable, sat me down one day and carefully gave me a good insight into the lurking dangers involved; and, after that lesson, heck, was I really careful!

A point was reached when every commodity was in short supply, especially money, and my father used to say of these times, 'If you ever want to know the real value of money, go and try to borrow some.' All the same, everyone rallied around to help each other, like my mother, who took it upon herself to range far and wide throughout the parish on her bicycle, bringing her thick, homemade farmhouse soup to the sick, infirm and elderly. She would first of all procure marrowbones from the butcher and boil them all down before adding a series of fresh vegetables and seasoning from the garden; and, when eventually this concoction was allowed to stand and cool, it would take on the rich consistency of jelly.

Mum had a very large, white, enamel jug with a blue lid into which the soup contents would be spooned; next, the whole ensemble would be firmly wedged into the front pannier of her cycle; and then off she would merrily go irrespective of the weather. My father used to say my mother's soup was of such a rich delicacy it just 'stuck to your ribs' and he felt sure it was seen in the neighbourhood as a kill-or-cure measure. He added, usually in a very low voice so my mother would never hear, that he felt sure most of the recipients would leap from their deathbeds and manifest a miraculous recovery rather than have to face eating the 'rich, rich jelly concoction'.

In spite of all the difficulties, this remained a happy and significant time when most people lived by the seasons, with the fishermen from nearby Saints Bay Harbour selling their freshly caught mackerel from door to door. It was a period when we could all go onto the cliffs blackberrying for an afternoon, returning home tired but jubilant to bake a juicy apple-and-blackberry pie. It was a time of caring and honesty, when the milkman would pour our fresh and creamy Guernsey milk into a covered jug we used to leave outside on our hedge each morning. It seemed to me as if we were living in the far-off mystical days of King Arthur's Camelot, where it was always fair and sunny, and it rained only at night when I was sound asleep. My most treasured memories are of long-lost summer days when our house was filled to the brim with roses and laughter.

I eventually started at St Martin's Primary School – well, almost, as the original school had been completely wrecked by the Germans and couldn't be used for quite some time, until the necessary repairs had been completed. Our class was then temporarily located in what had once been a private residence in previous and much happier times. It wasn't too far away from my own home and I loved walking there at schooltime. On leaving home in the early morning, I would walk along the green and leafy lanes, and at the old granite-built well I would take to the charming bridle path, and I can well remember the gentle grazing Guernsey cows, the wild daffodils and golden buttercups.

The problem with all this, though, was my school cap, not just because it had my initials on the front emblazoned in gold ribbon, but mainly because I just hated caps. Although the initials SM stood for St Martin, I was endlessly teased that it stood for Stephen Matthews. I did everything I could to lose it: I left it on buses, I tucked it down the side of cinema seats, and once in sheer desperation I even threw it onto the roof of the girls' toilets at the school, but somehow it always came back to haunt me. One thing I really enjoyed at school during this time, though, was the rich bottle of Guernsey milk provided in the mid-morning break. But what I didn't like was that, after drinking the milk, we had to rest at our desks with our heads on the surface for at least thirty minutes. My suggestion that if we could start school thirty minutes later we wouldn't need to rest at all was not greatly appreciated by any of the teachers.

The friends we made at school were friends for ever. None of us had anything of value and we had no status; our parents were struggling to reconstruct their lives and businesses. But we were all friends and we were happy. We safely roamed the cliffs together. It has always struck me as paradoxical that you are often at your happiest when you have nothing. Not only did we have free range of the cliffs and valleys but we also knew where every abandoned German defensive trench position and bunker lay hidden, ripe for exploration.

Sometimes, in the school holidays or at weekends, I was allowed to visit Fort George, a collection of old British army garrison buildings, built between 1780 and 1812. The fort had been originally constructed in anticipation of an invasion from nearby France during the Napoleonic conflict and was of strategic importance as it stood high on a pinnacle overlooking St Peter Port with unrestricted views out over the adjacent islands. After the invasion of 1940, the Germans significantly strengthened and reinforced the whole of the area with a honeycomb of tunnels, bunkers and machine-gun nests. As a point of history, the fort was of significant importance to the German hierarchy because they soon constructed a massive radar installation designed to provide them with an early warning system, but this was bombed in 1944 by the US Air-Force in order to destroy it ahead of the main Allied D-Day landing on the adjacent French coast.

After our return from exile, Fort George had already reverted to being War Department property, and as such members of the public were prohibited from entering upon this private and secret domain. Luckily for me, though, the commanding officer was a Major Harry Evans MBE, one of our many cousins. I suppose Uncle Harry would be described today as being a man's man. He gave me unrestricted access to the fort and I could wander where I wanted, but I had first to let him know as soon as I arrived. He usually sat in his impressive office alongside the ancient guardhouse, and over a cold drink and a biscuit I had to tell him where I was going – just in case I got lost. I happily roamed the tunnels and concrete bunkers, visited the ancient citadel and examined the German graffiti that adorned the walls. I was at my happiest when I could take my picnic lunch and spend the whole day mooching over old and modern military history, although I found the German cemetery in the grounds of the fort a very sad and depressing place. Uncle Harry always took a great interest in the things I found and allowed me to keep many of these items, such as a pair of German barbed-wire cutters manufactured in 1933 as a throwaway item on the battlefield; I still have this pair today, which remain in constant use despite being eighty-three years old. Still, he made sure any grenades, shells and ammunition were left in place, to be carefully removed and disposed of by his engineers.

Daggers, bayonets, helmets and sometimes a Luger pistol had

to be handed in at the stores, and regretfully I wasn't allowed to keep any of this equipment. Sometimes Uncle Harry would come with me to explore some of the bunkers, and once he allowed me to keep several German field telephones which I managed to get into working order with the help of my dad. Gradually my hoard of German components and equipment built up into a formidable array, and I began to turn my attention to some of the German military radio parts that had been left lying about by the capitulating Germans. At this juncture Uncle Harry decided to introduce me to one of his Guernsey engineers, a wonderful man called Frank Mourant, who was also a celebrated radio amateur (radio ham) in the island, and, on top of that, he allowed him to examine and repair some of my finds, in the workshops, which included several of the German military transmitters and receivers I had recovered from various bunkers together with a host of associated material such as cables, valves and batteries. Frank Mourant owned a large German BMW military motorcycle (Model R75) that he had 'liberated' from the Axis forces, but what really really impressed me was the fact that it even had a reverse gear!

Gradually my growing collection of electronic equipment became too difficult to manage in my bedroom, so one day my dad gave me access to the garden cabin he had originally built before the war in the garden at Dallington – in spite of my mother's misgivings in that she would now have nowhere to store her potatoes, and what about my schoolwork? The two of us set to, building shelves and worktops, and Dad even installed an electricity supply for me. Up to this point I had been using a variety of accumulating batteries that seemed to require continual recharging in order to operate the radios successfully, but now Frank Mourant gave me a transformer to reduce the current to just the right level. I was in seventh heaven, and could spend many peaceful hours listening either to radio hams worldwide or to shipping. I had been cautioned never to use the transmitters as I was required to have a licence issued by the Government; however, one day the temptation proved too difficult to resist and I switched on my latest acquisition, a very powerful German naval set that had been built built in 1936.

I twiddled the dials, balanced the receiver and transmitter bands together and then broke into a communication I heard, thinking this was a local radio amateur. What a shock to discover I was speaking to a US coastguard operator in New York Harbour. Abruptly disengaging myself from this wavelength, I immediately moved on to another, this time a very reassuring voice, and again I cut in, only to hear the same voice suddenly say: 'This is Pan Am Flight 701 in mid–Atlantic. Please identify yourself.' At that point I called it a day and never used the transmitters again.

There was one very sad episode which occurred when I was visiting Fort George for the day, with my haversack of sandwiches and cold drinks. Just as I was passing a green-painted wooden building, I heard a voice say: 'Hello, how are you?' I turned around to see a young man standing in the window area, so I stopped and we had quite a nice chat about all sort of things, including the latest football news, and it was obvious he knew who I was. Later in the afternoon, at the end of my jaunt when I was just catching up with Uncle Harry, I asked him who the young man was in the green wooden building, and he told me it was his only son, who had contracted tuberculosis and as a result had to be isolated in that building, with his food passed to him through the door or window. Auntie gave the impression of being a detached yet kind lady, and even at my young age I realised her deepest thoughts were elsewhere – with her son, who wanted for nothing but his freedom. After that I would make a point of visiting him, and we talked of many things through an open window; however, I was never sure how he really felt, because here was I free to roam at will, while he was a prisoner living behind stark wooden walls.

In those holiday breaks, I also enjoyed the treat of going out on visits with my father on our bicycles as he went about his business. He was never described as the boss, CEO or the MD but always as 'the Skipper'. If I had a chance I would spend time with some of the craftsmen who worked for the company, such as the cheerful and conscientious Hedley Ogier, who taught me how to saw wood properly, with the exhortation to 'bend your thumb and use it to control the flat of the saw'. Then there was the energetic Dick Luscombe, who took enormous trouble teaching me how to load a brush with paint and how to paint in the correct manner. 'It's all in the wrist action,' he would say.

And there was also the magnificent stalwart Wilson Thoume, kind and sanguine, who showed me how to make cement 'just like your mother makes a cake! Mix all the ingredients together well, then make a little hole in the centre and pour in the water'. This more than anything else has served me well over all the intervening years.

George Baudains was the firm's driver and my friend. George had always been a special person and one of the few who didn't take kindly to being addressed as 'Uncle'. He once said to me, 'You can just call me George, because that is what I am, pure and simple – just plain, honest George.'

When my father told me we were going to visit him at home one day, because he hadn't been at all well, I wasn't overly concerned, imaging he was suffering from nothing more than a cold or a touch of influenza. But being shown into the bedroom by Auntie Queenie, I could see immediately he was seriously ill and totally lacking in strength and vitality. When Auntie Queenie left the room to make some tea, George said he would like to speak with my father on a very personal matter. My father told me to leave the room and wait outside but George said, 'No, let the nipper stay. We've been together in far happier times and I would just like him to stay now.' George went on to explain that he knew his time on earth was now drawing to a close, and he wanted to ask a favour of my father. He reached under one of his pillows and drew out a battered and crumpled brown envelope and gave it to my father. He explained he had been keeping some of his wages back each week without telling anyone because he wanted Queenie to have a really good holiday when he had gone. He asked my father to keep the money for him and to make sure Queenie had a good break after the funeral. Dad told me a week or so later that George had died quietly in his sleep.

# AFTERWARDS

More than anything else, I loved meeting people out and about in the parish. For instance, there was Alf Saunders, the St Martin gravedigger, and periodically I would sit alongside him in the cemetery as he took a brief rest from his digging. Often he would muse about those parishioners who now occupied their allotted space in the graveyard. 'I helped plant your granddad just over there,' he might say, or things such as, 'If it continues raining like this, it's going to be more of a launching than a burial.'

His favourite sport, though, was often reserved for his regular visits to the local hostelry, called the Beaulieu Hotel, at the height of the visitor season, where, on cue, the barman would tell the visitors that Alf had been a great administrator during the war, and as such had many Germans placed under him! On being pressed with a large number of beers by the visitors, Alf would admit to a shocked and incredulous audience that dealing with the Germans in his professional capacity had been a sheer delight and a great pleasure, and he only wished he could have got his hands on many more of them. It was only when the free whiskies began to appear that he would finally admit to one and all that he was actually the parish gravedigger.

Then there was the wonderful Henry Davey, the St Martin undertaker, who had a riotous sense of humour. Dad and I were once waiting at a bus stop when Henry came by in his old and battered black hearse and offered us a lift into town. Dad sat in the front with Henry while I had to clamber into the back, although I was pleased to see there was no coffin or occupant in place.

The conversation was always lively. 'Did you know old Mr Le Sauvage is dead?' Henry asked.

'No,' said my father. 'Is that right?'

'Well, it had better be,' replied Henry, ''cos I've already screwed the lid down.'

After a few minutes my father said to Henry, 'Do you know, Henry, this hearse is really draughty and it rattles a great deal?' to which Henry politely replied, in something of a serious tone, 'Cecil, you're probably quite right, but, do you know, you're the only passenger who's ever taken a ride in my hearse over the years that has had the opportunity and the temerity to complain!'

Gradually, the regular bus services came back into operation; with no cars being available for quite some time, life progressed by bus, bicycle or Shanks's pony. Our St Martin bus route had two remarkable drivers. There was the quiet but charming Mr Lanchberry, who would ensure his passengers were well looked after, and then there was the ebullient Mr Guilbert, who in action was a true wonder to behold. If he liked the passengers he would wait patiently until they were seated before moving off. On the other hand, if he didn't like them, usually because they were either rude or dismissive, he would wait until they reached the top step of the bus, then release the clutch and gun the engine, often sending passengers pirouetting down the aisle to the back of the bus. If my mother was returning from town on his bus, fully laden with parcels, Mr Guilbert would ignore the regulation bus stop and park in the roadway just outside our house. He would then help my mum down and carry her parcels inside, in spite of any build-up of traffic outside.

# AFTERWARDS

With food and money still being in short supply and severely rationed, my mother resorted from time to time to a centuries-old peasant dish known as the Guernsey Bean Jar. This was in reality a type of cassoulet that has to be made in a large earthenware pot and cooked continuously for some ten hours on the basis that the longer it takes to cook the better it tastes. My mother used to make it with haricot beans and butter beans, then added a hock of pork or pig's trotters that had plenty of meat and fat on the bone. Then she would contribute a shin of beef, diced carrots, several large onions, salt and pepper and a teaspoon of mixed herbs together with two bay leaves, although it all depended on just how well-off we were that week. The contents were then put into the pot and covered with either water or stock.

The whole rigmarole would start just after lunch on a Friday and by about 5 p.m. the top of the earthenware pot was covered by thick brown paper, which was tied securely around the rim with string. We then wrote our family name across the top of the paper in ink, by which time it was my job to take it up the road to Senner's Bakery. In the meantime, I had acquired a 'buggy' made out of four old discarded pram wheels fixed to a plank of wood, together with a wooden box with the front panel removed so it acted as my seat. This buggy had become my pride and joy and it was never a chore to run errands with my special four-wheeled contraption. If things were going well and there was a little more cash in the family kitty, my mother would give me the money not only to pay the baker for cooking the bean jar but also to purchase one of his famous ginger cakes.

First of all, Mr Senner used to place the bean jar in his cooling-bread oven to be duly collected early the next morning. However, I really didn't like ginger cakes very much; on the other hand, I adored his fabulous walnut cakes with the delicious cream topping. On returning home I would merely say Mr Senner had run out of ginger cakes, and soon we were tucking into the wonderful walnut delight. All went well for several journeys, but I think my mother had become a little suspicious by now and, without telling me, one day she telephoned the bakery in advance of my arrival, to make sure there was a surfeit of ginger cakes all ready and waiting.

When I finally returned home and came through the door bearing the usual walnut extravaganza, my mother picked up the cake and hurled it across the kitchen, where it smashed against the tiles and spread across the wall. She said, 'Now take it back and change it for the ginger one.' Then almost in the same breath she started laughing. My father came in to see what all the noise was about and then he too started laughing. We started to scrape the cake off the glazed tiles in between fits of giggling, but after that I thought it would be judicious if I learned to enjoy ginger cakes in future.

In these early days money was such a precious commodity, and most times, if we had bread for tea, then we could have either jam or butter to spread on it, but not both. I remember once cajoling my mother into sparing a few pence to buy some lemonade, and I suspect now it was in some desperation that she took out her purse and opened it to show me a solitary sixpenny piece lying in one of the compartments.

'And that has to last me the rest of the week!' I felt so terrible, I never asked her for any money again.

One Saturday afternoon I went to the harbour in St Peter Port to catch the small motorboat carrying tourists around Castle Cornet and on to Fermain Bay. I noticed a man of rather small stature, sporting a ginger beard. He was wearing a seaman's jacket, trousers and boots and the whole ensemble was topped off with a well-worn naval skipper's cap. However, the one item that greatly intrigued me was the small terrier dog peeping out from under the man's jacket. It all seemed rather reminiscent of the pirate stories portraying Long John Silver, and this man even flew the skull-and-crossbones flag from the masthead of his moored fishing boat, *Martha Gunn*.

Later that evening when I was recounting this remarkable story to the family at dinner, my father said, 'Ah, yes, that must have been Bonnie Newton.' Although I don't remember now, I must have passed some unflattering remarks, because early the following Sunday morning my father asked if I wanted to go to town with him, and I readily agreed as the only alternative was to attend chapel and Sunday School. First of all we went to the harbour area, then walked around the harbour bulwarks until we reached the ship's chandler near the Model Yacht Pond, which was run by a Walter Le Moitié. Although we were still some way off, we could see that Mr Le Moitié was standing outside his place of business and talking to Bonnie Newton. Well before we reached them, my father told me the following story.

Bonnie Newton had been born in Alderney, a lovely island lying to the north of Guernsey, and he had been given his name by a Scottish lady then living on the island, who had said he was just a wee bonny baby. Over the years Bonnie Newton developed an unsurpassed knowledge of local and French waters and later joined the Royal Navy in 1940 as a volunteer rating. After only a short period he joined the Special Operations Executive and carried out armed raids on German-occupied Brittany, and in doing so rescued many Allied airmen and French families under threat by the Gestapo. On various occasions, Bonnie and his party collected numerous German military prisoners and during one raid his band captured the entire seven-man German crew of the Casquets Lighthouse, which lay in the English Channel just off the Alderney coast.

For his courageous actions, Bonnie was awarded the Distinguished Service Cross; later, when he moved with British forces to Corsica and Italy, the Italians awarded him their Italian Star Medal; and in 1944 the French awarded him the Croix de Guerre and their Silver Star in full recognition of his outstanding courage and valuable services to France. This story made a great impact on me and throughout the coming years I never again referred to him as 'Bonnie' but always as 'Skipper Newton'. As my father said at the time, 'We all have one great lesson to learn in life and that is never to judge a book by its cover.' Sadly, Skipper Newton died suddenly in 1962 when I was out in Africa, but he was certainly a larger-than-life character the island has sorely missed.

Family progress materialised with the coming of our first car. My father came home one morning driving an ancient, green Standard 8 saloon car, built in 1936, which even had a temperature gauge fixed outside on the top of the bonnet. The seats were in matching green leather, although it was somewhat cracked. I was mildly disappointed, as I had expected to see a large black Wolsey 20 in a similar style to the local police cars.

My mother enthused over the car and the seat coverings, but all I could see was the 'down-at-heel' green leather upholstery. Nevertheless, it now meant we could go to the cinema whenever we wanted to, irrespective of the weather conditions. Preference was always given to British-made films, which were inevitably made in black and white, but we didn't really mind. After the show, we would clamber back into the car and head for the local fish-and-chip shop, where our order ('with plenty of vinegar and salt, dear') was first wrapped in greaseproof paper and then wrapped up again in newspaper. Then we would drive helter-skelter for home for a fish-and-chip supper on our laps as we sat around the blazing coal fire.

The summers were wonderful, especially when it was time for the St Martin Agricultural and Horticultural Show; it always seemed to be held on a hot summer's day. The event had started way back in 1908 with many successful shows taking place in the lush and wide-open fields attached to Sausmarez Manor. There would be tea and beer tents, sideshows, various stalls and marquees that held all the vegetable, fruit and flower exhibits of those proud and dedicated gardeners seeking to win cups and certificates.

The advertisements heralding the forthcoming South

Show, as it was colloquially known, would spur me to go into training for several weeks before the appointed day. I would hang a dartboard up in the garage at home and then spend many hours perfecting my aim and throwing technique. All of this was necessary before I could even contemplate enjoying the benefits of the show, as I had a definite mission to fulfil. I knew there would be one particular stall there containing a dartboard surrounded by a massive heap of prizes. There would be a playing card, usually the three of diamonds, pinned to the board and the idea was to throw a dart and hit one of the three small diamonds to win a prize – which was no easy task.

Success meant a prize of one's choice, and the prize I craved most was a Gillette safety razor and a packet of blades. I had to win before my mum and dad visited the show, usually at around 5 o'clock in the evening. Somehow I always managed to acquire the razor, although quite often only after a great many throws, which took most of my pocket money and probably cost much more than the razor was actually worth, but that just didn't matter to me.

Invariably, there was the family ceremony afterwards, when I would hand the razor over to my father, and later, back at the house, my father would create much ado in throwing the old razor out and then unpacking the new one ready for use. Such wonderful days!

My mother continued to play bridge on Thursday afternoons with her three regular partners. They all took it in turn to host the weekly event in their own homes, where they generally tried to outdo each other in providing the best and most original afternoon teas, in spite of all the food shortages and rationing. We could tell when the bridge afternoon was due at our house because baking started several days before the scheduled event, with the resultant delicacies wrapped in fancy coloured paper, layered into a variety of biscuit tins and stored in the cool larder.

On the appointed day my father and I would make sure we were at home by 4.30 p.m. My father had a small lean-to greenhouse with wooden sides, which shielded us from any observations from the main house; and it was his job to get everything ready. He would provide the stools and make a pot of tea for himself and cocoa or an orange drink for me.

It was then my job to raid the pantry – no easy task, as I had only a short time before my mother would come out into the kitchen to make the tea for her bridge-players. The secret lay in very quietly helping ourselves to only a few morsels from each tin and then rearranging the remaining goodies to fill out any of the empty spaces. At that juncture, I had to move quickly and silently back to the greenhouse so we might enjoy the first feed without interference. Usually at a time between 5 and 5.15 p.m., I would be called in to meet the players and endure virtually the same questions from the same people each time. 'How are you doing at school?' (Fine.) 'What's your favourite subject?' (History.) 'Do you like playing sports?' (Do I just!) At this juncture my mother would usher me out with a trolley of the remaining food, and usually the selection reflected the least favourite items. So then back to the greenhouse for our second feed.

This ritual took place once a month over many years and never varied in content, and I have often wondered if my mum was ever aware of what went on in the pantry and the greenhouse.

Someone very important must have died in the parish of St Martin, because it was stipulated that the Rabey clan should attend the funeral '*en masse*', and Great-Uncle John suggested to my mother I should attend what was to be my first funeral. It was also strongly suggested I should have my first pair of long trousers; my mother, knowing I would soon outgrow the trousers, obtained a second-hand pair, far too large for me, so they were duly sent for alteration. The seamstress also knew the trousers would eventually have to be let out again as I was a fast-growing lad, and so she gathered in as much of the waste material as she could and fixed this all firmly together under the crotch of the trousers. This provided my father with endless amusement in later years, as he used to comment that he wasn't sure if I was then doing a fair imitation of a drunken sailor, and, anyway, this was surely another reason for the root cause of my funny walk in later life!

Everything was set fair for the great day of the funeral, except for the fact that Great-Uncle Walter didn't possess the obligatory black bowler hat. However, we had one in the loft, which was quickly retrieved, although it turned out to be far too large for Walter's head, so much so that the bowler kept falling down over his eyes until it simply rested on top of his ears. Not to be put off, my mother quickly overcame what she perceived to be only a very minor difficulty by forming a band of newspaper around the internal rim of the hat until she had secured a good tight fit.

I remember nothing at all of the service but only the gathering in the St Martin cemetery afterwards, with the Rabeys all lining the gravel pathway to the graveside. The ancient Rabey brothers stood in a straight line, looking extremely smart and dressed in their Sunday best attire, and, as the coffin approached, they doffed their bowler hats as one man, in a solemn mark of respect for the late departed. Everything was perfect except for poor old Great-Uncle Walter, who was left standing stiffly to attention with a crown of crinkled newspaper resting majestically on top of his head like a halo. I thought this was such a wonderful experience that I offered to go to any other funerals in the future, especially as I now had the long trousers to go with it, but my suggestion wasn't at all well received by my mother.

In those challenging but halcyon days before the onslaught of television, life revolved happily around both the parish and the chapel. I had to attend morning service at Les Camps Methodist Chapel each Sunday, often with my mother, then Sunday School in the afternoons, then the evening service with the whole family, where we had our own pew. I have some hilarious and heartwarming stories of my times at chapel, but I need to pay homage to all those people who worked tirelessly on behalf of their congregation and donated their time, energy and money in Christian endeavour. Many of these wonderful people even tithed their income to the administrators so the chapel and the manse could be properly maintained and provision made for the living of the appointed Methodist minister.

My mother possessed an exceptionally good singing voice, albeit somewhat vibrant. She had taken professional singing lessons when young and was often called upon to sing a solo for the congregation such as 'O for the Wings of a Dove', and on these occasions she would march boldly to the front of the chapel in preparation for her offering. While all this was going on, my father would quietly whisper in my ear such sentiments as, 'Get ready to duck in case your mother shatters the glass chandelier when she hits the high notes!'

At one time as a young boy I joined the choir, though only for a very brief period. I feel fairly certain I was not chosen for my vocal skills, but probably only to make up the numbers, coupled with the fact that I had a mop of angelic blond hair. However, our nemesis arrived shortly afterwards in the guise of the Salvation Army band, who very kindly came to our chapel to play carols just before one Christmas. Once they were announced and welcomed from the pulpit, their diminutive conductress stood on a wooden box that had been placed in front of the first row of pews, so she could command both band and choir in their seasonal musical offerings.

Everything went rather well at first, with the initial rendition of 'Silent Night', but disaster struck in the middle of 'Ding Dong Merrily on High', and a ding-dong it soon became! By now the conductress was well into her rhythm, but soon her own natural exuberance took over and, with one mighty upward sweep of her baton, she teetered, overbalanced and then suddenly jack-knifed backwards over the front pew and all but disappeared from view. All that remained in focus from my elevated position in the choir stalls was a pair of feet sticking up in the air. I was confronted with a surreal scene, reminiscent of a Salvador Dalí painting, as portrayed by a voluminous pair of bright-pink elasticated bloomers which firmly gripped the conductress's kneecaps, then dark-brown wrinkled surgical stockings topped off by a pair of suede brogues pointing outwards.

In the midst of this confusion, the trombone player hit the highest note of his career as the remainder of the orchestra readily abandoned their instruments in order to extricate the stricken conductress from her pew. Thankfully, the poor lady wasn't hurt, but, unfortunately for me, at that precise moment I just caught sight of my father's beaming face and twinkling eyes and I was completely lost with laughter, so my days in the choir came to rather an abrupt end.

On the way home I had to face my mother's wrath and the fact that this time she was truly, truly mortified. Well, that was until we reached halfway home, when she started to laugh until the tears ran down her face. But I learned one invaluable lesson, which is that for every chaotic and difficult moment in life there is always a silver lining: and for me, no more choir practice was the cherished silver lining.

Just like Mend and Darn Day, Shoe Day came around once a month, when all the family's footwear was brought out for inspection. The ones needing attention and repair were bundled up with explicit notes attached to the laces, and I would be instructed to take them around to the local cobbler, Mr Lewis (never 'Uncle'). Accompanying the package would be a selection of vegetables from our garden, and I was instructed to hand these personally to his wife, Auntie Adele, whom I liked enormously. My mode of transport had been upgraded to a second-hand bicycle on the understanding that, if I passed the school examination to Elizabeth College, in a year or two I could have a brand-new model. So, with detailed lists and money in my pocket, I was eagerly prepared to run the errand.

I would usually cycle up the road to the Old Mill and then down the hill until I reached the Queen's Hotel. I often passed by this hostelry very quickly because my mother was wont to emphasise the point: 'The Queen's is a real den of iniquity as they have a public bar, where people stand drinking all day.' Periodically I had to stop off at Taylor's Cycle Shop to buy torch batteries. The emporium was run by Mrs Taylor and her son Charlie. Charlie dispensed petrol from a pump that had a moveable arm that swung out into the road, and he also sold and mended bicycles, while Mrs Taylor ran the shop and took the money. They were always helpful, always kind and always cheerful.

After visiting Taylor's it would be time to head to the nearby post office, and just across the road from there, in Rose Cottage – so aptly named, as it had delicate Albertine roses growing over the door – I would quite often see the petite figure of Miss Mary Le Messurier sitting in front of a wide-open lattice window, thumping out various hymns on her harmonium, although the tune invariably seemed to be the same: 'Nearer, My God, to Thee'. I used to think at the time that, living right next door to the chapel, she couldn't be much nearer to God than that.

Several doors further along, Monsieur Rudolf of Switzerland operated his exclusive and expensive hairdressing salon, which meant my mother went there only for very special occasions. His opening remarks always seemed to be the same: 'Oh, *mon Dieu*! What 'as Madame done to 'er tresses, *n'est-ce pas*?' My father used to say in a jocular fashion that quite possibly Monsieur Rudolf was really 'Arry 'Iggins from 'Ackney in London's East End, but I never ever found out.

Next on my list was one pleasant important task, which was a visit to Valpy's hardware shop just a little further up on the opposite side to the post office. The shop was run by George Valpy, unfailingly resplendent in a long brown dustcoat and often assisted by his daughter and a white Scottish terrier. This visit was important to me because I needed to buy all the screws and nails required by my father for our afternoon's work at home. The instructions would be precise: a dozen countersunk brass screws, size 6, a pound of oval three-inch nails, and so on. Each item was weighed and put into its own paper bag with the details and price written on the outside. In between, Mr Valpy would ask about the health of my mother, father and brother, and even when I left he would walk to the door with me and wave goodbye.

The Lewis family lived in a delightful, traditional Guernsey farmhouse built out of locally quarried granite, near the Old Post in St Martin, just off the main road in a side street running down to the nearby parish church. The cobbler's workshop was attached to the main house and was also built in matching granite, with dressed-stone lintels and quirky oak beams, and usually there would be a fire burning in the open hearth. It appeared to me that Mr Lewis lived in a happy and contented environment, losing himself in a long-forgotten world he instinctively knew would never return.

Coming into the workshop from the glare of the hot sun, the place would seem to be in a state of perpetual semi-darkness. He was surrounded by his beloved tools of the trade and other accoutrements, and coloured strips of leather hung down in festoons from the dusty oak beams; but the one thing I really liked about the workshop was the junk and the cobwebs and the wonderful smell of leather.

Sometimes, he would be sitting either at his bench or last, smoking his pipe, and Auntie Adele, always wearing her floral kitchen apron, would bustle in and out with cups of tea and messages from his loyal customers. After carefully examining my parcel and noting the instructions, he would often say, 'Tell your mother the brown shoes need to be soled and heeled – so you can come again next Thursday.' And that was that, as he would immediately return to his workbench and continue his slow and methodical line of work.

Periodically, both of us would just sit there together for quite a long time drinking our tea and not speaking, and then, suddenly, he would look up and say something like, 'You know, I well remember the day when you and your mum and dad walked by here on your way to Germany and with you carrying that heavy old kitbag all the way down the hill to the waiting coaches near the church, and I thought then this would be the end of our world.' Later, if I had enough money left over from all my various transactions, I would stop off back at the bakery and take my time in selecting a mouthwatering cream bun.

It is now, as I write, seventy-four years since we were wrenched away from the island and illegally deported to Germany. So what of Biberach today? All the old concentration-camp barrack blocks have now been demolished and the spoil removed, together with my 'pirate treasure', and in their place new imposing buildings have been constructed to create an impressive police university. Biberach nowadays is a neighbourhood of real friends, where those few surviving prison inmates from far-off days can meet in more tranquil surroundings with the hospitable folk of Biberach, to enjoy their overwhelming hospitality and kindness and to thank God we all survived, and where Britons and Germans still marvel together at the traumatic events that occurred and swirled around them so many decades ago.

# AUTHOR'S NOTE

Since finishing the manuscript for the book, I found an old notebook of my father's dated 1944. In this he wrote down the poem by James Buckham, which reads:

There are many helpful things to do along life's way
(Help to the helper, if we but knew) from day to day!
So many troubled hearts to soothe,
So many pathways rough to smooth,
So many comforting words to say,
To those that falter along the way.

And then I read of some of his innermost thoughts, thoughts of a man I loved and saw as an indefatigable spirit, imbued with energy and humour in all situations and who always looked for the best in everyone. Yet, behind the laughter and the smiles, these thoughts persisted, highlighting the frightening times we lived through:

'It is snowing and I am so tired today, I just fell asleep.'

'I went to bed at 00.30am. I am so restless but I must hide my feelings somehow.'

'I want to do what is right but this life is all wrong.'

'A terrible day and I feel so homesick.'

Stephen Rabey Matthews
2016

# ACKNOWLEDGEMENTS

It is an impossibility to name everyone who has freely given so generously of their time and efforts to ensure this book was published, but it does give me a marvellous opportunity to record my deep appreciation for all their assistance. However, I would especially wish to acknowledge the help and support of the following:

Firstly, I am totally indebted to Sir Richard Collas, Bailiff of Guernsey, and Norbert Zeidler, Lord Mayor of Biberach-an-der-Riss, Germany, who have kindly written forewords to the book.

## GUERNSEY

Tom Remfrey, chairman, Guernsey Deportees Association, a much-valued friend of long-standing.
Editorial team of the Guernsey Press Co. Ltd

Jurat Rev. Peter Lane and Wendy Lane
Fellow members and friends of Guernsey Deportees
Association
President and fellow members of the Channel Islands
Occupation Society
States of Guernsey Museum
States of Guernsey Culture & Leisure Department
The Priaulx Library
Leonard Percy Tippett, a nephew of the courageous Annette
Le Page, an integral part of the story

## UNITED KINGDOM
James Hodgkinson, Editor at John Blake Publishing, for his
sheer professionalism, creativity and enduring patience
Dr Gilly Carr (Cambridge University), in connection
with Guernsey deportee Byll Balcombe and my engraved
German-issue mug

## GERMANY AND BIBERACH-AN-DER-RISS
Reinhold Adler ('Adi'), local historian and the fount of all
knowledge, for his friendship and assistance over the years
and for granting me unfettered access to his considerable
archives of photographs and documents
Rotraud Rebman ('Rebbie'), a wonderful Christian lady
and friend who acted as interpreter and adviser on all things
to do with Biberach
Stefan Rasser, for his help and assistance in rediscovering the
camp escape tunnel and for permission to use photographs
from the collection of the late Michael Kraft

# ACKNOWLEDGEMENTS

Christa Neher-Ort, granddaughter of Franz Laib, deputy commandant of Biberach Camp

Dr Gerhard and Uschi Küenler, for their sparkling hospitality, kindness and deep friendship over the years, and especially for initiating me into the intriguing delights of Swabian cuisine

Sabine Engelhardt, head of the Biberach-an-der-Riss Cultural Office

Helga Raiser and Claudia Zweil, joint presidents of the Biberach Friends of Guernsey Association

Biberach friends – I also owe a great debt of gratitude to the many people of Biberach who have combined as friends to make me feel so welcome and quite at home in Biberach

## USA

Prof. Henry Joshua, whom I met, unknowingly, at Biberach railway station in 1945 after he and the surviving members of his family had been sent to Biberach from the death camp of Bergen-Belsen

# SOURCES

Eileen Florence Matthews: War diaries and personal hand-written notes of the time from 1940. This also includes considerable original official documents, photos and artwork executed by local artists, which remain in the Matthews Family Archives

Cecil Frederick Matthews: International Red Cross Notebook/Calendar for the year 1944

*Isolated Island*, V.V. Cortvriend, Guernsey Press Co. Ltd, Guernsey (1945)

*Islanders Deported*, Roger E. Harris, C.I.S.S. Publishing, Essex (1980)
– a number of passages have been reproduced by kind permission of the author, Roger E. Harris

# THE DAY THE NAZIS CAME

Guernsey Press Co. Publications
– certain passages in various publications, periodicals and
journals have been reproduced by gracious courtesy of the
Guernsey Press Company Limited

Lastly, my own website, complete with more information
and photographs, is available for readers who are curious to
learn more: http://stephen-r-matthews.wix.com/author